FRED & JOYCE BEDARD

FIRST STEPS

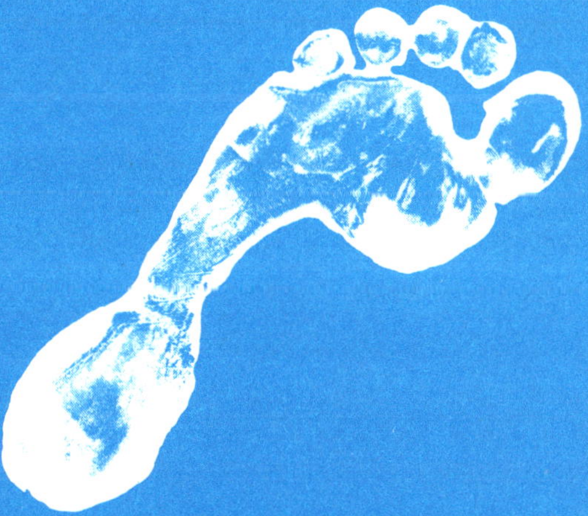

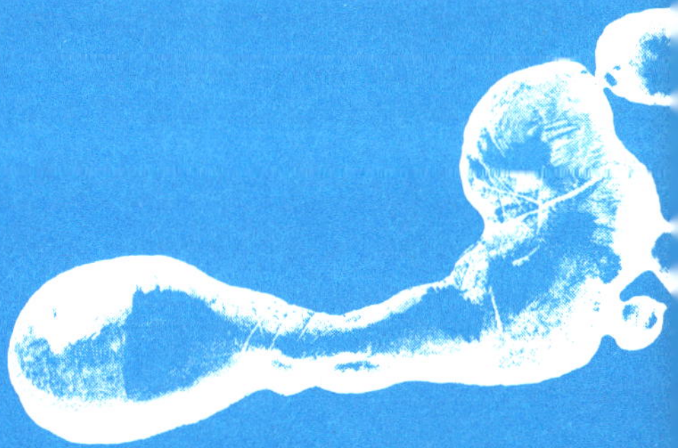

AL-ANON...

35 years of beginnings

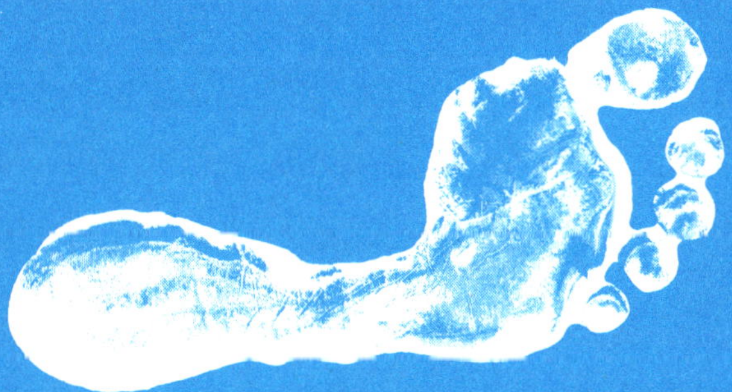

Post Office Box 862
Midtown Station
New York, New York 10018-0862

First Printing, April 1986
Library of Congress Catalog Card
No.85-073691
ISBN-910035-57-5

Approved by
World Service Conference
Al-Anon Family Groups

Printed in the United States

Other books by Al-Anon Family Groups:

AL-ANON FAMILY GROUPS (formerly living with an Alcoholic)
AL-ANON FACES ALCOHOLISM
THE DILEMMA OF THE ALCOHOLIC MARRIAGE
ONE DAY AT A TIME IN AL-ANON (Daily Readings)
FORUM FAVORITES (vols. 1 & 2)
ALATEEN-HOPE FOR CHILDREN OF ALCOHOLICS
LOIS REMEMBERS (a biography by our co-founder)
AL-ANON'S TWELVE STEPS & TWELVE TRADITIONS
ALATEEN—a day at a time
AS WE UNDERSTOOD...

The Al-Anon Family Groups are a fellowship of relatives and friends of alcoholics who share their experience, strength and hope in order to solve their common problems. We believe alcoholism is a family illness and that changed attitudes can aid recovery.

Al-Anon is not allied with any sect, denomination, political entity, organization or institution; does not engage in any controversy, neither endorses nor opposes any cause. There are no dues for membership. Al-Anon is self-supporting through its own voluntary contributions.

Al-Anon has but one purpose: to help families of alcoholics. We do this by practicing the Twelve Steps, by welcoming and giving comfort to families of alcoholics, and by giving understanding and encouragement to the alcoholic.

The Suggested Preamble to the Twelve Steps
Al-Anon Family Group Headquarters, Inc.

Preface

This is more than a book of historical fact; it is a love story—one that comes alive through the untiring efforts, quiet strengths and loyal dedication of a handful of individuals who, from small beginnings, created a movement that would reshape the lives of hundreds of thousands.

With 1986 marking the 35th anniversary of the Al-Anon Family Group fellowship, we look back in gratitude to our founders as we tell their stories and at the same time preserve our heritage.

As Lois W., our co-founder, stated at the 1980 International Convention held in New Orleans, Louisiana, "Anyone can start something, but it takes many people to keep it going." Hence, a tribute must also be made to *all* members of Al-Anon and Alateen for preserving the principles set forth by our pioneers and for assuring a future filled with many FIRST STEPS.

Myrna H., General Secretary
Al-Anon World Service Office

Contents

God grant me the serenity
to accept the things I cannot change,
courage to change the things I can,
and wisdom to know the difference.

Chapter One
Search For Recovery

"Damn your old meetings," said Lois W. as she threw a shoe at her husband, Bill. Late in 1935, this unexpected response to Bill's personal search for recovery from alcoholism led Lois to recognize the need for her own recovery. What Lois did not—could not—know at that moment of spiritual awakening was that she and Anne B. would found the world-wide fellowship of Al-Anon.

In the 16 years between Bill's founding of Alcoholics Anonymous (AA) and Lois's establishment of the Al-Anon Family Group Clearing House, spiritual awakenings happened spontaneously and simultaneously to other wives of AA members all across the country. One of them was Annie S., wife of AA's other founder, Dr. Bob. Unfortunately Annie died before independent family groups were united under the Al-Anon umbrella. But with Lois, Annie was to lay a strong foundation for the Al-Anon fellowship.

Many other pioneers, some of them thus far unrecognized, worked quietly and courageously to organize Al-Anon Family Groups, giving support and encouragement to others as they sought spiritual recovery for themselves. It is because these pioneers gave of themselves, their experience, and their optimism—especially their optimism—that Al-Anon has been able to develop from a handful of wives gathering together while their husbands attended AA meetings, to a separate world-wide fellowship of well over 25,000 groups. The Al-Anon journey has been made possible by the personal contributions of many people, both known and unknown. Some of these people have been mentioned in the pages of this book, but many have not. Their contributions were not documented because, at the beginning, Al-Anon's potential for growth went unrecognized. This book is their collective story.

Both Lois W. and Annie S. had their own personal strengths long before they encountered alcoholism. Lois, in her own book, *Lois Remembers*, describes the strong influence of her mother:

"Absolutely without self-consciousness and totally selfless, Mother loved people and people loved her. Everyone told us youngsters that Mother was the loveliest person they knew. Her features were somewhat plain, but they were framed by curly, burnished-blond hair, and her outgoing spirit charmed everyone and made her beautiful."

Dr. Bob And The Good Oldtimers hints at the early influence of Annie S.' family:

"She was small and reserved but had a cheerfulness, sweetness, and calm that were to remain with her throughout the years. She had been reared within a family of railroad people. It was a very sheltered atmosphere, although there wasn't much money at that time. Annie, who abhorred ostentation and pretense, always pointed out that she attended Wellesley on a scholarship, because her family couldn't have afforded to send her there otherwise."

Both women also possessed a personal dedication to their husbands that never wavered in the face of difficulties. It is fair to ask whether AA could have been so successfully launched without the support of Lois in New York and Annie in Akron, Ohio. The real evolution of Al-Anon began, however, when such women as these two were able to look beyond their husbands' alcoholism to focus on their own development as people. Annie translated her beliefs into action. Her coffee pot at AA meetings is legendary. Knowledge of how quietly and effectively Annie gathered about her those in need, sharing with them some spiritual principles has come to us through the writings of others, such as her son, Bob Jr.:

"Mother [who] had been raised in a sheltered atmosphere as far as worldliness was concerned, obtained a scholarship to Wellesley college and graduated there. She was teaching school when she and Dad were married. By nature and environment a rather timid person, she could nevertheless rise to great heights if she thought the occasion warranted. I am thinking of the times when she thought the AA program was in danger of being diverted by some of the eager-beaver or big organizer-type members who showed up from time to time and tried to mold the movement along the lines that suited them the best. When this happened, Mother would be ready to do battle with anyone for the principles that she believed were right. I have also seen her rise out of her quiet disposition in defense of Dad or myself personally. Her shyness and unworldliness were a source of constant delight to Dad who loved to bring home some unconventional item to shock her and watch her reactions. Mother always had a very deep loyalty to our family and later to the AAs which made no personal sacrifice too great. She just would not spend any money on herself in order to help the family get the things that she thought they needed.

"Her sense of humor made it great fun to play tricks on her and all of us spent a lot of time doing it because her reactions were so good. Although it was very foreign to her own upbringing, Mother was extremely tolerant of the ways of others and just would not criticize but always sought to excuse the actions of others by some means. Her advice was never given on the spur of the moment but was reserved until she had had time to pray and think about the problem. As a result, her answer was given in a very loving, unselfish way and served to steady Dad to a very great degree.

"They were always a very devoted couple, dedicated to each other and I have never seen them have an argument. Her passing was a very great shock to Dad from which he never fully recovered."

This was a very close family, and recollections of Annie coping with her husband's erratic behavior, sometimes hilariously, have been recorded by Bob Jr.:

"I remember one time my mother became so desperate that she took me upstairs and said, 'Now, I'm going to take a drink of whiskey, and when he comes home tonight, you tell him I'm drunk.' She took a drink of it and tried to act like she was drunk. It ended up in quite an uproar and didn't accomplish much. I don't think he thought she was drunk. He was just embarrassed by the show she was putting on. But you can see how desperate she was to show him what he was doing to himself. I don't think she ever had a drink before or after."

By 1933, Dr. Bob's position at Akron City Hospital was on the line, and there was talk of his dismissal. At home Annie was paying the household debts out of Christmas-present money.

During the same period, hardly by coincidence, rubber company president, Harvey Firestone, grateful because the Oxford Group, a Christian movement founded by a Lutheran minister, had helped his alcoholic son, invited some 60 group leaders from England to Akron for a ten-day house party. The event was well publicized. Annie, by this time was ready to try anything. When she heard of the Oxford Group, she persuaded her husband to begin attending meetings.

Annie and Dr. Bob joined the Oxford Group at West Hill for two and one-half years. Henrietta Seiberling, also a member, initiated the historic encounter between Dr. Bob and Bill W. Henrietta recalls that a friend, Delphine Weber, asked her one night in March or April of 1935, "What are we going to do about Bob S.?"

"What's wrong with him?" Henrietta asked.

"He's a terrible drinker," Delphine replied, noting that he was having problems at the hospital and was practically bankrupt because of his drinking.

"I immediately felt guided that we should have a meeting for Bob S. before Bill W. ever came to Akron," said Henrietta. She went to fellow Oxford Group members, T. Henry and Clarace Williams and asked whether it would be possible to use their home as a meeting place. They readily agreed.

T. Henry and Clarace opened their home as a Wednesday night meeting place for the "alcoholic squad" as it was later called. They met with the other members of the Oxford Group at the Williams' from the summer of 1935 to 1939.

Ernie G., AA's fourth member, recalls a conversation he had with Bill: "In those days, everybody had a nice, soft seat, because there weren't too many of us. Clarace Williams never had to use more than a couple of straight chairs. There was you, Doc, Bill D., me, and Phil S. The rest were Oxford Groupers, what few showed up—13 or 14 all told." (In the beginning, the others would have included T. Henry and Clarace, Henrietta Seiberling, Annie S. and Henrietta D.)

This Akron group is widely regarded as the first AA group. But tension began to grow between the "alcoholic squad" and other Oxford Group members. The alcoholics began gathering after the meeting at Kessler's Doughnut Shop to talk together. In January, 1940 Dr. Bob moved the meeting to his house on Ardmore Avenue, and then to the King Street School. So the Akron connection with the Oxford Group, as vital as it had been in the beginning was loosened, as the "alcoholic squad" moved on.

Annie followed her husband to the King Street School group. Along with the other wives, she began preparing the refreshments. This non-alcoholic kitchen brigade was allowed, as one AA member put it, "to wash dishes, make coffee, organize picnics and things like that." But Annie did more. She would put her own personal beliefs into practice for the benefit of others. According to an early AA member, Dan K:

"Annie always looked to the newcomers. She'd spot you, and after the meeting, she would go to your table and introduce herself. 'I want to welcome you and your lovely wife to Alcoholics Anonymous. We hope you'll keep coming back.'"

Dorothy S.M., one of AA's first woman members, said to Bill:

"You remember how Annie always called everybody by their first name? She could remember them. She knew all the children they had. It was that terrific personal interest she took in everybody. Even when she was almost blind, there at the last, she'd go up to them, and even if she couldn't distinguish who they were, she could tell by their voices, and she would recall every single thing about them.

"She used to gather clothes for anyone who didn't have anything to wear. I had a summer coat, and I had to wear it as a winter coat. Annie ripped the fur off somebody's old suit, and we sewed that on, and I had a winter coat. Then came summer, and we just ripped off the fur collar and put on a white collar. She did things like that for everybody."

Annie and Dr. Bob's house became a hostel for would-be AA members. Annie never declined to help, though some candidates for sobriety were more successful than others. At one time, Annie quietly persuaded a violent house guest to put down the carving knife he was intending to use on her.

Annie's caring is remembered with gratitude by an early AA member, Archie T:

"A very great privilege was mine. I was literally taken off the street and nursed back to life by Annie S. Bob will know when I say this, that I am not minimizing his part in my recovery. When a couple undertakes the sort of job that Annie and Dr. Bob took on when they took me into their home, it is the wife who is going to bear at least a slightly heavier part of the burden. This is particularly true when the recipient of such an extraordinary act of kindness is not only jobless and penniless, but too ill to get out of the house during the day and hunt for work. Such was my case: and so great was Annie's love, so endless her patience with me, so understanding her handling of me, that ten months later I left the house a new man, perhaps imbued with just a few grains of love, patience and understanding."

Annie can also be credited with the evolution of Al-Anon slogans which perhaps developed out of her devotional life and Dr. Bob's personal maxim to *keep it simple* . Bob E., treated by Dr. Bob at Akron City Hospital for his alcoholism and a member of the Wednesday night meeting at the Williams', reminisces about Annie:

"She had a quiet, soft way of making you feel at home. I shared a good many of my life problems with her. She read the Bible and counseled with me. She tried to keep things simple, too. I told her about being nervous and demoralized. She gave me a couple of phrases to say whenever I got downhearted or confused or frustrated. One I remember is: God is love. I used it consistently."

Annabelle G. has a telling story about another early use of the Al-Anon slogans. She was the wife of one of Dr. Bob's successful Twelfth-Step calls (the carrying of the AA message of recovery from one alcoholic to another).

"Dr Bob called Maybelle L. (Tom's wife) and told her, 'Get a hold of that dame (Annabelle) or her husband will be drunk before he's been out of the hospital two hours.' So you can see what I was like.

"She called me and asked me to come over. I was canning peaches and couldn't be interrupted. She said, 'What is more important, peaches or your husband?'

"'Well, if you must know, the peaches,' I replied. But I went over anyway. And I hadn't been there more than a few minutes before Doc and Annie came in."

"I couldn't let go," Annabelle said. "Maybelle took me upstairs, and I poured my heart out to her. Why don't you just surrender him to God?' she said. *'Let go and let God.'*

"That night, I couldn't sleep, and all of a sudden I said out loud, 'All right God, I can't do anything. Maybe You can. You can take over.' I felt such peace I went right to sleep."

Apart from her great personal kindness, Annie S. was a woman of faith. She believed in reading her Bible, praying, and that "Faith without works is dead." Perhaps Annie was given the first insight as to the significance of the Twelve Steps of AA as a way of life, and the possibility that the spiritual principles of what was later to become Al-Anon could be the foundation of a world-wide fellowship. As with many private people, the extent of her contributions to Al-Anon was never acknowledged during her lifetime. It was only when she died suddenly of a heart attack in Texas on June 1st, 1949 that a true appreciation of her as a person found expression.

ANNE S[redacted]

(March 21st, 1881—June 1st, 1949)

"She greeted strangers, and listened for their names."

SOMEHOW we believe Dr.Bob's beloved Anne would prefer this simple tribute beyond all others. It was written by one who knew her well. It came from the bottom of a grateful heart which sensed that extravagant language and trumpeting phrases would serve only to obscure a life that had deep meaning.

It is doubtful if now, only one year after her passing, that the true significance of Anne S[redacted]'s life can be realized. Certainly it cannot yet be written, for the warmth of her love, and charm of her personality and the strength of her humility are still upon those of us who knew her.

For Anne S[redacted] was far more than a gracious lady. She was one of four people, chosen by a Higher Destiny, to perform a service to mankind. How great this contribution is, only time and an intelligence beyond man's can determine. With Dr. Bob, Lois and Bill, Anne S[redacted] stepped into history, not as a heroine but as one willing to accept God's will and ready to do what needed to be done.

Her kitchen was the battleground and, while Anne poured the black coffee, a battle was fought there which has led to your salvation and mine. It was she, perhaps, who first understood the miracle of what passed between Bill and Dr. Bob. And, in the years to follow, it was she who knew with divine certainty that what had happened in her home would happen in other homes again, again, and yet again.

For Anne, understood the simplicity of faith. Perhaps that's why God chose her for us. Perhaps that's why Anne never once thought of herself as a 'woman of destiny' but went quietly about her job.

Perhaps that's why, when she said to a grief-torn wife, "Come in, my dear, you're with friends now—friends who understand" that fear and loneliness vanished. Perhaps that's why Anne always sat in the rear of the meetings, so she could see the newcomers as they came, timid and doubtful . . . and make them welcome.

There's a plaque on the wall of of Akron's St. Thomas hospital dedicated to Anne. It's a fine memorial. But there's a finer one lying alongside the typewriter as this is being written—letters to Dr. Bob from men and women who knew and loved her well. Each tries to put in words what is felt in many hearts. They fail—and that's the tribute beyond price. For real love, divine love, escapes even the poet's pen.

So, in the simplest way we know, and speaking for every AA everywhere, let's just say 'Thanks, Dr. Bob, for sharing her with us.' We know that she's in a Higher Group now, sitting well to the back, with an eye out for newcomers, greeting the strangers and listening for their names!

Annie's experience in Akron was paralleled by Lois' in New York. Both women expressed their caring in ways which reflected their individual temperaments. In Lois' own words:

"My daydreams as a young girl were of changing bad people into good ones. My mother seemed to have this gift; everyone who had intimate contact with her was the better for it, I felt.

"With this background was it any wonder that I thought I could inspire Bill to stop drinking and that I kept trying for seventeen years?

"After Bill sobered up, it was a great blow for me to realize that he did not need me in the way he had before. My primary aim in life, helping Bill achieve sobriety, had been cancelled out. I had not yet found anything to take its place. Slowly I recognized that because I had not been able to 'cure' Bill of his alcoholism, I resented the fact that someone else had done so, and I was jealous of his newfound friends. Little by little, I saw that my ego had been nourished during his drinking years by the important roles I had to fill: mother, nurse, breadwinner, decision maker. As we had no children, the mother role was very necessary to me. Also my ego was bolstered by my ability to support us both, however meagerly, and to make the family decisions that Bill was incapable of making. I had felt myself very much needed.

"When Bill stopped drinking, no doubt I continued trying to run things, and it took me a long time to adjust to the role of partner.

"After a while I began to wonder why I was not as happy as I ought to be. A surprising display of temper over nothing pulled me up short and made me start to analyze my own attitudes. By degrees I saw that I had been wallowing in self-pity, that I resented the fact that Bill and I never spent any time together anymore, and that I was left alone while he was off somewhere scouting up new drunks or working with old ones. I felt on the outside ..."

Several years later, the Clearing House Newsletter would put into words this common experience among family members of recovering alcoholics.

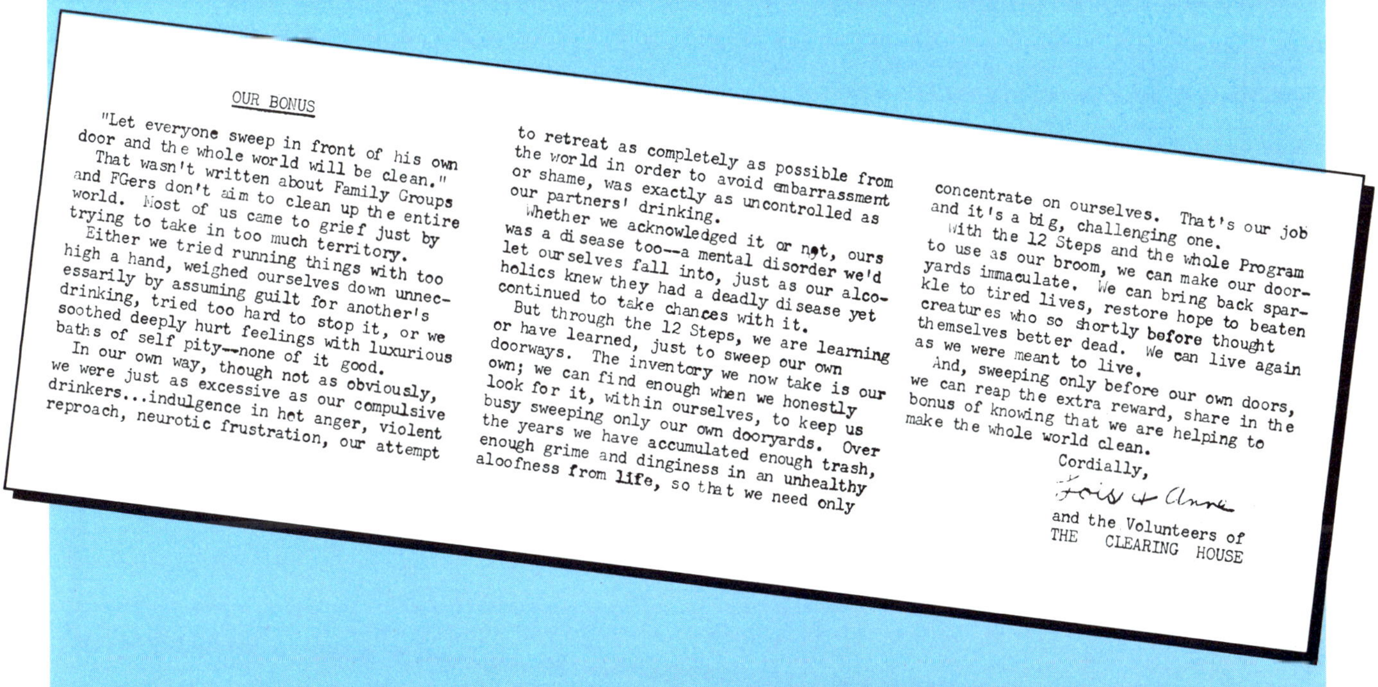

OUR BONUS

"Let everyone sweep in front of his own door and the whole world will be clean."

That wasn't written about Family Groups and FGers don't aim to clean up the entire world. Most of us came to grief just by trying to take in too much territory.

Either we tried running things with too high a hand, weighed ourselves down unnecessarily by assuming guilt for another's drinking, tried too hard to stop it, or we soothed deeply hurt feelings with luxurious baths of self pity--none of it good.

In our own way, though not as obviously, we were just as excessive as our compulsive drinkers...indulgence in hot anger, violent reproach, neurotic frustration, our attempt to retreat as completely as possible from the world in order to avoid embarrassment or shame, was exactly as uncontrolled as our partners' drinking.

Whether we acknowledged it or not, ours was a disease too--a mental disorder we'd let ourselves fall into, just as our alcoholics knew they had a deadly disease yet continued to take chances with it.

But through the 12 Steps, we are learning or have learned, just to sweep our own doorways. The inventory we now take is our own; we can find enough when we honestly look for it, within ourselves, to keep us busy sweeping only our own dooryards. Over the years we have accumulated enough trash, enough grime and dinginess in an unhealthy aloofness from life, so that we need only concentrate on ourselves. That's our job and it's a big, challenging one.

With the 12 Steps and the whole Program to use as our broom, we can make our dooryards immaculate. We can bring back sparkle to tired lives, restore hope to beaten creatures who so shortly before thought themselves better dead. We can live again as we were meant to live.

And, sweeping only before our own doors, we can reap the extra reward, share in the bonus of knowing that we are helping to make the whole world clean.

Cordially,

Lois & Annie

and the Volunteers of
THE CLEARING HOUSE

OUR LARGE PLACE

"I called upon the Lord in distress. The Lord answered me, and set me in a large place." Psalm 118 - 5

Like so many of us, did you begin life as a confident, out-going person with a family which meant the world to you, with a wide circle of friends, interested in everyone from the grocer to the paper boy?

And, over the years of living with a problem too great for you, did you gradually shut yourself away from your own family, friends, casual acquaintances and any contacts which could be avoided, no matter on how flimsy the pretext?

That's what most of us did. We didn't quite realize just how we were narrowing our world until one day realization came that we had built a solid wall between ourselves and our family, our friends and anything and everything outside the tight shells in which we had encased ourselves. Our shells were closer and more confining than those of snapping turtles. Porcupines were soft, confiding pets compared with the bristling creatures we'd become.

For shorter or longer periods, we lived withdrawn. For most of us, the first AA contact pierced the wall but it was only breached, not demolished. The understanding instantly felt among other husbands or wives, faced with identical problems, gave us hope. But, as it should be, AA was designed for alcoholics; the help we got was indirect and only partial.

In our Family Groups, however, we find the complete help we so desperately need. The application of the program, while it is still the same program, is designed for us, the sober members of families damaged by alcohol. Here is our opportunity to discuss just how the Steps apply to us, how they are best interpreted for non-alcoholics, and we are constantly reminded to practice this program "in all our daily affairs."

We come to the Family Group in great distress; we learn to call on the Higher Power as we understand that Higher Power, and the immediate hope, release from tension, and the new aim and insight gained from meeting with other members, gives us the knowledge that indeed the Lord has answered us & set us in a large place.

From the narrow, pressing walls we have built, we see the day when our alcoholics are again their true selves instead of unhappy slaves to such incomprehensible, compulsive drinking. And it isn't too long before we've torn down our walls ourselves, cast off our shells--even tho for a few, our alcoholics may still persist in drinking. Truly, we are in a large place, with understanding, hope and faith to keep us in it.

Cordially,

Margaret D.

For Lois, Anne
and the Volunteers
of THE CLEARING HOUSE.

KNOWING OURSELVES

This month's Stopper is particularly apt for this issue of the Forum because it fits so well with the Fourth Step. The fact that it was written for a pamphlet on mental health gives it even more significance as it broadens the application, not just to us, but to anyone struggling with a big problem.

We all know dimly that progress comes only with dissatisfaction; man grew tired of living in caves so he built himself a house; skins and furs were stiff and clumsy so he wove supple cloths for his attire; the spoken word was too difficult to be his only means of communication so he devised the alphabet and written messages.

Back of all these was dissatisfaction, discontent with present circumstances, or actual pain. Little as we like to acknowledge it, we must sometime realize that pain is a necessary part of our growth.

Children sometimes grow so quickly they have actual "growing pains," which are lightly dismissed by thoughtless persons. But they are not fun for the one enduring them. Neither is the pain of spiritual growth which, also, can be attained only through dissatisfaction, unhappiness and a wish to progress.

If we remain dissatisfied and unhappy, spend all our time in discontent with our lives, we are wasting the opportunity to grow in stature. Life without pain to spur us on would be static and sterile.

Through suffering, if we accept it as the goad it is meant to be, we can grow, can achieve an understanding that success is not just in material things, in living a pleasant, happy life--nice and comfortable as that would be--but in overcoming our own defects of character, in suppressing our selfishness and in living for others rather than ourselves.

No one knows better than we the pain of living with an alcoholic problem, but we who honestly try to practice all 12 Steps in all our daily affairs, know also that that pain is the price we pay for a better and deeper understanding, a richer and more meaningful life.

Cordially,

Margaret D.

For Lois, Anne and the Volunteers
of the CLEARING HOUSE.

What Lois and other wives like her discovered was that they needed the same tools of recovery as their husbands in AA. Once family members adopted this set of spiritual principles, personal growth was assured.

While Bill was still drinking, Lois had begun the search for recovery. Together they found a resource close to what they were looking for in the Oxford Group, at a time when Dr. Bob and Annie were already attending these meetings.

Bill stumbled into the first Oxford Group meeting early in December, 1934 after he and Ebby T. had had their historic encounter. When Ebby told Bill that he had "got religion," Bill decided to find out what it was all about from the mission where Ebby said he had found sobriety. In *Pass It On*, the author says:

"For Bill, the turning point came one afternoon. In a maudlin, self-pitying mood, he decided to make his own investigations. It was to a rescue mission operated by Dr. Sam Shoemaker's Calvary Church, at Fourth Avenue (now called Park Avenue South) and East 21st Street, near Gramercy Park that Bill went. The church operated a more respectable hostel called Calvary House, next to the church itself, but it was the one on 23rd Street that was aimed at helping the down and-outer. Between 1926 and 1936, more than 200,000 men are said to have visited the mission."

When Bill left Towns Hospital for the last time on December 8, 1934, never to drink again, he and Lois returned to Calvary House at Calvary Church to attend Oxford Group meetings. Dr. Sam Shoemaker was a leading figure in the Oxford Group movement at the time. He was later to break with it in 1941, as did Bill and Lois, but not before becoming a close personal friend to Lois and Bill.

Bill also acknowledged AA's debt to Dr. Carl Jung, the eminent psychiatrist, in an exchange of letters in 1961. Roland H., a "hopeless" alcoholic, had been advised by this Swiss psychiatrist, whom he had consulted, that nothing short of a religious conversion experience could help him in his recovery from alcoholism. It was a sober Roland who contacted Ebby T. and intro-

THE OXFORD GROUP

'And it shall be in the last days, saith God, I will pour forth of my Spirit upon all flesh: and your sons and your daughters shall prophesy, and your young men shall see visions, and your old men shall dream dreams.'—ACTS ii. 17.

YOU cannot belong to the Oxford Group. It has no membership list, subscriptions, badge, rules, or definite location. It is a name for a group of people who, from every rank, profession, and trade, in many countries, have surrendered their lives to God and who are endeavouring to lead a spiritual quality of life under the guidance of the Holy Spirit.

The Oxford Group is not a religion; it has no hierarchy, no temples, no endowments; its workers have no salaries, no plans but God's Plan; every country is their country, every man their brother. They are Holy Crusaders in modern dress, wearing spiritual armour. Their aim is 'A New World Order for Christ, the King'.

The Oxford Group is often confused in the minds of strangers with the Oxford Movement. The former which, by accident rather than by design, uses Oxford as the nominal centre for its activities in England, is a campaign for the renaissance of the practice among men of the truths of simple Christianity; the latter is a Catholic renaissance within the Church of England.

The Oxford Group works within churches of all denominations, planning to bring those outside back into their folds and to re-awaken those within to their responsibilities as Christians. It advocates nothing beauty of thought, word, and deed. They may not be so unattainable as we may suppose, but very few can or have ever lived lives of Absolute Honesty, Purity, Unselfishness, and Love. 'For all have sinned and come short of the glory of God', St. Paul tells us. It is doubtful if even a mystic, giving up his life to pious contemplation, lives a life founded on these four points in their fullness. It is a matter of argument whether his shutting himself away from human contact is Absolute Love for his fellow men; it certainly seems to the uninitiated to be selflessness in a negative form. The saints of this world, past and present, are those who whilst still leading a helpful material life for other people fight relentless warfare against their own temptations and the dire results of Sin in other people. They are the Saint Georges who persistently strive to kill the dragon of Sin which will not lie down and die gracefully. Daily they are singed by the fiery breath from the dragon's devouring jaws, crushed to earth by his huge unwieldy body; but they rise again, pick up the sword of a Christian life dropped when they fell into Sin and, by God's grace, forgiven their fall, they commence once again their fight for Absolute Honesty, Purity, Unselfishness, and Love.

duced him to the Oxford Group.

Bill never did *directly* acknowledge AA's connection to the Oxford Group movement, although several references were made to it in *AA Comes of Age.* Founded by a Lutheran minister, Dr. Frank Buchman, in its early days the Oxford Group movement had been likened to first century Christianity, holding simple meetings for small groups of people. But by 1936, so popular had it become that a meeting of 10,000 Oxford Group members was held at Stockbridge, Massachusetts. With the meeting came political commentary that attracted adverse newspaper publicity. Because of the controversy, Oxford University requested that the name be dropped, and in 1938 the Oxford Group became, Moral Rearmament, or MRA.

The origin of much of the Al-Anon program can be traced to AA's beginnings. A brief look, however, at some Oxford Group ideas from *What Is The Oxford Group,* written anonymously and published by Oxford University Press in 1933, will show how the movement foreshadows some familiar Al-Anon spiritual principles and meeting formats. Al-Anon members will substitute the words "Higher Power" for "God" and "Holy Spirit," and "character defect" for the word "sin."

It was the Oxford Group meetings that Lois was "cussing" when she threw her shoe at Bill, not AA. At first, like Annie and Dr. Bob, Lois and Bill found support among the Oxford Group members. Bill told the story of his conversion while at Towns Hospital, and he and Lois attended some Oxford Group house parties. But the split between Bill's need to work with other alcoholics and the Oxford Group came early on. In Lois' words:

"The Oxford Group, as we knew it back in the early months of 1935, worked in teams of six to a dozen, sitting quietly together like a Quaker meeting and listening for the guidance of God for each one. Bill belonged to a team for a while, but I didn't. The rest of the team would get guidance for him to work with such and such a person in order to 'bring him to God.' Bill usually had different guidance and felt no identity with the person they selected. He became a bit annoyed at being told what to do. He knew he could be far more useful working with alcoholics, with whom he could identify."

To make matters worse, Bill began to be successful with his alcoholics and a few of them remained sober for a while. Jack Smith, one of Dr. Sam Shoemaker's assistants, brought the conflict into the open when he referred to Bill's meetings in front of other Oxford Group members as being 'held surreptitiously behind Mrs. Jones barn.' Alcoholics living at Calvary Mission were told not to go to Bill's house on Clinton Street. Lois and Bill continued to attend Oxford Group meetings, but Bill's conviction grew that he must associate with his own kind. He and Lois finally severed the connection in 1937. Dr. Bob and Annie were to continue until 1939. Writing about it years later to an AA member in Richmond, Virginia, Bill says:

"I am often asked why I do not publicly acknowledge my very real debt of gratitude to the Oxford Group[OG]. The answer is that, unfortunately a vast and sometimes unreasoning prejudice exists all over this country against the OG and its successor, MRA. My dilemma is that if I make such an acknowledgement, I may establish a connection between the OG and Alcoholics Anonymous which does not exist at the present time. I had to ask myself which was the more important: that the OG receive credit and that I have the pleasure of discharging my debt of gratitude, or that alcoholics everywhere have the best possible chance to stay alive regardless of who gets the credit." To that, we can add their families, too.

Chapter Two
AA Wives Meet Together

During those early days of Oxford Group meetings and working with Bill to sober up alcoholics, Lois saw no separation between her husband's recovery and her own. Many wives were to follow their husbands into AA and went along on Twelfth-Step calls. Gradually, as AA groups grew larger, alcoholics sought out other alcoholics with which to share their program. This was especially true when women joined AA. Non-alcoholic wives, welcome at meetings, congregated on the

The non-alcoholic wife's quandary

MANY wives of alcoholics are in this wife's quandary: "Although my husband has been sober for two years now, in AA, he is very nervous and irritable with me and the children, and I am afraid he will drive them away. I do so want peace and harmony at home."

We who live with alcoholics have the opportunity, at least, to put the 12 Steps of AA to practical use. To this wife we can only say that peace and serenity, like sobriety, are found only within ourselves. Her husband, although sober, has not followed the 12 Steps on to the further growth in which he would not be forced to take refuge from his inner difficulties in irritability. Instead of getting drunk and shouting at his family he is being irritable and shouting. And, just as he had to seek AA in the first place through his own volition, so will he have to realize, of himself and by himself, his need for further help from the AA Program in other directions than sobriety. Sobriety was apparently a stopping-place for him instead of being one of the steps toward happiness and integration.

This wife cannot deal with his irritability any more than she once could deal with his drunkenness. Of course she wants a peaceful, harmonious home for her children, and she feels that they have a right to such a home. Since she cannot change her husband, the change in the conditions in her home will have to come about through herself. It is not enough to blame her husband for those conditions of discord. It could be that she is herself contributing to that discord by her own attitude.

It is perfectly natural on her part to be tempted into resentment, but having followed the 12 Steps of AA herself, along with her husband, in the earlier days of his acquaintance with AA, she cannot now be comfortable harboring it.

(Haven't we all sighed at times in utter exasperation, "Oh, if I could only go back to being angry and critical and feel that I'm *right* in being so!")

But no, we're haunted by our own better selves! Once inoculated with AA we can never again say to another, "You're to blame!" without hearing an inner voice prod us in the ribs, "Whoosh! Look who's talking...the pot calling the kettle black again!"

This husband is irritable because of inner conflict which he cannot yet resolve. The wife is resentful, likewise, and apprehensive, living in the tension of anxiety because of inner conflict which she has not yet resolved. And that must be her starting point.

What are the conflicts within her which are "touchy" to her husband's shouting at her and the children? Would his shouting be so unbearable if her own attitude of tension and at least implied criticism did not provide the atmosphere in which the children's responses are more negative than they otherwise might be?

If the children are driven away it is because that is their pattern of life. Nothing can stop them. After all, children run away from the best, as well as the worst, of homes. It could be that she is overly protective and solicitous, and it might be that which they must break away from. Very often, where there is anxiety in the mother and tension toward an irritable husband, the children's reaction is to escape the anxiety and tension rather than the irritability. The shouting and harshness are at least out in the open; they can cope with it. But tension is a pervasive, smothering sort of thing that wraps itself around and through their daily lives in invisible, baffling cords of steel.

We all want our children to be spared troubles and difficulties and discords; if we are not wise we try to protect them too much. Children are individuals who are setting out on their own paths of destiny; we are given their care for a few years in which to do our best for them. But which is our best, to wear ourselves – and them – out trying to spare them all discord, or to show them, by example, how to retain and reflect inner serenity in the face of discord? They will be confronted with troubles and difficulties all their lives; if they learn from us that serenity and poise and quiet peace do not depend on outer circumstances or on the emotions and moods of other people they are protected from hurt by the armor of God. For nobody can dwell serenely in the security of inner peace without "abiding in the shadow of the Almighty...His truth shall be thy shield and buckler."

Our problems and our lives require constant re-affirmation of the principles embodied in the 12 Steps of AA. We cannot stop at any point. The AA Program, a way of vital, spiritual growth, is a pilgrimage for all of us, non-alcoholics as well as alcoholics; when we reach a point where the going is rough it is a sign that we are off the road. In all the turmoil and confusion, then, we have one shining beacon light to steer by: the way of life pointed out in the 12 Steps of AA.

—*R.G., San Francisco, California*

I Am Confused

Wherein A Wife Wonders Why Understanding Must Be One-Sided

I have read and tried to live by the Twelve Steps. I may be reading and studying them with blinders, but I can't for the life of me find a line in them that says we have to devote all of our leisure hours to our AA friends. Surely, there is time to be found for others...surely there is other conversation than AA. There are millions of things going on in the world but to listen to our living room conversation one would think that *all* the world revolves around Alcoholics Anonymous, its group politics, its clubroom problems, whether Joe Blow really wants the program or whether he's just flirting with it and..."Didn't you think he looked like he was on pills the other night?"

Is this what it means to be restored to sanity? Somehow I can't believe that it is. Yes, Jim's home sober now, sometimes, but that's the only difference. He's hitting AA just as hard as he ever hit the bottle. And I'm worried. Before someone jumps up and says that I'm resentful, I'll say it myself. Maybe I am. I think worried is a better word. I'm worried because I see him developing into a man with a one-track mind. I'm worrying because my children have no more father now than they ever had and, above all, I'm worried because I don't know how to help.

From all that I can hear or gather from what I read in the *Grapevine* or other literature aimed at the non-alcoholic, I'm supposed to jump on the bandwagon, too. I'm told that I should straighten out my character defects. Well, I'm trying, but if it means incarcerating ourselves in the silken web of group hypnosis I don't care for some, and I can't believe that Jim's sobriety depends upon it. I have a strange notion that both his sobriety and our peace of mind lies in the study and the living of the Twelve Steps, and the "practicing these principles in all our affairs."

So far I haven't reached the point of confusion where I've done anything drastic..and I mean drastic. I know of one wife who is becoming a closet drinker, another whose public antics are causing some conversation and still another who stuck her head in the gas oven.

From where I sit at present, it looks to me like I am again trapped. When Jim was drunk I had the choice of taking him or leaving him. I took him. Now, again, I have the choice of taking him or leaving him. I'll no doubt take him, but I'm fighting like a steer against becoming such a serene glob of humanity that I can tolerate anything. It occurs to me that I was cut out for neither martyrdom nor sainthood.

Don't think that I don't want my husband sober. I do. But I do also want him restored to sanity. Therefore I am confused. Does being restored to sanity mean that he must substitute one over-indulgence for another? And that again, *all* the understanding must come from me? Or does it mean that now with the help of God and these Twelve Suggested Steps we can and should, at long last, fit into our small niche in the wonderful world in which we live?

Can someone unconfuse me?

Anonymous, New York.

sidelines and, while making coffee for the AA group began to share their common problems and to explore some common solutions. These steps toward the formation of groups for families happened quietly but consistently, wherever AA prospered.

In the years from 1934 to 1937, Lois threw herself into an entirely new way of life which had come about with Bill's sobriety. At her home on Clinton Street, she and Bill enthusiastically tried to love other alcoholics into accepting the AA program. Russ R., who lived with Lois and Bill for over a year describes what happened:

"All of us were living rent-free, food-free, everything-free in Clinton Street, and Lois was doing all the work. She was working in a department store during the day and cooking for us and providing all the money the whole house had."

But others like Lois were confused when sobriety did not bring harmony and happiness at home. Wives expressed their bewilderment in articles contributed to the magazine, *AA Grapevine.*

Until 1939, nothing that the "alcoholic squad" did together had been written down. There were no tools for recovery other than meetings and working with other alcoholics. Frank Amos, who was sent to Akron in February, 1938 by John D. Rockefeller, describes how 50 men and two women found recovery from alcoholism, and gives us an interesting glimpse into the development of the spiritual principles of AA:

"An alcoholic must surrender himself entirely to God, realizing that in himself there is no hope.

"He must have devotions every morning—a 'quiet time' of prayer and some reading from the Bible and other religious literature. Unless this is faithfully followed, there is grave danger of backsliding.

"He must be willing to help other alcoholics get straightened out.

"It is important, but not vital, that he meet frequently with other reformed alcoholics and form both a social and a religious comradeship."

When Bill wrote the Twelve Steps of Recovery for the AA "Big Book" (copyrighted as *Alcoholics Anonymous*) later that year, he was relying on the word-of-mouth experiences of the first 100 sober alcoholics, the Oxford Group philosophy and the writings of William James. The understanding of the medical aspects of alcoholism came from Dr. Bob and Dr. Silkworth. The "Big Book" included two chapters written by Bill for "Wives and the Family Afterward." Lois says that when she suggested shyly to Bill that she write these chapters, he turned her down, for reasons that were never entirely clear.

Once the "Big Book" was published in April, 1939, wives could learn first hand of the spiritual principles of AA, without attending AA meetings. Living with AA members gaining in sobriety by practicing the Twelve Steps, the wives more and more wanted the same quality of life for themselves. Lois describes it another way:

"In the beginning AA was a family affair. Many of the wives tried to live by the program themselves and made much progress, but this was in a general way only. There was nothing to help them understand their own reactions. There was little sharing of experience. The later formation of the Family Groups filled this gap."

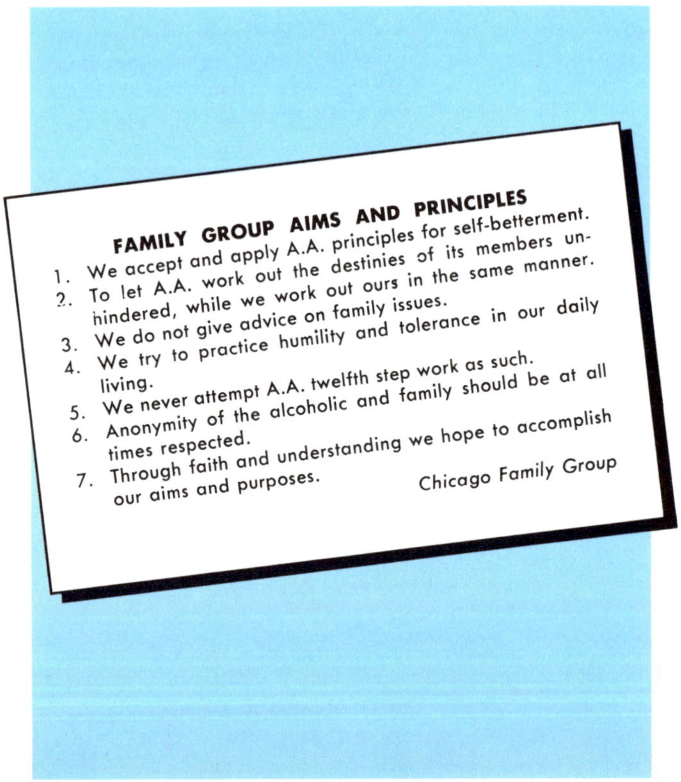

FAMILY GROUP AIMS AND PRINCIPLES

1. We accept and apply A.A. principles for self-betterment.
2. To let A.A. work out the destinies of its members unhindered, while we work out ours in the same manner.
3. We do not give advice on family issues.
4. We try to practice humility and tolerance in our daily living.
5. We never attempt A.A. twelfth step work as such.
6. Anonymity of the alcoholic and family should be at all times respected.
7. Through faith and understanding we hope to accomplish our aims and purposes.

Chicago Family Group

BEGINNING
of
St. Paul Al-Anon
Minnesota

In the early spring of 1952, after attending an open AA meeting of the Midway AA group, several of the wives of the AA group members visited with each other over coffee. The next day one of the wives called me and asked me if I had noticed anything about our conversation the night befor? It turned out that I had picked up on some of the same things that she had. What we had observed was the fact that, as wives of alcoholics, we were expressing feelings of fear, anxiety frustration, self-pity etc. We didn't like where we were at, however, we didn'tknow how we could rid ourselves of these distructive feelings either. As we continued to talk we discussed how we had noticed that our spouses had changed some things in their lives through the practice of the 12 Steps of AA. Due to this we wondered if thoes same 12 Steps might help us to eliminate some of these negative emotions or feelings from our lives and maybe even help us to find some Peace of Mind.

As a result of that conversation, and after talking with some of the other wives, we decided to meet once a month in our homes to study the 12 Steps and how we might apply them to our lives and to share our experiences in doing so.

After a few years of meeting in our homes and working with the 12 Steps in our lives, one of our members said she had attended a meeting held by other family members, at 2218 AA Club in Minneapolis and that they told her they were registered in New York at a Family Groups Clearing House there. We wrote to the Clearing House and received the reply that there were many other Family Groups through out our Country and Canada, and that they had banded together under the name of the Al-Anon Family Groups...explaining that the term Al-Anon stood for Alcoholics Anonymous in a short form, and that we were welcome to register as a Al-Anon Family Group. We did this and so became the first registered Family Group in St. Paul Minnesota, and were known as the St. Paul Al-Anon Family Group.

A few years later we started to have people join us who were still living with a person with active Alcoholism and because they did not always feel they could use their homes for meetings to be held in ...we made the decision to find a permanent meeting place. We rented a room from the East side AA Club and began meeting there once a month.

When we first started to meet in 1952, it so happened, that all our husbands were members of the Midway AA Club.... so we called ourselves the Midway Wives Group, however by the time we registered with New York, our members came from different parts of St. Paul, and many had loved ones who were members of AA at other AA Clubs in St. Paul.

By 1962 there were Al-Anon groups meeting at several different AA Clubs in St. Paul and the following Al-Anon groups had formed... Down Town Al-Anon, Northwestern Al-Anon and the original St. Paul Al-Anon group was now known as the East Side Al-Anon group.

About this time a few of us from the East Side group deceided to rent a meeting room from the Midway AA Club as they now had a building to meet in. So in 1962 the Midway Al-Anon group was formed, and we had come to a full circle from where Al-Anon had started in St. Paul.

From there Al-Anon in St. Paul continued to grow and Alateen groups were formed as time passed .... until today there are around one hundred and forty Al-Anon/Alateen groups in the St. Paul Area.

Submitted by

Lucille C[redacted]

A member of the first
St. Paul Al-Anon group
and a member of the
Midway Wed Afternoon Al-Anon
group today...............

June 7, 1982

Chapter Two/AA Wives Meet Together

Filling the gap for wives of AA members became the first spiritual struggle for independent development by the family groups. Following the lead of AA, they began to write down their thoughts. This was the beginning of an independent literature. To coin a phrase from the book read by Bill in Towns Hospital, there were varieties of religious experiences.

A-A Auxiliary

722 N. W. G[redacted] STREET
PORTLAND 9, OREGON

1. **Love is very patient,**
2. **Love is very kind.**
3. **Love knows no jealousy,**
4. **Love makes no parade.**
5. **Love gives itself no airs,**
6. **Love is never rude,**
7. **Love is never selfish,**
8. **Love is never irritated,**
9. **Love is never resentful.**
10. **Love is never glad when others go wrong,**
11. **Love is always gladdened by goodness,**
12. **Love is slow to expose,**
13. **Love is eager to believe the best,**
14. **Love is always hopeful,**
15. **Love is always patient,**
16. **Love never faileth.**

SOUND HOMES THROUGH WIVES' APPROACH TO A.A.

"SOMEBODY CARES"
(Motto)

The Wives Meetings of A.A. are held for the purpose of showing the wife how she can be of help to her husband in overcoming his problem of alcohol and at the same time promoting a spirit of cooperation in the home that will show the whole family "the A.A. Way of Life" is the answer to any problem - whether it be alcohol, disposition or what.

When we study the FOURTH STEP step and honestly take a moral of ourselves, we soon discover the first step is easy to take.

...nce admitting we too have been wrong to a degree, then we ...h the rest of the program, and soon find that once again we ...n. interest at heart, and work together as God intended a ...e and family should do.

...is the privilege of any group to function as they see fit. ...the less organization the better, remembering A.A. is an ...an organization.

...ave not found it necessary to have any leader, secretary

...s in turn take over meetings and money is NOT needed if ...d in homes. If held in churches or public places, we ...tary contributions forthcoming when necessary.

...r the new A.A. wife probably has not too much money on ...d any embarrassment if not asked to contribute.

...ting can be taken care of by a study of one of the ...y part of the Love Chapter, which is found in 1st. ...er 13. We find Moffat's version very helpful - in ...a tremendous help to our groups.

...member may see fit to share some of her constructive

...necessary that only one person talk at a time, thus ...portunity to hear all that may be said.

...sponsibility of the one in charge of the meeting ...lso to check ANY MENTION OF HUSBANDS remembering ...purpose of overcoming our own defects of character.

...re opened with a moment's silence - followed by ...ed with the Lord's Prayer said in unison.

DO'S AND DON'TS FOR AN ALCOHOLIC'S WIFE

1. DO show an interest in everything your husband is doing.
2. DO show a loving care.
3. DO ask their opinions - they love it.
4. DO make them feel important.
5. DO appear happy and detached.
6. DO be cheerful.
7. DO cooperate.
8. DO be patient.
9. DO attend the open meetings.
10. DO - "THINK"

1. DON'T bring up the past.
2. DON'T say "you are a fine example".
3. DON'T argue.
4. DON'T show that you know too much about the program.
5. DON'T have a martyr's attitude.
6. DON'T be indifferent.
7. DON'T be smug.
8. DON't nag.
9. DON't worry.
10. DON'T hurry.

REMEMBER: "BUT FOR THE GRACE OF GOD."

The wife of an alcoholic from San Francisco, California, Ruth G. was far ahead of her time. After initiating a lively correspondence with AA's Alcoholic Foundation, forerunner of the AA General Service Office, to register her San Francisco AA Family Club, Ruth conceived the idea of starting a magazine for family group members. Energetic and creative, Ruth G., for the first time, linked newly formed family groups through the *San Francisco Family Club Chronicle,* later to be called *The Family Forum.* Lois says of her:

"Without her, early Al-Anon could never have gained the impetus it did. The wife of an alcoholic on the West Coast, Ruth spent much time and thought on the magazine. Its pumpkin-colored sheets were filled with editorials, correspondence from families of alcoholics, appropriate quotations from the Bible, Marcus Aurelius Antonius, St. Francis of Assisi, Nietzsche, ancient Chinese philosophers and even Machiavelli. It also contained some cleverly drawn cartoons."

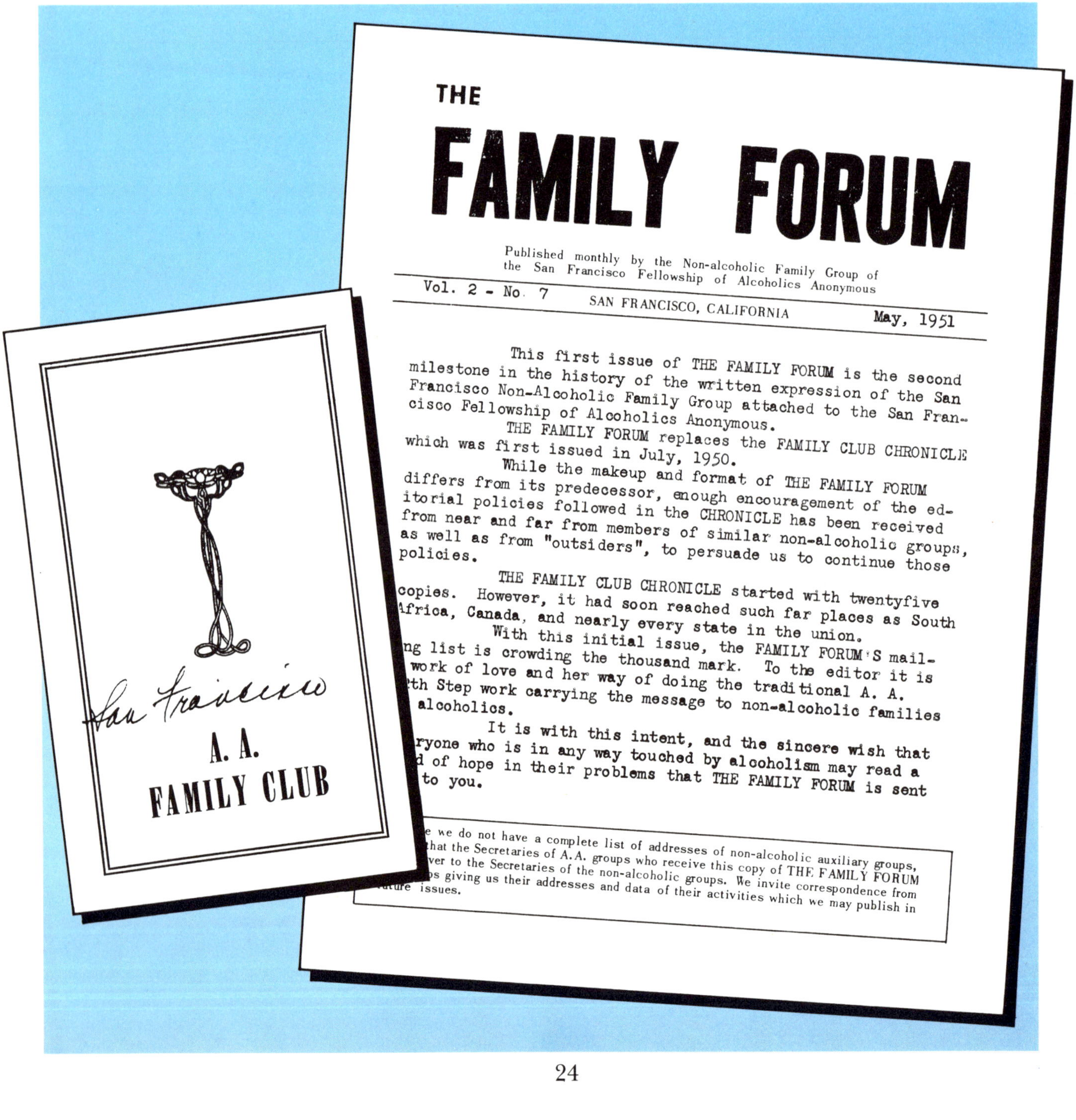

San Francisco
A. A.
FAMILY CLUB

THE
FAMILY FORUM

Published monthly by the Non-alcoholic Family Group of the San Francisco Fellowship of Alcoholics Anonymous

Vol. 2 - No. 7 SAN FRANCISCO, CALIFORNIA May, 1951

This first issue of THE FAMILY FORUM is the second milestone in the history of the written expression of the San Francisco Non-Alcoholic Family Group attached to the San Francisco Fellowship of Alcoholics Anonymous.

THE FAMILY FORUM replaces the FAMILY CLUB CHRONICLE which was first issued in July, 1950.

While the makeup and format of THE FAMILY FORUM differs from its predecessor, enough encouragement of the editorial policies followed in the CHRONICLE has been received from near and far from members of similar non-alcoholic groups, as well as from "outsiders", to persuade us to continue those policies.

THE FAMILY CLUB CHRONICLE started with twentyfive copies. However, it had soon reached such far places as South Africa, Canada, and nearly every state in the union.

With this initial issue, the FAMILY FORUM'S mailing list is crowding the thousand mark. To the editor it is work of love and her way of doing the traditional A. A. th Step work carrying the message to non-alcoholic families alcoholics.

It is with this intent, and the sincere wish that ryone who is in any way touched by alcoholism may read a d of hope in their problems that THE FAMILY FORUM is sent to you.

e we do not have a complete list of addresses of non-alcoholic auxiliary groups, hat the Secretaries of A.A. groups who receive this copy of THE FAMILY FORUM ver to the Secretaries of the non-alcoholic groups. We invite correspondence from ps giving us their addresses and data of their activities which we may publish in ture issues.

At one time, Ruth G. discussed with Lois the possibility of writing a book for non-alcoholics, but the scheme appears to have died on the vine. She continued to write extensively in her magazine. When Margaret D. took over the editorship of the *Al-Anon Clearing House Newsletter* in June, 1954, permission was obtained from Ruth G. to use the *Family Forum* name. Since, by that time Ruth was no longer publishing her magazine, she kindly agreed. A tribute to Ruth and the first Family Group magazine, clearly a forerunner of all the *FORUMs* to follow was made in the April, 1954 *Newsletter.*

Ruth G.'s *Family Forum* was one way in which Family Groups could discuss together how to adapt the AA principles to meet their own needs. Here one began to see a significant difference in thinking among Family Groups at that time. One group of wives saw their role principally as that of supporting their AA husbands in their recovery, while another group saw their primary purpose as seeking recovery for themselves. Both groups called themselves AA Auxiliaries, AA Family Groups, or other names implying a very close association with AA. All the family groups embraced AA's Twelve Steps and began adapting their wording according to individual "group conscience."

NAA

Austin, Texas

TWELVE SUGGESTIONS FOR NON-ALCOHOLICS

1. I will accept the fact that alcoholism is an illness and should be treated as such.

2. I realize that only with help of a Higher Power can we be restored to normal living.

3. Each day I will make a conscious effort to give thanks for our blessings and ask for guidance and wisdom in our daily living, remembering to say "Thy Will be done."

4. I will make a searching inventory of myself and also of my reactions to the behavior of an alcoholic.

5. I admit that I was wrong in my understanding of an alcoholic, being thankful that it is an illness instead of pure cussedness.

6. I will do all in my power to assist any one to follow the A.A. program.

7. I will humbly ask for help to recognize and to remove my shortcomings and the defects of my character.

8. I will try to hold neither bitterness nor resentment about the past. I would not censor any person suffering from any other sickness, for sacrifices or unhappiness I may have experienced as a result of their illness.

9. I will try to make amends for my mistakes and will con stantly be on the alert to make sure that I think of alcoholis as an illness with a definite behavior pattern.

10. I will continue to take personal inventory and ma sure I am reacting toward alcoholism as an illness, rememb ing "But for the Grace of God."

11. I will seek through prayer and meditation to impr my conscious contact with God, praying for knowledge of H will for me and the power to carry that out.

12. Having had this spiritual awakening through the help and the fellowship of A.A. and N-A.A., I will try to carry the message to others and to practice these principles in all our affairs.

A TRIBUTE TO THE FAMILY FORUM

Ruth H., of San Pedro, Cal., asked that we include the following in the Newsletter:-

"Our groups in this area still remember with fondness, Ruth G. of San Francisco, editor of the old Family Forum. We feel, if she knows about the Newsletter she would be happy, indeed, to see her dreams of the Forum materialize in this way. Ruth worked unstintingly for the unity and growth of our Al-Anon Family Groups, and in this Newsletter, we are happy to see her 'theme' being carried out.

If this Newsletter should reach a group in Ruth G.'s vicinity, please pass it on to her, with the love and good wishes of the Harbor Groups, San Pedro, Cal."

OUR TWELVE STEPS

1—I admitted I was powerless over an alcoholic and that our lives had become unmanageable. (Hadn't I spent .... years trying to change an alcoholic without success? Hadn't I used pleas, reproaches, love, hate, threats and reasoning, calmness and rage; all to no avail? Hadn't I wept, laid awake nights, worried and prayed? Certainly both of our lives had become unmanageable in the chaotic state in which we were living.)

2—Came to believe that a Power greater than ourselves could restore me to sanity. (If I was to be restored to sanity, it must be through a Power greater than myself, for certainly I was on the verge of insanity after living for............ years with an alcoholic. What else could a life that is made up of fears, suspicion, antagonism, dishonesty and distrust be, if not insanity.)

3—Made a searching and fe... inventory of myself. ... made some shocking di... found that over a peri... while living with an a... the accompanying w... distress and unhappin... the natural result of... that I had built up a ... ing that was no credi... character.)

4—Made a decision to turn my life over to God *whether I understood Him or not.* (Why should I attempt to understand God? I know that much of my confusion over religion had been due to the belief that I should accept a given interpretation of Him, and I was unable to accept these interpretations, and that now I would turn my life over to this Power or Force of God, whether I understand It or not.)

5—Admit to God, myself and other human beings the nature of my mistakes.

a. I had become apprehensive of the future.

b. I threw up a cloud of fear and worry that engulfed me every time I was away from my husband or he away from me.

c. I mistrusted him and I showed this mistrust.

d. I had become irritable and nervous.

e. I had grown less affectionate (thru repulsion).

f. I condemned rather than praised.

...ove all, I had developed a self-... ...t pride that was driving ... friends and

8—I am willing to make amends for the mistakes of the past, to constantly be on the alert for any destructive habits, such as nagging and criticizing.

9—When wrong, I will promptly admit it. (This is hard to do, for usually we think we are right. I was wrong to show my distrust, even though I felt it. I was wrong in my understanding of an alcoholic; in fact, I was wrong in my whole attitude of living.)

10—I will continue to take personal inventory. (This I must do to keep me from developing those defects of character, which through habit, may creep back into my life. I must re-educate myself. I must grow with my husband. I must constantly be honest with myself.)

11—I will seek through prayer and meditation to improve my conscious contact with God. (I am conscious of this Power many times during the day, and through this contact I am eliminating pettiness, distrust, fear, antagonism and self-pity from my life.)

12—Having had this spiritual experience through the help and fellowship of A.A. and having had my heart ...rmed and my soul fed by friendli-... as exhibited in this ... earnest desire

---

Mrs. Ruth [redacted]
962 [redacted] Avenue
San Francisco, Calif.

August 17, 1950

Dear Mrs. Glowacki:

Your letter addressed to the A.A. Grapevine has been referred to us and may we express our appreciation of this.

We were very glad to get news of the San Francisco Family Club, founded in September 1945. While these Associate A.A. Groups do not register with us in the usual sense of the word, yet we attempt to keep a record of information regarding their plan, methods of procedure and all other pertinent data. Therefore, we are glad to have this on our records and will add the name of the San Francisco Family Club to our list of Associate A.A. Groups. I imagine that you are familiar with the pamphlet put out by the Group in Long Beach, California, a copy of which is enclosed, but if not you might wish to obtain more from Mrs. Florence [redacted], 3305 East [redacted] Street, Long Beach. Also, you might care to write Mrs. Nettie A. [redacted], 3200 [redacted] Avenue, Richmond, Virginia who would be most happy, I am sure, to write you concerning the Richmond Auxiliary Group. They too have literature. Also, you might write to Secretary, 1601 Avenue [redacted], Lubbock, Texas.

There was a state-wide conference held at Mitchell, South Dakota November 19th and 20th, 1949 and a mimeographed report was made of this. The Sunday A. M. meeting was called "Non-Alcoholic Wives Meeting". Perhaps a copy of this would prove helpful. These copies can be obtained at a price of $.25 each by writing Clare [redacted], Box [redacted], Mitchell, South Dakota. Clare is the Treasurer of the local Alano Society.

I read with interest the pamphlet you enclosed and feel that the Statement of Aims and Purposes of your Family Club is a very fine one. Great interest seems to be taken in these Groups all over the United States. Enclosed with my letter, you will find our latest list of these Associate Groups. Perhaps this will prove helpful to you.

Best wishes to you and all in the San Francisco Family Club.

Cordially yours,

Virginia [redacted]
Corresponding Secretary

VT/drd
Enclosures

Family Groups first came to light when the secretary of one such group corresponded with the AA Alcoholic Foundation. Frequently, they forwarded a group donation. The first Family Group is generally thought to have formed in Long Beach, California. It was closely followed by others in Cleveland, Ohio, Chicago, Illinois, Denver, Colorado, San Pedro, California, Kansas City, Kansas, Amarillo, Texas and Toronto, Ontario. There are others with a similar claim to fame, but whose beginnings have not been so carefully recorded. The San Diego, California group was sharing its fifth anniversary celebration in the *Grapevine* as early as 1951.

Grapevine

Amarillo, Texas
November 18 –

Alcoholic Anonymous
New York, N.Y. –

NOV 24 1947

Gentlemen –

Will you please send what information reprints of talks, literature and most effective procedure of conducting Ladies auxiliary, which you have available for that purpose, to a.a. Club House, 2024 Washington, Amarillo, Texas. Address it to Ladies auxiliary there – Please send statement for this information and literature along together and remittance will be promptly made to you –

Very truly,
Mrs. Harvey E. [redacted],
President - Ladies Auxiliary of a.a.

Washington
Duxbury, Mass.,
Jan. 11, 1950.

Miss Marion M[redacted]
National Foundation Alcoholics Inc.
General Headquarters
415 Lexington Ave.
New York 17, N.Y.

Dear Miss Mallet:

I am seeking information on the "Non-Alcoholics Anonymous" Movement, which I understand is now about a year old. Is there any literature on this movement, and could you tell me something about the beginning and development? I am especially interested in where and how it began and the location of community chapters. Mrs. Elizabeth D. W[redacted] of the Boston Committee on Education for Alcoholism suggested I write you.

I should greatly appreciate any information you can give me.

Sincerely yours,
John H. [redacted]
John H. C[redacted]

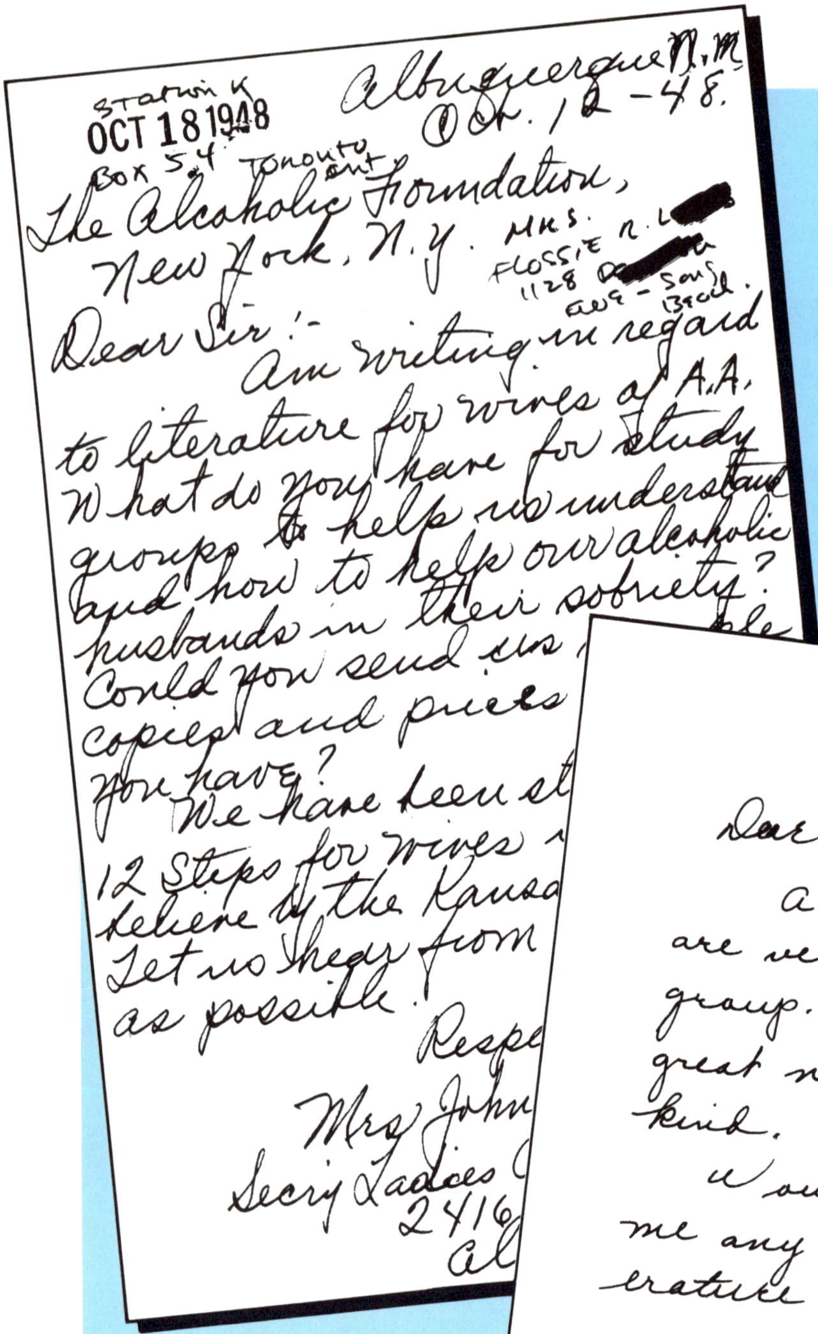

STATION K
OCT 18 1948
BOX 54 TORONTO ONT

Albuquerque N.M.
Oct. 12-48.

The Alcoholic Foundation,
New York, N.Y.

MRS. FLOSSIE R. L[redacted]
1128 D[redacted]
AVE - SONS BROCK.

Dear Sir:-
Am writing in regard to literature for wives of A.A.
What do you have for study groups to help us understand and how to help our alcoholic husbands in their sobriety?
Could you send us ...ble
copies and prices
you have?
We have been st
12 Steps for wives
believe of the Kansa
Let us hear from
as possible.

Respe

Mrs John
Secy Ladies
2416
Al

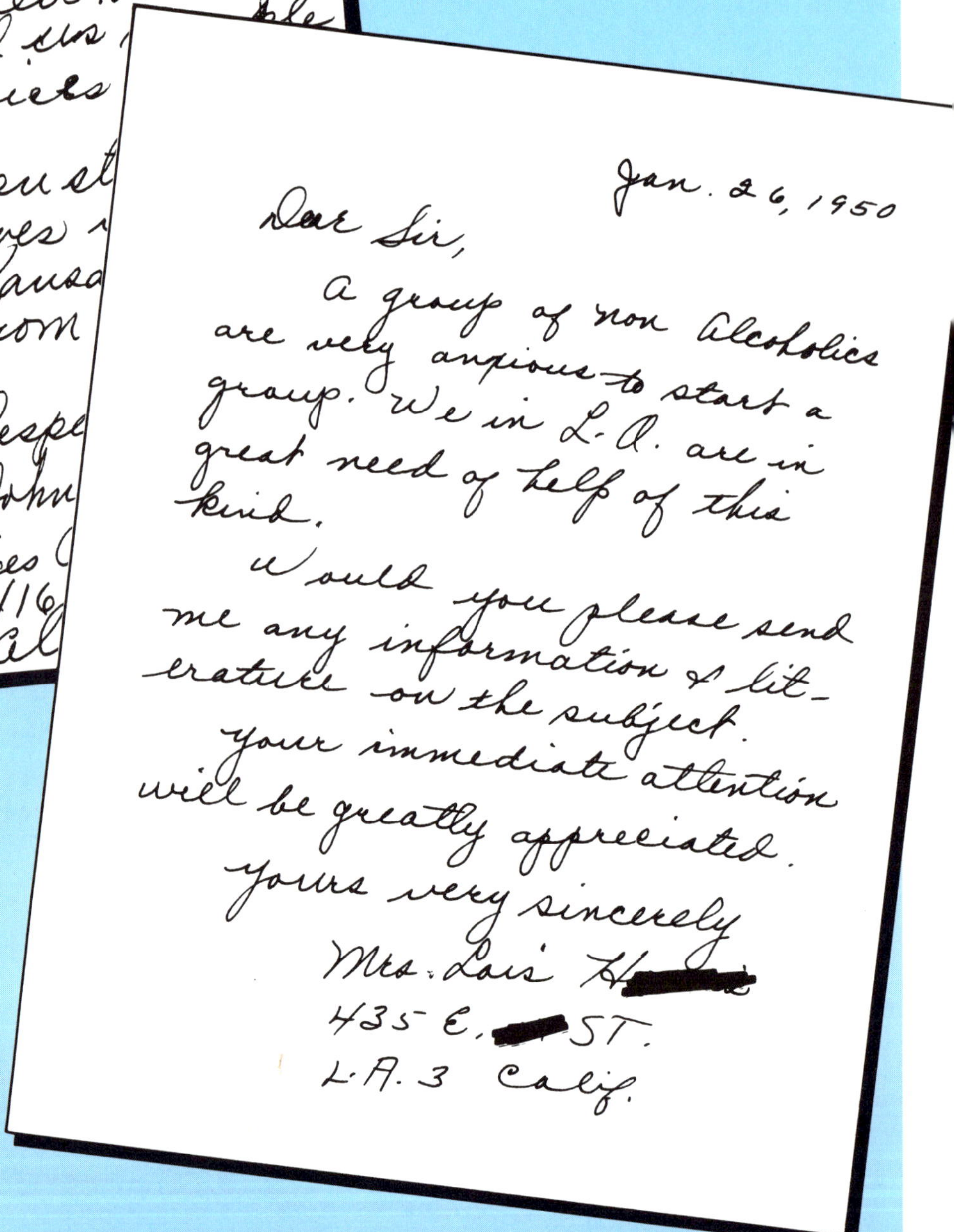

Jan. 26, 1950

Dear Sir,

A group of non Alcoholics are very anxious to start a group. We in L.A. are in great need of help of this kind.

Would you please send me any information & literature on the subject.

Your immediate attention will be greatly appreciated.

Yours very sincerely
Mrs. Lois H[redacted]
435 E. [redacted] ST.
L.A. 3 Calif.

Pierre, S. D.
Feb. 3, 1950

Alcholic Foundation
New York, N. Y.

Dear Folks:

We are organizing an A. A. Wives group here. We don't have a drinking problem, ourselves but but our belong to A. A.

We were wondering if you have any information on organization and activities of such a group. Any and all help that you can give me on this will be greatly appreciated.

Hoping to hear from you soon, I remain

Sincerly,

Mrs. S. F J[redacted]
P. O. Box [redacted]
Pierre, S. D.

San Pedro Calif
727 W 36th St
9/20/45

Alcoholic Foundation Inc.

Enclosed you will find a M.O. for ten dollars ($10.00) a voluntary contribution from the San Pedro Group of Non Alcoholics

We are sincerely and eagerly trying to do our part in the work carried on by A.A. and hope to make our contribution larger soon.

Sincerely

Mrs Helen E P[redacted]
Treasure of Non Alcoholics.
727 W. [redacted] St
San Pedro
Calif.

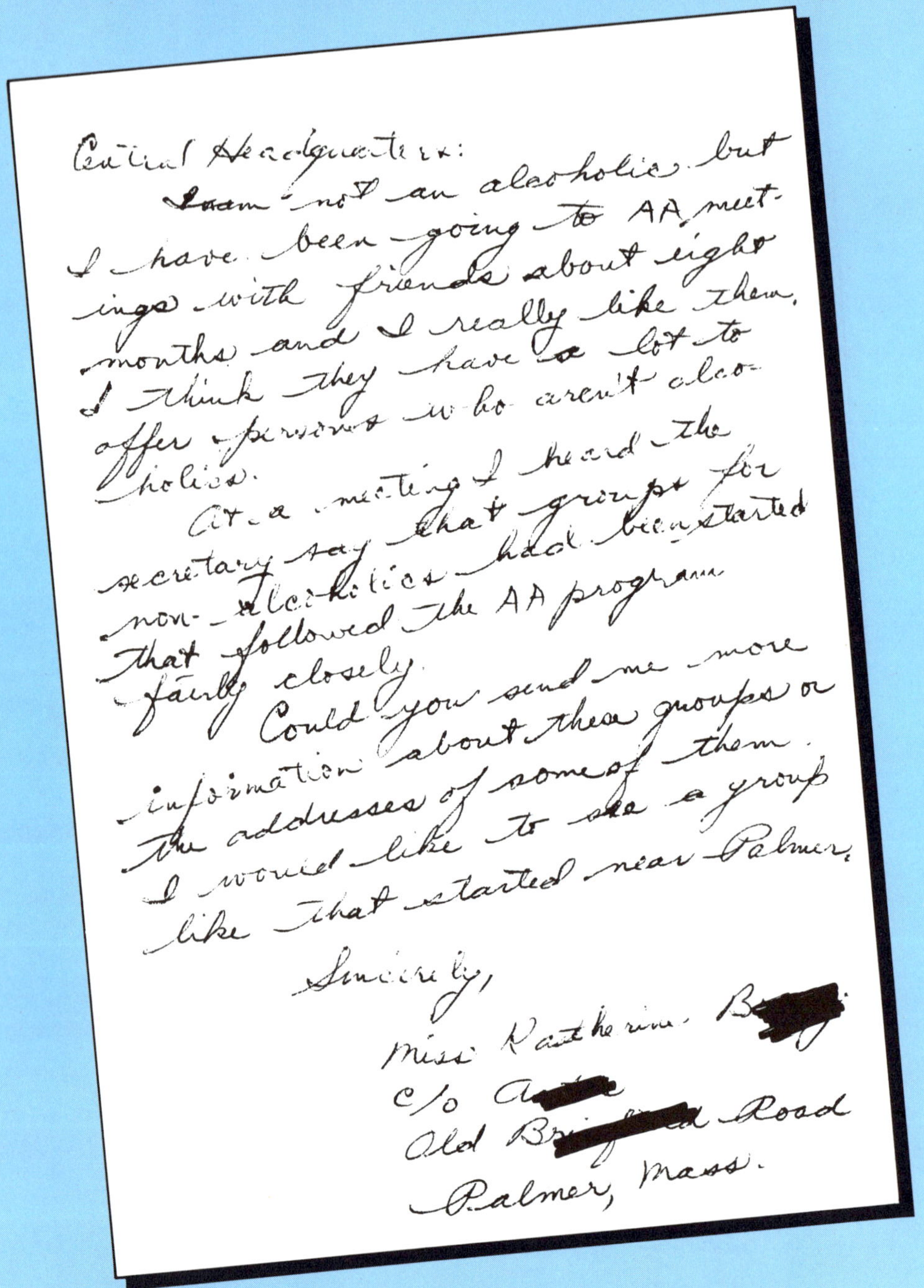

Central Headquarters:

I am not an alcoholic but I have been going to AA meetings with friends about eight months and I really like them. I think they have a lot to offer persons who aren't alcoholics.

At a meeting I heard the secretary say that groups for non-alcoholics had been started that followed the AA program fairly closely.

Could you send me more information about these groups or the addresses of some of them. I would like to see a group like that started near Palmer.

Sincerely,

Miss Katherine B[redacted]
c/o A[redacted]
Old Br[redacted] Road
Palmer, Mass.

Although AA welcomed the development of Family Groups, their inclusion did pose certain problems, since Bill had never intended that the AA program be extended to non-alcoholics. A reply to a Family Group member in Torrance, California in 1950 shows the direction in which AA was moving.

"We want to thank you for your recent letter and the cooperation indicated by the enclosed contribution of $5 to us. We are returning this to you, since some months back, the Trustees of The Alcoholic Foundation passed the resolution that money be accepted from AA groups only."

At the same time, AA continued to encourage participation by wives and other family members through separate articles in the *AA Grapevine.*

ENCOURAGEMENT
for New Members' Wives in NAA

I AM the wife of an ex-drunk and I mean ex, thank goodness, for he has been a member of Alcoholics Anonymous for the past four years. Before this I had many years of worry and unpleasantness caused by his drinking.

Today I have found *my* place also in the Alcoholics Anonymous organization by joining the NAA Group, and I am happy to tell how much it has helped me.

After my husband joined AA I was glad to go to meetings with him, and help in any way I could, but I soon learned that this was his program. I read the Twelve Suggested Steps and tried to practice some of the principles and such sayings as "easy does it," "first things first," as well as the prayer which starts "*God grant me the serenity...*" I did get much out of all the meetings, but felt that my husband was getting something more from the program which I needed too, which was fellowship and understanding. This caused me to feel a little left out until I joined the NAA Group, and here I found not only fellowship, but the privilege of asking questions as to how best I could help my husband and myself straighten out some of our problems. I discovered that these women and men had some of the same difficulties to overcome as I, and so I was able to profit from the way they had solved their problems.

I learned to be more unselfish by trying to help others, which gave me a feeling of being a part of the program pattern.

We also have our Twelve Steps to live by.

In the group we make many friends, to whom we feel close enough to call on when things are not going too smoothly. But the most important function of NAA is to encourage the wives of *new* AA members. Often they come in confused and desperate, not knowing what it is all about, and never sure whether their husbands are really sincere. They want desperately to understand; but they haven't got used to this new life yet, and it seems impossible that it can be true – they think, in fact, that it must be too good to be true.

Once they have been made to see more clearly how they can help at home they begin to have a glimmer of hope – hope that perhaps they *can* be a real help through understanding and patience.

Above all we must take an active part if we want to grow with our husbands, and thereby gain more understanding and peace of mind.

If you have a NAA Group, attend the meetings as often as possible.

— *Mrs. C.J., Miami, Florida*

However, as Family Groups began to grow at a rate that was astonishing, it seemed that something special was happening. And what these Family Group members— including wives of still drinking alcoholics—had learned together, they were willing to share. So began a movement within the family groups themselves similar to the Twelfth-Step principle of AA.

Chapter Three
Family Groups: Developing A Network

When Lois and Anne B. began working together at Stepping Stones (Lois and Bill's home in Bedford Hills, New York) to answer Family Group inquiries first sent to the Alcoholic Foundation, the step began a process of separation from AA. The result was the formation of Al-Anon with Lois and Anne B. as co-founders. Bill was made aware of the extent to which the Family Group movement was growing when traveling from AA group to AA group. He suggested to Lois that she take over the leadership of this offshoot of AA. Lois immediately asked Anne B., her friend and neighbor and founder of Westchester's first Family Group, to help her. Anne agreed. One year later Anne was to become a leader among the first group of dedicated volunteers at the Al-Anon Clearing House, later known as Al-Anon Family Group Headquarters and the Al-Anon Family Group World Service Office (WSO).

Anne B. was born in Brooklyn and was by her own admission a very sickly child. She said she had every known childhood disease all in one year, including diphtheria. Her sister died of heart disease when she was twelve years old, leaving Anne an only child. When Anne was eight, she contracted St. Vitus' Dance, a nervous disorder, and it was the family doctor who suggested a move to the country for the sake of Anne's health. She moved with her family to Chappaqua, New York. Many years later she was to become a friend to Lois and Bill.

Anne refers to the fact that she had a difficult time being close to her mother. Perhaps for this reason, she married young. Anne met Devoe B. at Baptist Sunday School when she was 17, and married him two years later. Anne was proud of the fact that Devoe was a self-employed businessman, and the youngest man to secure a bank loan to get himself started. Devoe owned his own garage and sold and serviced high-priced foreign cars until the outbreak of World War II.

According to Anne, Devoe did not try alcohol until he was 30 years old. For no particular reason, one night Devoe stopped at the local bar to have a drink after he locked up the garage and before he started for home. He never did get home as he intended, Anne said. During the time of his four trips to Towns Hospital, and the ten years in AA before Devoe found sobriety, Anne turned constantly to Lois as the wife of another alcoholic. Lois, always a fine example of the Al-Anon program in action, said that Anne helped her rather than the other way around. There were many times when four AA couples, including Anne and Devoe, and Lois and Bill spent social Saturday evenings together.

When the Clearing House was established, Anne became chairman of the Prison Groups Committee, forerunner of the Institutions Committee. Although Anne wrote to prisoners as early as 1955,

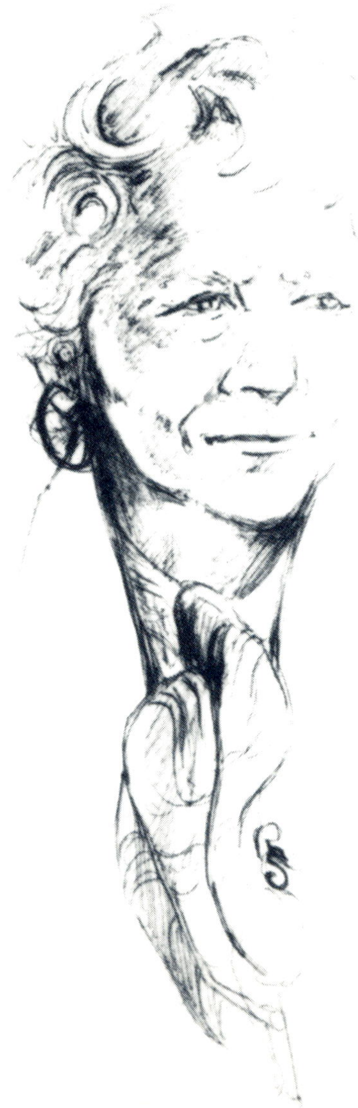

she did not assume the Committee chairmanship until 1958. In describing Anne and her work with the Prison Groups Committee, the July, 1984 issue of *Al-Anon In Institutions* says:

"This Committee was contacted by AA Groups in prisons and was sent lists of men who wanted their families to receive information about Al-Anon. Anne contacted families in this way and also through wardens. She was in direct contact with prison wardens when she received a letter from an inmate seeking help. At that time she directed them to AA for information on alcoholism and she would send along the name of a local Al-Anon group for family members. When she wrote to a prisoner and his family, she always wrote to the warden telling him about Al-Anon.

"In 1957, Anne wrote to an inmate in Walla Walla, Washington, 'When I receive a letter like yours, it makes me realize more and more how important the work I am trying to do with the families really is. It inspires me to keep on with it.'

"In 1960, a prisoner from Rahway, New Jersey wrote, 'Mrs. B., I would like to hear from you; your letters and the letters I receive from AA members have made a very deep impression on me. It made my time go a lot faster thinking of the wonderful friends I have at a time like this Mrs. B., may the good Lord bless you for your kind heart and thought in bringing happiness to an alcoholic.'

"A quote from a letter Anne wrote in 1965, to a member in California, extending hope and confidence: 'Sometimes it's wise not to become resentful and go about doing the things that you think are useful and important. In time they will see the results and become understanding. One of the hardest lessons we have to learn is to be patient. So keep on with your project and you will be given rewards for your efforts.'

"Because of the Al-Anon contact, officials from Wisconsin and Indiana prisons wrote that 90% of the inmates whose families were contacted by Al-Anon stayed sober. They felt this was due to the understanding and help the family gained from contact with Al-Anon and they expressed their gratitude."

The reasons Anne chose to share Al-Anon with alcoholic inmates is one key to her own personality. She had for a long time found herself a prisoner to her own personal fears and inadequacies, developed early in childhood. The Twelve Steps were able to show her a way out. In a talk given at the Clearing House, Anne said:

"I had lived in ignorance of the universal law of love, but here were the Twelve Steps of AA, the tools by which to work. They are the tools of wisdom to open the door of the prison, so that I can walk out into the light. They give me the faith, tolerance and courage to go on, and not turn back.

"AA has helped me understand alcoholism and see the rainbow that stands for hope. I am grateful for the ability to pass on the message of hope to anyone who needs a helping hand."

Anne's extraordinary gift of service to Al-Anon came from someone who always described herself as an introvert and had difficulty speaking in public. Her talks are typed out in full, usually in capitalized letters. She looked to others for approval as a public figure, especially to Lois and Bill. She once had to talk in front of Bill, and when at the end of the meeting he told Anne that she had conducted herself like a pro, she fairly burst with pride.

Anne and Lois also traveled together to other meetings—something Anne describes as quite an adventure in those early days.

"We would go all over, no matter what the weather was. One time Lois and I were supposed to go to a New Jersey meeting and stay overnight. I left all the details to Lois, even the driving. When we finally got there, they looked at us with very startled faces because we were a day too early. We were just as startled as they were.... I spoke once in Louisville, Kentucky for fifteen minutes. Then I took a trip to Burlington, Vermont. They only let me talk for five minutes. I couldn't believe they invited me to come all the way up there just for five minutes. Sometimes several groups got together like a mini-conference. After I gave my little talk, the members would ask questions."

When Devoe died suddenly after ten sober years in AA, Anne married Howard,

A WHILE BACK I MADE MY DEBUT AS A LEADER AT ONE OF THESE MEETINGS AND MOST OF MY ATTENTION WAS DIVERTED TO A THUMPING HEART AND SHAKING KNEES, SO THIS TIME I BROUGHT NOTES.

THROUGH MY HUSBAND I CAME TO KNOW AA WHICH I NEEDED AND STILL DO. I WAS AN INTROVERT TO A GREAT DEGREE, FULL OF FEARS, AND COMPLEXES. I CLEARLY REMEMBER THESE FEARS WHEN I WAS THE YOUNG AGE OF 6, AND HOW LIFE BECAME COMPLICATED BY THE NERVOUS DICEASE, ST. VITUS DANCE.

THERE ALWAYS SEEMED TO BE A BARRIER B BETWEEN ME AND THE OUTSIDE WORLD. I LIVED SO FAR OUT IN THE COUNTRY THAT MY FRIENDS WERE FEW. I WALKED THREE MILES, ONE WAY, TO SCHOOL AND BECAUSE OF THE NEED FOR FRIENDSHIPS I WALKED THE SAME DISTANCE ON SUNDAY TO CHURCH.

UNTIL I MET MY HUSBAND, I ATTENDED SIX DIFFERENT DENOMINATIONS OF RELIGION, AND A FEW SINCE. I ALWAYS SEEMED TO BE SEEKING SOMETHING TO GIVE ME INNER PEACE.

MY HUSBAND BECAME ALCOHOLIC 12 YEARS

2

AFTER WE WERE MARRIED. I HAD NEVER HEARD OF THE WORD ALCOHOLIC AND I NEVER KNEW ANYONE THAT DRANK TO EXCESS. (HE NEVER TOUCHED LIQUOR AND HAD NO TOLERANCE FOR PEOPLE THAT DID).

I WAS ONE OF THE FORTUNATE ONES TO HAVE HAD FINANCIAL SECURITY, BUT MY MENTAL AND EMOTIONAL CONDITION WAS POVERTY STRICKEN. MY COMPASSION AND ANGER WERE OF THE SAME DEPTH SO THAT I WOULD GO FROM ONE EMOTIONAL EXTREME TO THE OTHER.

WHEN AA WAS PRESENTED TO US, I KNEW THAT IT WAS THE ANSWER TO WHAT I HAD BEEN SEEKING. I HAD LIVED IN IGNORANCE OF THE UNIVERSAL LAW OF LOVE, SO HERE WERE THE 12 STEPS * THE TOOLS BY WHICH TO WORK WITH. THEY ARE THE TOOLS OF WISDOM TO OPEN THE DOOR OF THE PRISON,- SO THAT I CAN WALK OUT INTO THE LIGHT. THEY HELPED ME TO UNDERSTAND ALCOHOLISM, - THEY GAVE ME FAITH, TOLERANCE AND COURAGE TO GO ON AND NOT TURN BACK. THIS PROGRAM GAVE ME A SPIRITUAL ASPECT THAT I NEVER EXPERIENCED BEFORE . I USED TO PRAY AND THINGS ALWAYS REVERSED

3

THEMSELVES, SO I STOPPED PRAYING. NOW WHEN I PRAY I GIVE THANKS FOR ALL I HAVE, ESPECIALLY THE LITTLE THINGS. AT THE PEAK OF THE ALCOHLIC CONFUSION, I BECAME AGNOSTIC, BUT I KNOW NOW THAT IT WAS ONLY A VENEER, BECAUSE I COULDN'T HAVE RETURNED TO THAT GREATER POWER SO READILY IF THE LACK OF FAITH HAD BEEN DEEPLY ROOTED.

BY TRIAL ANDERROR I DISCOVERED THAT I WASN'T USING THESE TOOLS TO THE BEST OF MY ABILITY. I WORKEDON THE 4 and 5 STEPS AND THEY SHOWED ME THE ROAD TO TRUTH AND HUMILITY.

ABOUT SIX MONTHS AGO I FOUND MYSELF IN A REBELLIOUS TURMOIL, WHICH IS A FORM OF DISCORD AND DISHARMONY, AND A FEAR. I RECOGNIZED THIS STATE OF AFFAIRS AND YET I COULDN'T DISPEL IT. ONE OF THE THINGS THAT HELPED TO MAGNIFY IT WAS THE GIVING UP OF CIGARETTES. THREE MONTHS LATER I BECAME AWARE OF THE CAUSE OF THIS REBELLION, BUT I WAS LOATHE TO GIVE IT UP. WHEN I FINALLY DID SURRENDER THIS CONDITION TO THE GREATER POWER

4

I FOUND A DEEPER INNER PEACE. IT SEEMS THAT EACH LESSON EXPERIENCED BRINGS FORTH A DEEPER UNDERSTANDING AND A TRUER FORM OF TRANQUILITY.

I AM GRATEFUL TO GOD ~~FOR~~ and to ~~GIVING US~~ BILL AND DR. BOB ~~TO SHOW~~ for giving ME THIS WONDERFUL WAY OF LIFE, AND I AM GRATEFUL TO LOIS AND ANNE S.- AND MANY OTHERS FOR GIVING ME THE COURAGE, HOPE AND FAITH TO KEEP GOING ON, AND I AM GRATEFUL FOR THE ABILITY TO PASS ON THE MESSAGE TO ONE WHO NEEDS UNDERSTANDING AND A HELPING HAND..

I WANT TO CLOSE WITH THIS VERY SHORT POEM THAT IS IN KEEPING WITH 12 step work

ONE SPOKE A KINDLY WORD TO DAY
WHEN MY NEED WAS SORE.
HE HAD NO WAY OF KNOWING QUITE
THE HEAVY WEIGHT I BORE:
BUT AT HIS UNDERSTANDING WORD
A CANDLE'S LIFTED SPARK
FLARED WARM AND GOLDENLY TO LIGHT
MY WAY ACROSS THE DARK.

DEAR GOD, SO VITAL WAS THAT WORD
I, TOO, WOULD SEEK THEM OUT
WHO WANDER LONELY THROUGH A NIGHT
OF FEAR AND GRIEF AND DOUBT.

SPEAK THROUGH ME, LORD, THAT I MAY SAY
THE WORD TO FREE AND BLESS:
A GENTLE WORD , A WORD TO LIGHT
THE ROAD TO HAPPINESS.

April 26, 1952. 1.

~~Our~~ Clearing House is now 1 yr. old. When you were here last year all we had was a PO Box. We have made rapid progress. After the Conf. a letter was sent to ~~the~~ 87 names listed at the A.A. F. These names were not al groups; many were individuals asking what the could do to help themselves, that is, find s one relief from the terrors of alocism. The Grapv published this letter ~~and~~ in the June issue. ~~Replies~~ came in fast and out of ~~the~~ 87 names that we wrote to, replied. I say ~~we, because~~ when Loise volunteered to be chairman, and who is better suited to be our leader, she asked me to help her. We worked here two days a week answering letters of inquiries from wives of AAs who were interested in starting a group, also an occassional husband of a lady AA; frequently an AA wrote in for literature about starting or sponsering a F.G. But the most stirring

2.

and heart rending letters are from the desparate wife of an alco who is not yet in AA.

Just recently we had one from a wice down south who has four children and contempl suicide. A number of wives have reported that through the F.G.s they found much serenity altho their husbands had not yet stopped drinking. In many cases the alco came into AA because his wife attended F.G. meetings. He noticed a change in her so he thot he would try it.

By Jan. 1952 the interest in F.G.s had grown enough to consider finding an office in NY where volunteers could be trained and take part in this work, until we could afford a paid part-time worker. The 24th St. Club offered their upstairs rooms and equip. Vol. from the 7 Met. area groups meet every We. Now we have 250 reg. F.G.s and there are probably many that have not reg. with us yet. Foreign groups.

3.

On Mar. 1 1952, we sent a bulletin to these 250 groups telling of our progress and future plans. As in AA we proposed no fees or dues but there are expenses to be met wo we aked these groups if they were willing to volunteer semi-annually one dollar a member. The response has been tremendous, greater than we anticipated.
~~Mostxofxthese POsxandxindivxxthatxwrite~~

The voluntary donations that have come in prior to this helped to pay for the literature we had printed and the office supplies.

Bill's cousin. She was to say afterward that she felt she had remarried too quickly. Anne moved to Connecticut where she went to AA meetings with her second husband, at his insistence. After a few years he and Anne parted company and Anne began to travel all over the United States. She spent six years in Florida where she took part in the foundation of Al-Anon in that state, and and then moved to Illinois and California. Although she no longer attended meetings, Anne always said that she practiced the Al-Anon principles in her life.

Anne and Lois met for the last time in Palm Springs, California in 1983. They reminisced about old times. Anne expressed her philosophy of life very simply then. She said, "I don't hold any grudges. I love people, good or bad." Anne died in 1984 as she had lived, quietly and peacefully, at the grand age of 84. Her tremendous Al-Anon legacy lives on.

World Service Office Highlights

INSIDE Al-Anon

April/May 1984
Vol. 6 No. 3

Anne B., Co-Founder of Al-Anon Passes Away in California

Anne B.'s great contribution to Al-Anon can never be forgotten, but it was her lovely personality that affected me most, as it did others. Without her help in the beginning, Al-Anon could not have grown so fast and so well.

As we think of Anne with love and gratitude now and in the days to come, let us renew our commitment to Al-Anon service in her honor.

Lois W.

Anne B., Al-Anon's co-founder, died as she had lived, quietly and peacefully. This shy, gentle woman with a soft twinkling laugh, who had chosen in later years to remain in the background, was instrumental in beginning a movement with worldwide repercussions.

But life had not always been so peaceful for Anne. After years of the turbulence of active alcoholism, a doctor who was a friend of the family suggested that there was "something new," that she and her husband, Devoe, might try before divorce. This "something" was AA. It was Thanksgiving, 1942. Countless numbers of families and friends of alcoholics now give thanks for this historic event, for it was shortly after that she met Lois and Bill. This led to a lifetime friendship and the development of the Al-Anon fellowship.

By 1949 there were several groups within the Westchester, New York area where Lois and Anne lived. They were called "AA Auxiliaries" and consisted mainly of wives of AA members. At this time, Anne began a group in her Chappaqua home where the members tried to achieve serenity by working the Twelve Steps which were sobering up their husbands.

But it wasn't until 1951 that Lois and Anne set up the Clearing House that was to unify these "AA Auxiliaries" which had sprung up throughout the country, giving birth to a new fellowship, later called the Al-Anon Family Groups.

Lois and Anne met for the last time in Palm Springs, California in June, 1983. In a taped interview Anne confirmed, "If I didn't have the peace of Al-Anon, I wouldn't be the person that I am now."

Anne passed away in her sleep on Friday, February 24th, 1984 at the age of 84 years in her Santa Paula home. Her remains will be flown to Chappaqua, New York to be placed beside her husband. Expressions of condolences sent to the WSO will be forwarded to her family.

At a time when Anne was active in Westchester's first Al-Anon group in Chappaqua, New York, Lois was traveling with Bill throughout the United States and Canada. These two self-styled motorcycle hobos had always found companionship in travel. Now, both of them were needed as leaders for two growing movements in search of identity.

By the late 1940's, AA regional conferences were springing up, bringing together the membership across a widening area. Wherever Lois and Bill traveled, they brought with them a spirit of unity, optimism, and a unique caring for each and every AA member and his family.

PROGRAM
OF
REGIONAL CONFERENCE

ROYAL YORK HOTEL • TORONTO • CANADA

March 3rd and 4th 1951

SATURDAY, MARCH 3rd

10.45 to 12.15—(Ballroom, Convention Floor)

"ANONYMITY"

Chairman—Gordon H., Toronto

(a) Why anonymity is important to the new member — John F., Oshawa, Ont.
(b) The responsibility of individual members regarding the anonymity of fellow members - - - - - William H., Buffalo, N.Y.
(c) Why anonymity is essential in our relations with the public. — Warren S., Ottawa, Ont.
(d) Spiritual significance of anonymity and the benefits derived therefrom. - - - - - - - - - Dr. Ed., Wellsville, N.Y.

10.45 to 12.15—(Concert Hall, Convention Floor)

"SPONSORSHIP"

Chairman—Carl J., Toronto

(a) Sponsorship defined—its purpose. - John C., Syracuse, N.Y.
(b) Importance of first contact with prospect. - Art R. Rochester, N.Y.
(c) Responsibility of sponsor to new member. Stan C., Hamilton, Ont.
(d) Benefits of sponsorship. - - - - - - Jim G., Sudbury, Ont.

1.15 to 3.30—(Concert Hall, Convention Floor)

GENERAL SERVICE CONFERENCE (Closed)

Host-Chairman—Morry G., Toronto

Speaker—Bill W.

1.30 to 3.00—(Ballroom, Convention Floor)

"RIGHT RELATIONSHIPS" (A.A. Wives)

Chairman—Lois W.

(a) Attitudes. - - - - - - - - - - Edith D., Toronto, Ont.
(b) Fellowship. - - - - - - - - Ruth J., Lowville, N.Y.
(c) Gratitude - - - - - - - Dorothy M., Toronto, Ont.
(d) Serenity - - - - - - - - Callista P., Buffalo, N.Y.

3.45 to 5.00—(Ballroom, Convention Floor)

"TRADITION"

Chairman—Bob B., Toronto

(a) Purpose of A.A. Traditions—Individual's Responsibility and Benefits. — Ed. F., Buffalo, N.Y.
(b) Group Conscience - - - - - - Earl M., Toronto, Ont.
(c) Our public relations policy - - - Bus. M., Toronto, Ont.
(d) Principles above personalities - - - Bud P., Rochester, N.Y.

3.45 to 5.00—(Tudor Room, Mezzanine Floor)

"THE WOMAN ALCOHOLIC"

Chairman—Margaret M., Toronto

(a) To what extent the judgment of society affects her acceptance of A.A. - - - - - - - - - - - - Margaret W., Buffalo, N.Y.
(b) The members' presentation of A.A. to the new woman. — Wyn D., Hamilton, Ont.
(c) The importance of anonymity to the woman at business. — Isabel B., Toronto, Ont.
(d) What A.A. offers the woman alcoholic - - Elva R., Buffalo, N.Y.

8.30 to 10.00—(Banquet Hall, Convention Floor)

OPEN MEETING

Speaker—Hamilton W., Buffalo, N.Y.

SUNDAY, MARCH 4th

10.30 to 12.00—(Ballroom, Convention Floor)

"SPIRITUAL SIDE"

Chairman—Gordon S., Toronto

(a) Definition of the term "Spiritual" in A.A. - Donald A., Erie, Pa.
(b) Presentation to the new member - Edward T., Syracuse, N.Y.
(c) Importance of recognition of a Higher Power in relation to our recovery - - - - - - - - - Bill B., Toronto, Ont.
(d) The spiritual principles embodied in the twelve steps as a guide to better living - - - - - - - - - Jack C., Windsor, Ont.

10.30 to 12.00—(Tudor Room, Mezzanine Floor)

"SPIRITUAL SIDE"

Chairman—Bill T., Toronto

(a) Definition of the term "Spiritual" in A.A. Ed. P., Toronto, Ont.
(b) Presentation to the new member - - Jim M., Custer City, Pa.
(c) Importance of recognition of a Higher Power in relation to our recovery - - - - - - - - Russell B., Jamestown, N.Y.
(d) The spiritual principles embodied in the twelve steps as a guide to better living - - - - - - Fred H., London, Ont.

BANQUET

12.30 p.m.—(Imperial Room, Main Floor)
1.00 p.m.—(Banquet Hall, Convention Floor)

Chairman—Morry G., Toronto

ENTERTAINMENT
GUEST SPEAKER

• Any registrants, who are not attending the banquet but wish to hear the guest speaker, are asked to assemble in the Ballroom (Convention Floor) not later than 1.45 p.m., on Sunday, March 4th, 1951. As soon as the banquet tables have been cleared away, these members and guests will be ushered to seats in the Banquet Hall.

ALCOHOLICS ANONYMOUS

Convention Address: P. O. Box 284, Raleigh, North Caro

1952 STATE CONVENTION BULLETIN #3
March 12, 1952

FIRST GENERAL SESSION
Friday evening, 7:45
Hugh Morson High School, Auditorium

COFFEE HOUR
Friday evening, 10:00
Hotel Sir Walter, Virginia Dare Ballroom
Admission by card

GROUP SECRETARIES' MEETING
Saturday morning, 9:30
Hotel Sir Walter, Raleigh Room

WOMEN'S AUXILIARY MEETING
Saturday morning, 9:30
Hotel Sir Walter, Cafe Garden

INFORMATION PLEASE
Saturday morning, 11:15
Hotel Sir Walter, Virginia Dare Ballroom

SECOND GENERAL SESSION
Saturday afternoon, 2:30
Hugh Morson High School, Auditorium

THIRD GENERAL SESSION
Saturday evening, 7:45
Hugh Morson High School, Auditorium

COFFEE HOUR
Saturday evening, 10:00
Hotel Sir Walter, Virginia Dare Ballroom
Admission by card

GROUP DELEGATES' MEETING
Sunday morning, 9:30
Hotel Sir Walter, Raleigh Room

CHURCH
Sunday morning, 11:00
Go to the church of your choice

FOURTH GENERAL SESSION
Sunday afternoon, 2:30
Hotel Sir Walter, Virginia Dare Ballroo

Fifth Annual North Carolina St
Raleigh: May 23, 24, and 25, 1952

ALCOHOLICS ANONYMOUS

Convention Address: P. O. Box 284, Raleigh, North Carolina

March 10, 1952

Send literature

Mrs. Lois W[redacted]
Post Office Box 1475
Grand Central Annex
New York 17, New York

Dear Lois:

At the Fifth Annual State of North Carolina Convention of Alcoholics Anonymous to be held in Raleigh on May 23rd, 24th, and 25th, we plan to direct an important part of the program to the activities and development of family groups.

It is therefore hoped that you will accept this invitation to attend the State Convention and speak on this subject.

By highlighting this theme, it is expected to develop an increasing interest in family group activities not only among those affiliated with the AA program in North Carolina but also in the large number that will attend from both South Carolina and Virginia.

If your heavy schedule will permit and you are inclined to speak at the Convention, it will be of material assistance to us in this and adjoining states in further developing family group activities.

It is hoped that you will agree to speak at the Saturday night meeting.

Our mutual friend, Lib S[redacted] of the Foundation, will speak Friday night, May 23, and will hold a forum with the Group Secretaries the next afternoon; so she will be traveling to Raleigh for the Convention and can accompany you.

Hopefully anticipating your acceptance of this invitation to speak at the Convention, I remain

Sincerely yours,

Haslin S[redacted]
Convention Secretary

HS:vp

Fifth Annual North Carolina State Convention
Raleigh: May 23, 24, and 25, 1952

Ans-yes

March 28, 1952
615 East [redacted] Street
Bronx 54, N.Y.C.

Dear Lois,

We wrote Bill about speaking for us on our 6th Anniversary at the South Bronx Group on June 7, 1952 and he had to decline & we understand his position. We were wondering if you would consent to speak for us. We would so like to have you. Its a big event for us and we are all so grateful to you & Bill for giving us A.A. Its so badly needed here

2

in the South Bronx.

I will arrange to have you picked up anyplace you name and also to take you back to your home.

Bill is cordially invited to just be a guest if he cares to. But if he dont we all understand.

Could you let us know soon?

Sincerely
Jimmy [redacted]
615 E. [redacted] Street
Bronx 54, N.Y.C.

Melrose 5-[redacted]

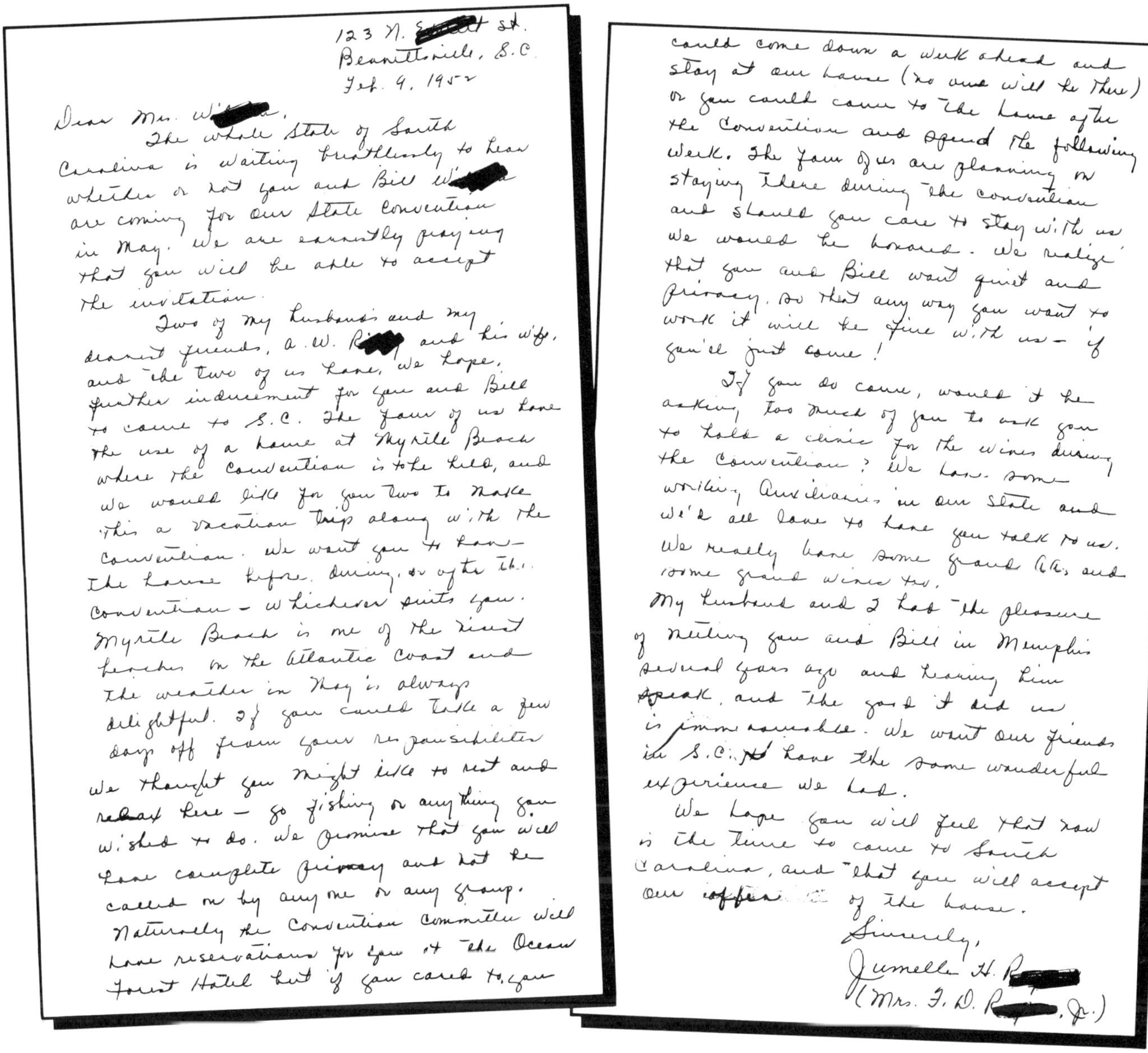
123 N. [redacted] st.
Bennettsville, S.C.
Feb. 9, 1952

Dear Mrs. W[redacted],

The whole State of South Carolina is waiting breathlessly to hear whether or not you and Bill W[redacted] are coming for our State Convention in May. We are earnestly praying that you will be able to accept the invitation.

Two of my husband's and my dearest friends, A. W. R[redacted] and his wife, and the two of us have, we hope, further inducement for you and Bill to come to S.C. The four of us have the use of a home at Myrtle Beach where the Convention is to be held, and we would like for you two to make this a vacation trip along with the Convention. We want you to have the house before, during, or after the Convention – whichever suits you. Myrtle Beach is one of the nicest beaches on the Atlantic Coast and the weather in May is always delightful. If you could take a few days off from your responsibilities we thought you might like to rest and relax here – go fishing or anything you wished to do. We promise that you will have complete privacy and not be called on by anyone or any group. Naturally the Convention Committee will have reservations for you at the Ocean Forest Hotel but if you cared to, you could come down a week ahead and stay at our house (no one will be there) or you could come to the house after the Convention and spend the following week. The four of us are planning on staying there during the convention and should you care to stay with us we would be honored. We realize that you and Bill want quiet and privacy, so that any way you want to work it will be fine with us – if you'll just come!

If you do come, would it be asking too much of you to ask you to hold a clinic for the wives during the Convention? We have some working Auxiliaries in our State and we'd all love to have you talk to us. We really have some grand AA's and some grand wives too.

My husband and I had the pleasure of meeting you and Bill in Memphis several years ago and hearing him speak, and the good it did us is immeasurable. We want our friends in S.C. to have the same wonderful experience we had.

We hope you will feel that now is the time to come to South Carolina, and that you will accept our offer of the house.

Sincerely,
Jumelle H. R[redacted]
(Mrs. J. D. R[redacted], Jr.)

Lelah J., a member of the AA Auxiliary in Brandon, Manitoba wrote in a letter dated February 16, 1948: "Our big day arrived and passed but we in Winnipeg are still in the clouds. Bill and Lois came, we saw, they conquered. There is no yardstick that can measure the tremendous good gained spiritually. Untold good came with them and they left it here, with us to feast on for days and days to come. Grettir was so overwhelmed with the grace, love and humility shown by Lois that he found no words to properly express his thoughts and properly introduce her at the banquet..."

If Bill was the AA promoter par excellence, then Lois must be the example of what a selfless alcoholic's wife could be, by putting the past behind her and living life on the same spiritual basis as her husband. Lois's willingness to share what she had found is expressed in her own words:

"On the trip Bill and I took around the country in 1943 to visit AA groups, I usually spoke briefly at the large open meetings, thanking the AA members for giving me such a wonderful program to live by. But at teas and luncheons for the families, I tried to make more personal talks, telling how important it was for me to live by the spiritual principles of AA and how I came to discover this. Recently I counted sixty-two places where I made talks during our trips around the country between 1939 and 1951. In some places where we visited, groups of the families of AA members had already been formed." A charming insight into Lois' straightforward approach to speaking comes in the form of a memorandum jotted down in her own handwriting on a piece of scrap paper.

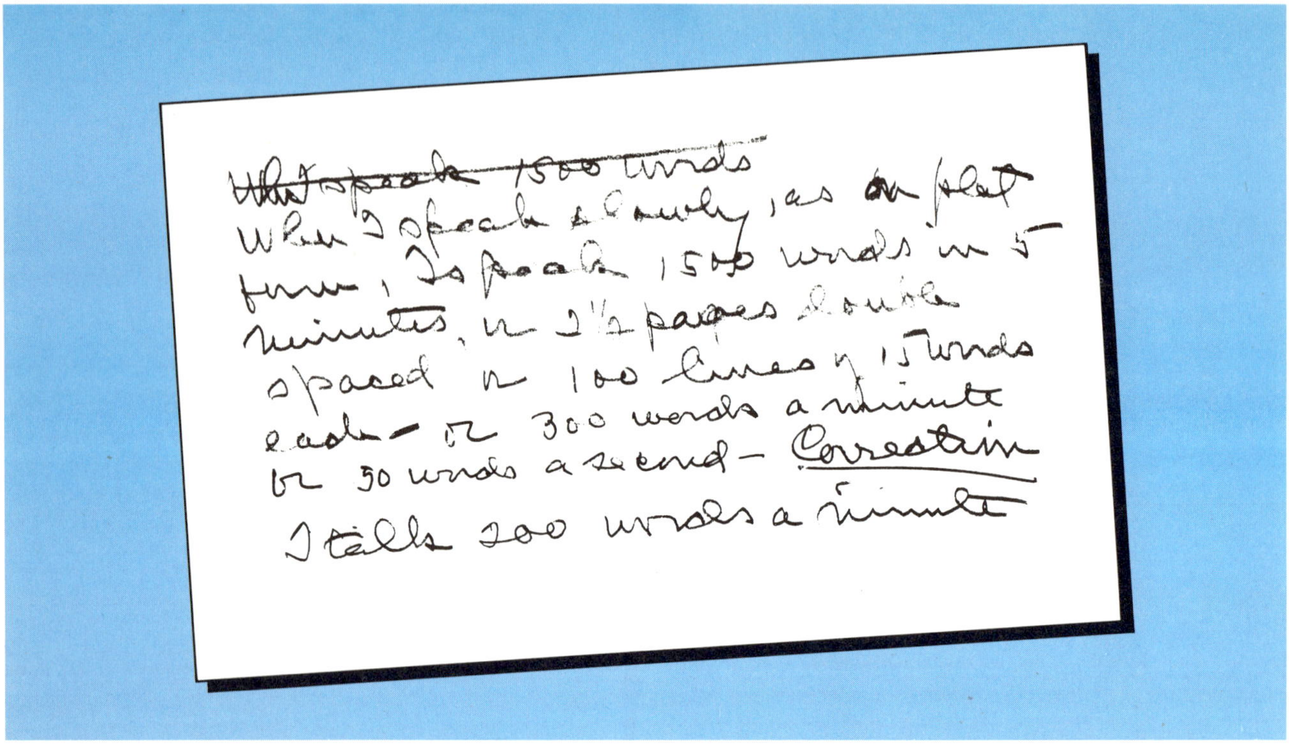
~~What speak 1500 words~~
When I speak slowly, as on plat-
form, I speak 1500 words in 5
minutes, or 2½ pages double
spaced or 100 lines of 15 words
each — or 300 words a minute
or 50 words a second — Correction
I talk 200 words a minute

This was the extent of Lois' planning. The rest of her talk came directly from the heart. In contrast to life on the road, Lois found an anchorage at last in her own home. Early in 1941, she and Bill bought Stepping Stones. Lois was ecstatic.

"How wonderful it was to have a home of our own! At that time in our lives a home was first of all a refuge from wanderings. And it gave us a chance to enjoy such interests as music, reading and gardening. All of these perfectly normal activities had been mostly denied us for a long time. It gave us particularly, an opportunity to be alone together and to plan for the future...."

For the next few years, Lois was to feel the pull between happy homemaking for herself and Bill, and accompanying her husband on his "missionary" tours across the United States to South America, South Africa and beyond. Everywhere they went, Family Groups were either forming, or growing larger.

1943 to 1951 were watershed years in the formation of Al-Anon. Suddenly, in 1951 the whole Al-Anon focus came together. It was Bill, always the visionary, who first saw the way ahead. Very simply, Lois describes how it happened:

"In 1950, Bill went by himself to the AA groups throughout the States and Canada to find out their feelings about establishing a General Service Conference for AA. He was surprised to run into so many Family Groups.

"Returning home, he told me about this budding fellowship and suggested I open a service office in New York, where these groups could register, receive helpful literature and become more unified. It would also be a place to which any distracted wife could cry out for help, and from which information could be spread to the public.

"Bill's suggestion did not appeal to me at first, because I was still excited about having a home of our own. Starting such an office would take too much time away from working in my garden and making useful things for the house. But as I began to think about the need, the idea grew more and more intriguing. At the close of the 1951 AA General Service Conference, I asked the wives of the Delegates to meet at Stepping Stones for lunch with the local Family Group members. All but two or three of the wives belonged to Family Groups in their hometowns and told about their meetings, as did our local members.

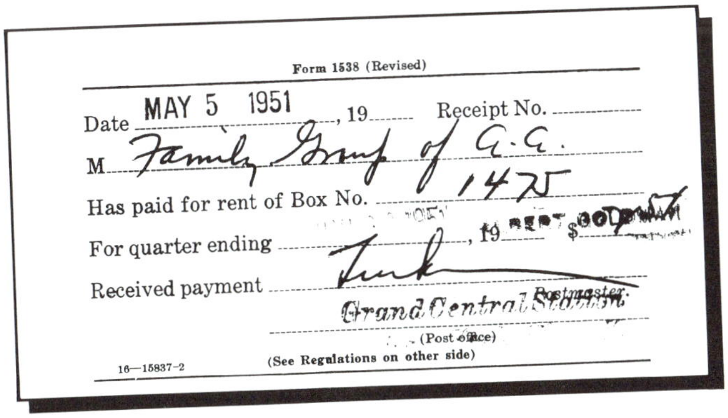

Form 1538 (Revised)

Date MAY 5 1951, 19 ____ Receipt No. ____

M Family Group of A.A.

Has paid for rent of Box No. 1475

For quarter ending ____, 19 ____ $ ____

Received payment ____ Postmaster.

Grand Central Station

(Post office)

16—15837-2 (See Regulations on other side)

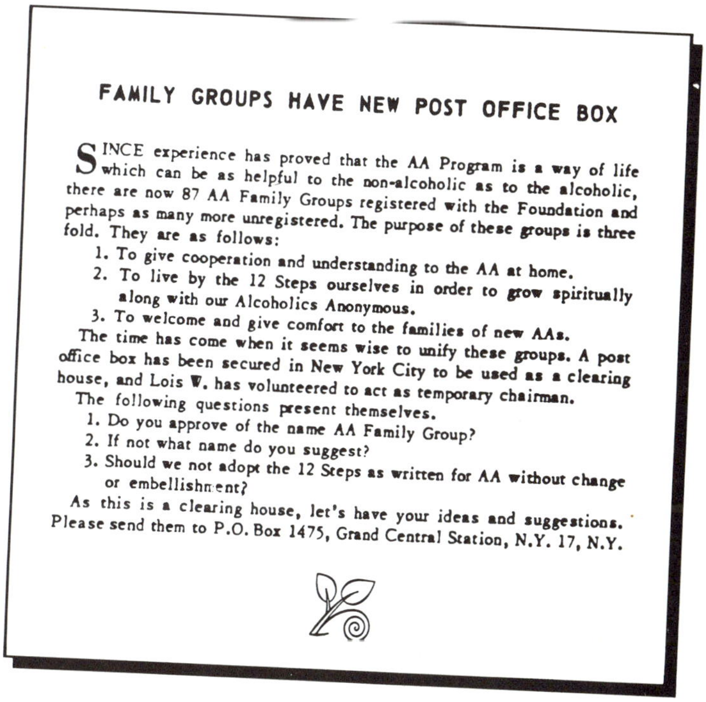

FAMILY GROUPS HAVE NEW POST OFFICE BOX

SINCE experience has proved that the AA Program is a way of life which can be as helpful to the non-alcoholic as to the alcoholic, there are now 87 AA Family Groups registered with the Foundation and perhaps as many more unregistered. The purpose of these groups is three fold. They are as follows:

1. To give cooperation and understanding to the AA at home.
2. To live by the 12 Steps ourselves in order to grow spiritually along with our Alcoholics Anonymous.
3. To welcome and give comfort to the families of new AAs.

The time has come when it seems wise to unify these groups. A post office box has been secured in New York City to be used as a clearing house, and Lois W. has volunteered to act as temporary chairman.

The following questions present themselves.

1. Do you approve of the name AA Family Group?
2. If not what name do you suggest?
3. Should we not adopt the 12 Steps as written for AA without change or embellishment?

As this is a clearing house, let's have your ideas and suggestions. Please send them to P.O. Box 1475, Grand Central Station, N.Y. 17, N.Y.

"It was then that I decided to open our own service office. This was three years after the death of Annie S."

The Alcoholic Foundation turned over to Lois and Anne B. its file of Family Group correspondence. The AA General Service Office was to continue to give the fledgling Al Anon guidance in the years to come.

During that first year, Lois and Anne worked upstairs at Stepping Stones. Lois rented a post office box, number 1475.

Having acquired a list of 87 Family Groups or individuals registered with the Alcoholic Foundation, Lois and Anne sent each a letter in May, 1951 expressing the resolve to unify these groups under one organizational umbrella. Lois was to act as temporary chairman of a committee. Anne would be its secretary, since she knew how to use a typewriter. The letter asked for approval of the use of AA's Twelve Steps, and a choice of name for this nameless organization—AA Family Groups was suggested. Finally, a response was requested to be sent to the post office box. Forty-eight groups responded. The movement was beginning to speak with a common voice.

Conscientiously, Lois and Anne recorded information received from these first 48 groups on three-by-five cards. An overwhelming proportion responded favorably to adopting the Twelve Steps of AA.

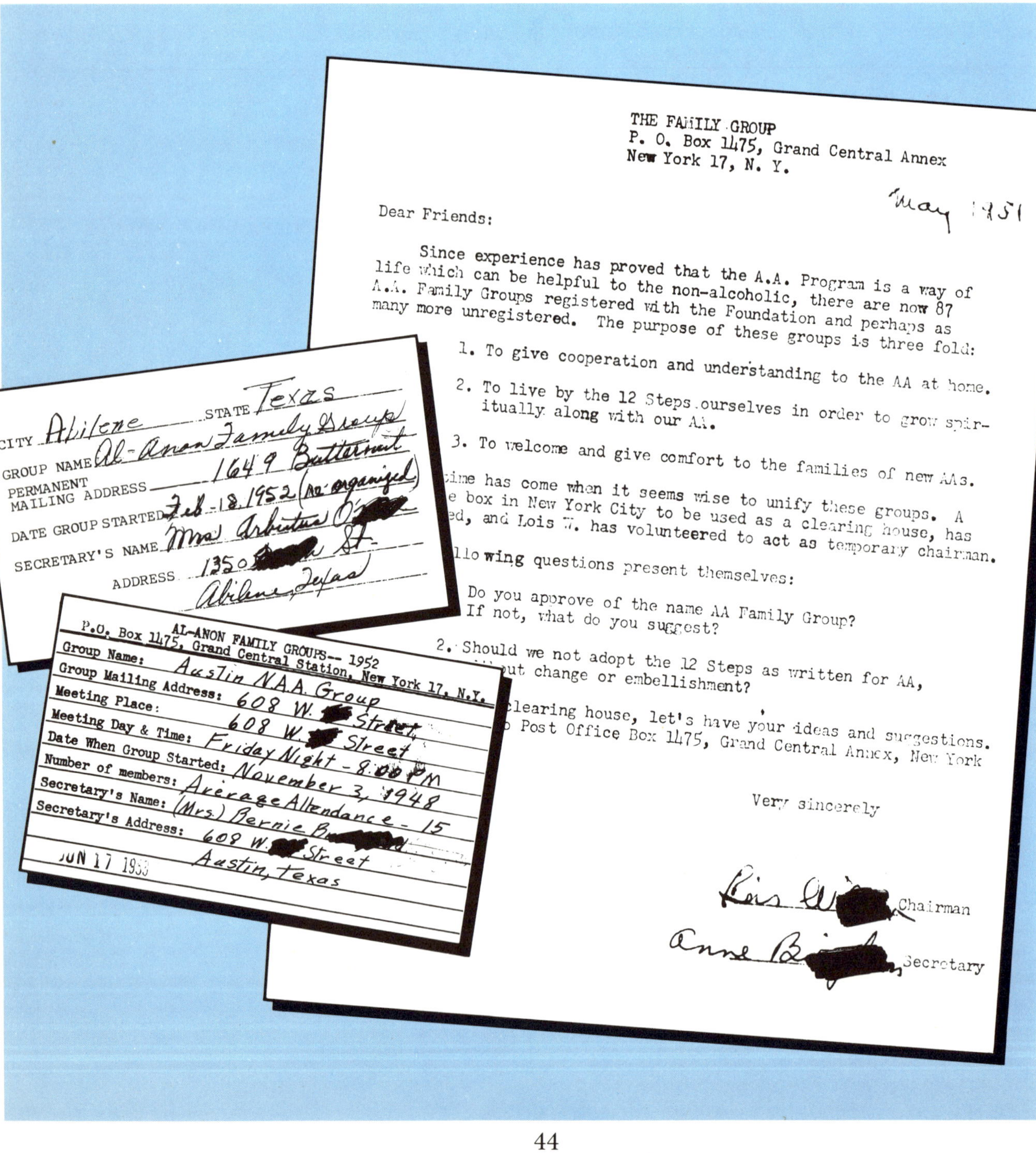

THE FAMILY GROUP
P. O. Box 1475, Grand Central Annex
New York 17, N. Y.

May 1951

Dear Friends:

Since experience has proved that the A.A. Program is a way of life which can be helpful to the non-alcoholic, there are now 87 A.A. Family Groups registered with the Foundation and perhaps as many more unregistered. The purpose of these groups is three fold:

1. To give cooperation and understanding to the AA at home.
2. To live by the 12 Steps ourselves in order to grow spiritually along with our AA.
3. To welcome and give comfort to the families of new AAs.

...time has come when it seems wise to unify these groups. A ...e box in New York City to be used as a clearing house, has ...ed, and Lois W. has volunteered to act as temporary chairman.

...llowing questions present themselves:

... Do you approve of the name AA Family Group? If not, what do you suggest?

2. Should we not adopt the 12 Steps as written for AA, ...out change or embellishment?

...clearing house, let's have your ideas and suggestions. ...o Post Office Box 1475, Grand Central Annex, New York

Very sincerely

Lois W[redacted] Chairman

Anne B[redacted] Secretary

CITY Abilene STATE Texas
GROUP NAME Al-Anon Family Group
PERMANENT MAILING ADDRESS 1649 Butternut
DATE GROUP STARTED Feb-18, 1952 (re-organized)
SECRETARY'S NAME Mrs. Arbutus O'[redacted]
ADDRESS 1350 [redacted] St.
Abilene, Texas

AL-ANON FAMILY GROUPS-- 1952
P.O. Box 1475, Grand Central Station, New York 17, N.Y.
Group Name: Austin N.A.A. Group
Group Mailing Address: 608 W. [redacted] Street
Meeting Place: 608 W. [redacted] Street
Meeting Day & Time: Friday Night - 8:00 PM
Date When Group Started: November 3, 1948
Number of members: Average Attendance - 15
Secretary's Name: (Mrs.) Bernie B[redacted]
Secretary's Address: 609 W. [redacted] Street
Austin, Texas
JUN 17 1953

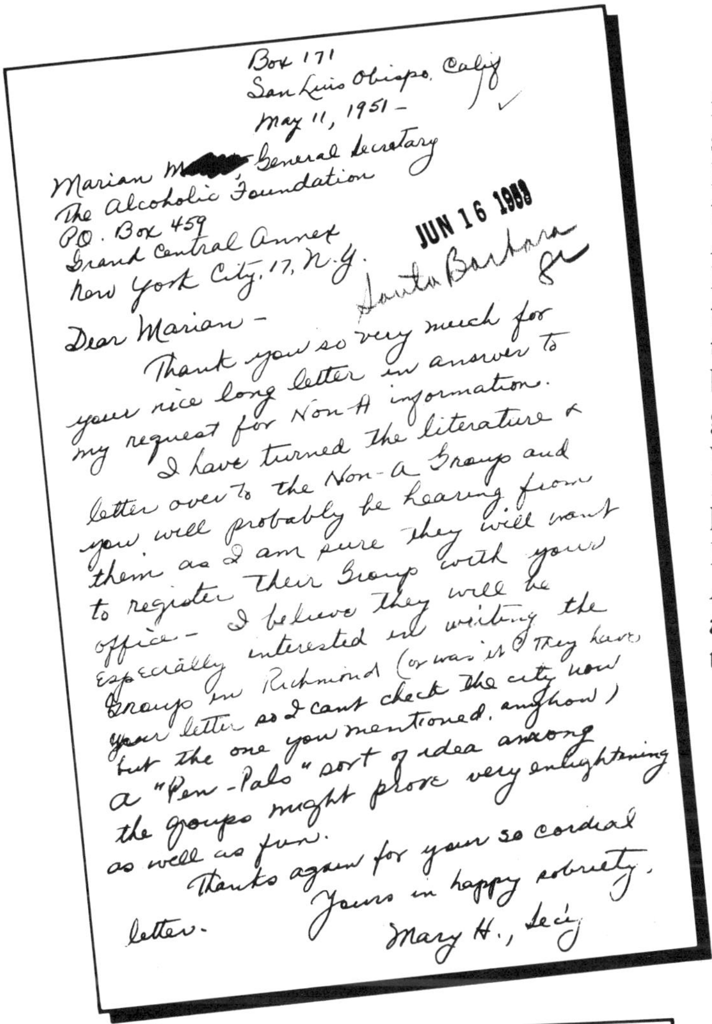
Box 171
San Luis Obispo, Calif.
May 11, 1951 –

Marian M[redacted] General Secretary
The Alcoholic Foundation
P.O. Box 459
Grand Central Annex
New York City, 17, N.Y.

JUN 16 19[illegible]

Santa Barbara

Dear Marian –

Thank you so very much for your nice long letter in answer to my request for Non-A information.

I have turned the literature & letter over to the Non-A Group and you will probably be hearing from them as I am sure they will want to register their Group with your office – I believe they will be especially interested in writing the Group in Richmond (or was it? They have your letter so I can't check the city now) but the one you mentioned, anyhow) a "Pen-Pals" sort of idea among the groups might prove very enlightening as well as fun.

Thanks again for your so cordial letter.

Yours in happy sobriety,
Mary H., Sec'y

As for the name, groups were imaginative but there was little consensus. Some suggestions were: "AA Helpmates" from Elmira, New York; "Triple A" from Edmonton, Alberta; "First Step AA" from Ann Arbor, Michigan; and "Non AA" from Long Beach, California. No one knows how the contraction of "Al-Anon" taken from the title of the AA Big Book seems to have been reached. It must have caught on gradually, since an Oklahoma City group was using another name as late as April, 1953, and Tucson, Arizona was printing literature under a different name in 1954. However, California already had an Al-Anon Council in June, 1953 and was going ahead with its own conference. Such was the pattern of growth in Al-Anon.

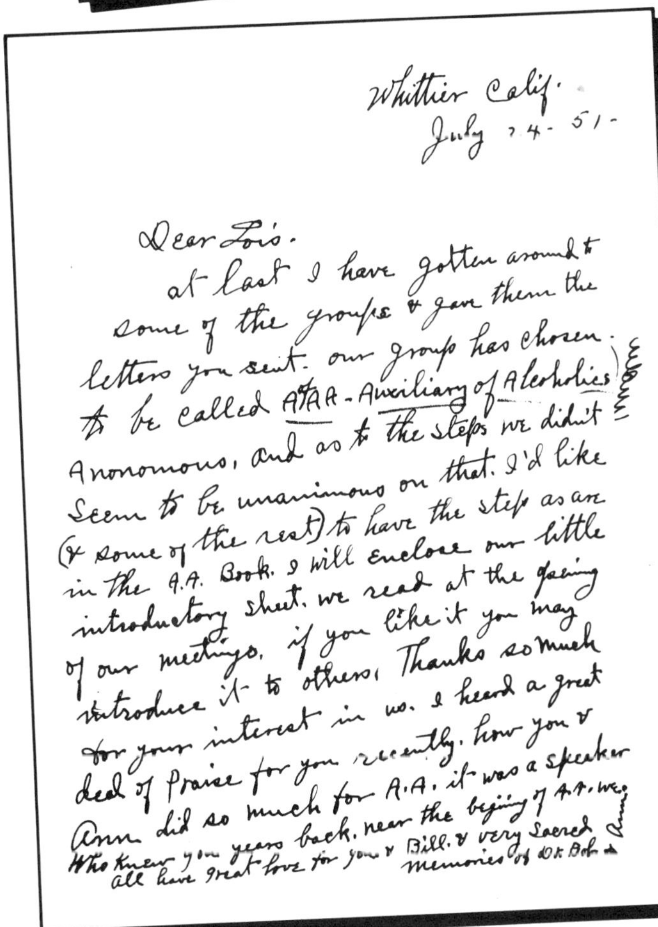
Whittier Calif.
July 24 - 51 -

Dear Lois.

at last I have gotten around to some of the groups & gave them the letters you sent. our group has chosen to be called A.A.A - Auxiliary of Alcoholics Anonomous, (Women) and as to the steps we didn't seem to be unanimous on that. I'd like (& some of the rest) to have the steps as are in the A.A. Book. I will enclose our little introductory sheet. we read at the opening of our meetings. if you like it you may introduce it to others. Thanks so much for your interest in us. I heard a great deal of Praise for you recently. how you & Ann did so much for A.A. it was a speaker who knew you years back. near the begining of A.A. we all have great love for you & Bill. & very sacred memories of Dr. Bob & Ann.

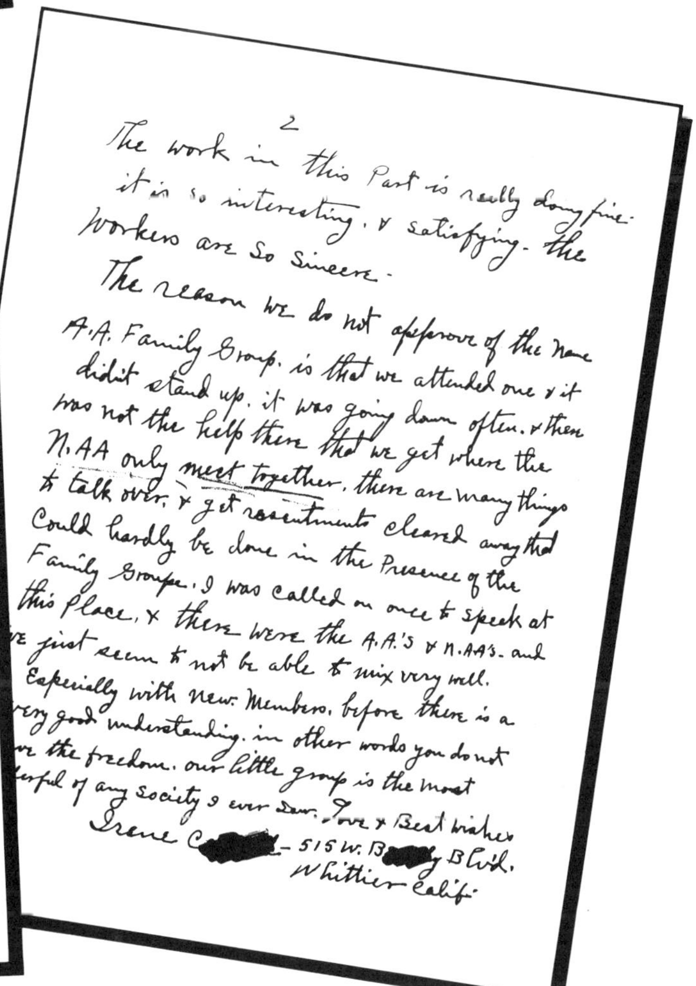
2

The work in this Part is really doing fine. it is so interesting. & satisfying. the workers are so sincere.

The reason we do not approve of the name A.A. Family Group. is that we attended one & it didn't stand up. it was going down often. & then was not the help there that we get where the N.AA only meet together. there are many things to talk over. & get resentments cleared away that could hardly be done in the Presence of the Family Groups. I was called on once to speak at this Place, & there were the A.A.'s & N.AA's. and we just seem to not be able to mix very well. Especially with new Members. before there is a very good understanding. in other words you do not have the freedom. our little group is the most wonderful of any society I ever saw. Love & Best wishes

Irene C[redacted] - 515 W. B[redacted] Blvd.
Whittier Calif.

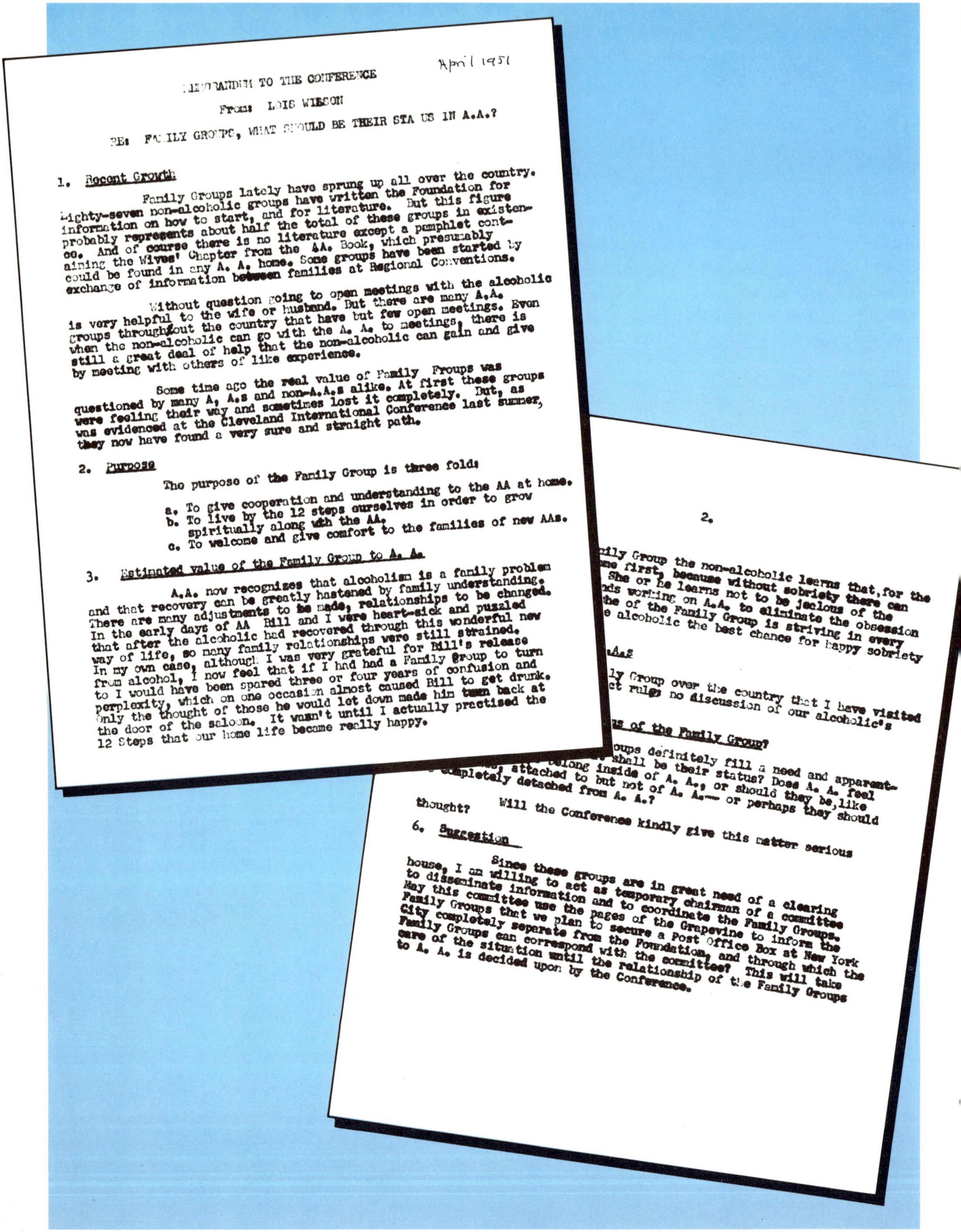

April 1951

MEMORANDUM TO THE CONFERENCE

From: LOIS WILSON

RE: FAMILY GROUPS, WHAT SHOULD BE THEIR STATUS IN A.A.?

1. Recent Growth

Family Groups lately have sprung up all over the country. Eighty-seven non-alcoholic groups have written the Foundation for information on how to start, and for literature. But this figure probably represents about half the total of these groups in existence. And of course there is no literature except a pamphlet containing the Wives' Chapter from the AA. Book, which presumably could be found in any A. A. home. Some groups have been started by exchange of information between families at Regional Conventions.

Without question going to open meetings with the alcoholic is very helpful to the wife or husband. But there are many A.A. groups throughout the country that have but few open meetings. Even when the non-alcoholic can go with the A. A. to meetings, there is still a great deal of help that the non-alcoholic can gain and give by meeting with others of like experience.

Some time ago the real value of Family Groups was questioned by many A. A.s and non-A.A.s alike. At first these groups were feeling their way and sometimes lost it completely. But, as was evidenced at the Cleveland International Conference last summer, they now have found a very sure and straight path.

2. Purpose

The purpose of the Family Group is three fold:

a. To give cooperation and understanding to the AA at home.
b. To live by the 12 steps ourselves in order to grow spiritually along with the AA.
c. To welcome and give comfort to the families of new AAs.

3. Estimated value of the Family Group to A. A.

A.A. now recognizes that alcoholism is a family problem and that recovery can be greatly hastened by family understanding. There are many adjustments to be made, relationships to be changed. In the early days of AA Bill and I were heart-sick and puzzled that after the alcoholic had recovered through this wonderful new way of life, so many family relationships were still strained. In my own case, although I was very grateful for Bill's release from alcohol, I now feel that if I had had a Family Group to turn to I would have been spared three or four years of confusion and perplexity, which on one occasion almost caused Bill to get drunk. Only the thought of those he would let down made him turn back at the door of the saloon. It wasn't until I actually practised the 12 Steps that our home life became really happy.

2.

…ily Group the non-alcoholic learns that, for the …me first, because without sobriety there can … She or he learns not to be jealous of the …ds working on A.A. to eliminate the obsession …he of the Family Group is striving in every …e alcoholic the best chance for happy sobriety

…A.s

…ly Group over the country that I have visited …ct rule: no discussion of our alcoholic's

…s of the Family Group?

…oups definitely fill a need and apparent… shall be their status? Does A. A. feel …ong inside of A. A., or should they be, like … attached to but not of A. A.— or perhaps they should … completely detached from A. A.?

Will the Conference kindly give this matter serious thought?

6. Suggestion

Since these groups are in great need of a clearing house, I am willing to act as temporary chairman of a committee to disseminate information and to coordinate the Family Groups. May this committee use the pages of the Grapevine to inform the Family Groups that we plan to secure a Post Office Box at New York City completely separate from the Foundation, and through which the Family Groups can correspond with the committee? This will take care of the situation until the relationship of the Family Groups to A. A. is decided upon by the Conference.

Lois and Anne continued to receive correspondence from new Family Groups, helped by an *AA Grapevine* article which appeared in June, 1951. By July, the number of groups registered had risen to 145. Leading among the states were New York with 20, California with 16, and Texas with 13. However, 39 states were represented, and in addition to 11 groups flourishing in Canada, others were registered in Australia and South Africa. A November, 1950 *AA Grapevine* article from a member in Cape Town describes for the first time Al-Anon members living with still-drinking alcoholics and with no ties to AA.

TUCSON, ARIZONA

The Tucson Triple A Family Group meets on the first and third Tuesdays of the month at 2 P. M., and the second and fourth Mondays at 8 P. M. When there is a fifth Tuesday in the month there is an extra meeting that afternoon. The address may be obtained by calling the Alcoholics Anonymous numbers in the telephone directory.

The opinions expressed in this booklet are our own and not necessarily those of any group or organization.

Revised Edition

Second Printing, 1954

June, 1953

Al-Anon Conference

Great strides have been taken by the Al-Anon Council since its inception less than twelve months ago. Vivienne F. of San Rafael, secretary of the Northern California Al-Anon Council reports that a very fine program has been scheduled for their meeting in Vallejo to be held at the same time as the Council meeting on June 13 and 14.

For the first time the sessions of the Al-Anon Council will also be extended into a period covering two days. This will allow the non-alcoholics to have their time occupied while the alcoholic mates are busy in their meetings.

Credit for the excellent program arranged falls to George S. Jr., of Yuba City, who is a member of the Marysville Al-Anon Group. He was assisted by Jim and Peggy L. of Vallejo and George of Santa Rosa.

The following is the schedule for Saturday June 13:

1:00 p.m. — Welcome Address, George S. Jr. of Marysville Al-Anon Group, Chairman.

1:05 p.m.—Summary of purpose of the N. C. C., George S. Jr.

1:10 p.m.—Guest Speaker, Mary J., Al-Anon Group, Sacramento.

1:45 p.m.—Report of activities on Al-Anon at the General Service Conference in New York, Alice B. of Roseville.

2:00 p.m.—Group Discussion, Marge M., Al-Anon Group of Sacramento, Moderator.

Sunday morning, June 14th, will see the session concluded with the following program.

10:00 a.m.—Guest Speaker, Andy of the Oakland Family Group.

10:30 a.m.—Conclusion of Group Discussion, led by Marge M.

If there are any of the non-alcoholic members that would like to bring up any questions, or problems, for discussion, it has been asked that they please send them to Marge M[redacted], 121 [redacted] Street, North Sacramento, California

THIS DAY

Publication of
Oklahoma City Family Group

Vol. 1 — April 1953 — No. 6

"IF GOD CAN SOLVE THE AGE-OLD RIDDLE OF ALCOHOLISM - - - HE CAN SOLVE YOUR PROBLEM TOO"

The above is quoted from the A.A. book, and is the foundation upon which we are trying to build a "Family Group". Through experience we have found whether our husbands are drinking or not, life is much better when we begin to apply spiritual principles to our own lives.

To some extent the families of alcoholics are sick and need the love and companionship of other families who have shared in the same problem. We believe that the family is a unit, and when we can do something to help ourselves, we will have helped our families.

We hope that you who will be forming family groups in your town will see the value of trying to make "YOU" a better person rather than the alcoholic. We believe that only God can change the alcoholic. We have learned that A.A. is not a "cure" for alcoholism but a Way of Life. And to quote the A.A. book again: "We urge you to try our program, for nothing will be so helpful to your husband, as the radically changed attitude toward him which God will show you how to have. Go along with your husband if you possibly can."

The three-fold purpose of the Family Group is:

(a) To grow spiritually through living the 12 steps of A.A.

(b) To give encouragement and understanding to the Alcoholic in the home.

(c) To welcome and give comfort to the families of A.A.

HAVING been the secretary of a group; and electing our secretary, treasurer, delegate and alternate in February, and having received the names of other secretaries of all groups, it occurred to me that if the serving officers of *all groups* were elected at the *same time* it would not only make it much easier for the General Service Headquarters in New York but would clarify matters greatly, particularly as to *who* is the secretary of a certain group.

For instance, if each Group would elect its officers in January, or any other month for that matter, for a six month period, or a year, whatever is the procedure of groups, the office in New York could then have a list of the serving officers which would be correct for at least a six month period.

As it is now, a list which might not be effective a month from today is sent from the New York office to secretaries of groups and the secretary might be out of office in a month, or a week, thus causing confusion not only in New York but with group secretaries and AAs who want to contact them.

I would like to hear through the Grapevine, what AAs everywhere think about it.

—— *W.J.C., Boston, Massachusetts*

WE have quite a large Auxiliary Group in Capetown, composed of wives of AA members, husbands of AA members, mothers and sisters of members, *and also* wives of excessive drinkers, who hope that their husbands will be induced to attend an AA meeting, or to contact a member of AA. It is about this last section that I have been doing a bit of thinking.

I am convinced from experience that the Auxiliary Group is an excellent thing for wives and husbands of members of AA. I also feel that the understanding and experience of such members has been of great help to other wives in the "section" I have singled out, who are having trouble through the excessive drinking of their husbands. But the point that worries me is: whether the Alky husband is likely to come along to AA with his problem because his wife has found the Auxiliary Group, or whether it is more likely that he will be less inclined to contact AA. It is common knowledge that we Alkies are "cagey" birds, and I can quite picture some of the Alkies I know, whose wives attend Auxillary AA meetings, meeting together at the bar and commiserating with each other about their wives attending meetings and "discussing their husbands with wives of some of those darned alcoholics." Is there any general understanding of membership of Non AA groups? Should they be confined only to wives and relations of AA Members? I would like to see some opinions on the question.

—— *R.H., Capetown, South Africa*

As the variety of requests continued to grow, Lois and Anne quickly identified the need for literature as an Al-Anon tool. Together they wrote "Purposes and Suggestions for Al-Anon Family Groups," which included the development of a new principle—focus on oneself, rather than the alcoholic:

"An Important Principle: To insure the success of the Family Groups there should be no gossip, nor complaints about the alcoholic's faults at meetings. Newcomers can quickly make friends with older members with whom they will invariably feel free to discuss their personal difficulties privately."

As more family members with alcoholics still drinking were entering Al-Anon, the pamphlet makes the distinction between help for still-drinking alcoholics and non-drinking family members:

"This leaflet is primarily for relatives of Alcoholics Anonymous. Should it fall in the hands of a relative of an alcoholic who has not yet contacted AA, that person can inquire from the Alcoholic Foundation, P.O. Box 459, Grand Central Station, New York, N.Y. for the location of the nearest AA meeting, where attendance is urged."

To further differentiate Al-Anon from AA, it can be seen that the word "alcoholics" has been dropped from the Twelfth Step for the first time.

4. <u>THE TWELVE STEPS OF A. A.</u>

These steps can be a way of life for the family of A.A.s as well as the alcoholic:

1. We admitted we were powerless over alcohol - that our lives had become unmanageable.
2. Came to believe that a Power greater than ourselves could restore us to sanity.
3. Made a decision to turn our will and our lives over to the care of God <u>as we understood Him.</u>
4. Made a searching and fearless moral inventory of ourselves.
5. Admitted to God, to ourselves, and to another human being the exact nature of our wrongs.
6. Were entirely ready to have God remove all these defects of character.
7. Humbly asked Him to remove our shortcomings.
8. Made a list of all persons we had harmed, and became willing to make amends to them all.
9. Made direct amends to such people wherever possible, except when to do so would injure them or others.
10. Continued to take personal inventory and when we were wrong promptly admitted it.
11. Sought through prayer and meditation to improve our conscious contact with God <u>as we understood Him</u> praying only for knowledge of His will for us and the power to carry that out.
12. Having had a spiritual awakening as the result of these steps, we tried to carry this message to others, and to practise these principles in all our affairs.

At Stepping Stones, Lois and Anne acquired the basis for an office—Anne's typewriter, a stapler, a file, and a supply of stationery and stamps. Expenses included paying for the box rental. Spontaneously, but hardly by coincidence, contributions for this work began trickling in from grateful people. The first on June 22, 1951, was from Sam K. of Lynn, Massachusetts. This was followed by others from Syracuse, New York, Montgomery, Alabama, and Yankton, South Dakota. Lois says, "We assumed our office would be supported by regular voluntary contributions as the AA office was. Whether or not this would work out we didn't know, as we hadn't yet asked for donations." Now that the Al-Anon Family Groups were "out of the red and into the black," as Anne put it, she and Lois had their own stationery printed. Although they worked hard with the 200 Family Groups now registered, including one group in Ireland, the mail was too voluminous for them to keep up with in the two days a week set aside. Lois and Anne needed more space, and more help. Also, both expressed the need for a policy "that would coincide with AA."

For these reasons, Lois and Anne called a meeting at Stepping Stones on November 17, 1951. To it they invited the chairmen and secretaries of the local Al-Anon groups. These members were first asked to poll their groups for additional volunteers to assist Lois and Anne, and second, they were asked to form themselves into a service committee to advise on policy. Bill spoke at the meeting, lending support to these Family Groups. He urged them to follow in the footsteps of AA by forming a foundation which would have, in his words, "unlimited potentialities." Anne echoed Bill's thought:

"A while back in June, an article came out in the *American* by Beatrix Fairfax. We have had a number of inquiries from that—our secretary Anne K. being one of them. So you see how helpful these groups can be. There are so many known cases where the alcoholic has come into AA because the wife attended these Family Group meetings and he saw the change in her."

The result of this historic meeting between the co-founders and local Al-Anon leaders was the establishment of the Clearing House with the move to the Old 24th Street Clubhouse in New York City, on January 9, 1952. At the start of a new year, not only did the movement have a name—Al-Anon Family Groups, but it had officers—Lois and Anne B. It also had an office of sorts, thanks to AA, with a two-drawer filing cabinet and a half share in a mimeograph machine. And oh, did it have a membership!

The Al-Anon Family Groups
P. O. Box 1475
GRAND CENTRAL STATION
NEW YORK 17, N. Y.

4 POINTS TO BE DISCUSSED AND VOTED UPON

1. Central policy needed for Family Groups that would coincide with A.A. - to have the office nar the Alcoholic Foundation.

2. What is the nxt step?
   a. Suggest that we have service committee to carry out decisions of this meeting. This committee to be elected at the end of meeting.
   b. Country-wide consultation. Notification of new plans by bulletin.
   c. Is it time to ask for funds? If so, when and how?

3. Pamphlet

4. Mechanism of setting up office in New York City.
   a. office or desk room
   b. equipment: desk, typwriter, file,
   c. volunteers: each chairman and sec

The Al-Anon Family Groups
P. O. Box 1475
GRAND CENTRAL STATION
NEW YORK 17, N. Y.

Nov. 17, 1951

Agenda of MEETING OF FAMILY GROUP CHAIRMEN AND SECRETARIES
at

OPEN WITH MOMENT OF SILENCE

REPORT OF SECRETARY ON CLEARING HOUSE

By Bill - OBLIGATION ON US IN THIS AREA SIMILAR TO THE OBLIGATION OF EARLY GROUP TO FORM FOUNDATION, AND UNLIMITED POTENTIALITIES

DISCUSSION OF POINTS TO BE BROUGHT UP:

1. Central policy needed for Family Groups that would coincide with A. A. To be near the Foundation.

2. What is the next step?
   a. Suggest that we have service committee to carry out decisions of this meeting. TO BE ELECTED AT END OF MEETING
   b. Country-wide consultation - notification of new plans by bulletin
   c. Is it time to ask for funds?
      1. office or desk room
      2. equipment: desk, typewriter, file and phone, stationery, PO Box
      3. ~~[illegible]~~

3. Pamphlet

4. Mechanism of setting up office in N. Y.
   a. office or desk room
   b. equipment: desk & typewriter
      tleephone
      file
      STATIONERY AND POST OFFICE BOX
   c. volunteers: chairman and secretary of groups to select workers

VOTING ON POINTS -
Leaflet re-effort - Gen. Plan Service U. P. 1000 @ 15.70
$4 - 63 $1
CLOSE WITH LORD'S PRAYER

Chapter Four
Al-Anon Clearing House

The Old 24th Street Clubhouse to which Lois and Anne B. moved on that celebrated day early in 1952 was a remarkable place. On June 18th, 1940 it had opened as AA's first clubhouse. There was a large room and a kitchen on the first floor. A steep stairway led up to a second floor where another large room was to serve as a recreation room for AA at night, and the Al-Anon Clearing House during the day. One of the two small rooms on the second floor had been temporary quarters for Lois and Bill after leaving Clinton Street. Lois had painted egg crates blue and hung them with curtains to become makeshift bureaus. Even in 1952, one of the rooms served as a bedroom for Bill when he returned from AA General Service Board meetings late, and couldn't make it back to Bedford Hills. He referred to the room as his "little cubicle."

The land on which the Clubhouse stood had at one time been owned by Clement Moore's family. (Moore is the author of the well-known poem, "The Night Before Christmas.) A carpenter's shop and stable were first built on the site, and during Prohibition they became a combination tea garden and speakeasy. The building was later purchased by the Illustrators Club, and the skylights in the upstairs room and pine paneling downstairs were added. In 1952, the building was run by the Seamen's Group of AA. In keeping with the Traditions, Al-Anon immediately began paying a nominal rent for office space in return for some dubious services from the janitor and social visits by Larry, the Clubhouse's resident artist and AA member. Margaret D., one of the first volunteers to work at the Clearing House, described how it was.

"Larry M., a commercial artist, would work until he got enough money to give himself a vacation by coming over to our upstairs room. He loved Al-Anon. He would paint all day, and never interrupt us. He was a real help.

"We had a brute of a skylight that worked on some chains. If you didn't stop it at a certain place, it would come whamming down. There were two small windows on one side and a skylight on the other. You would think that we had cross ventilation, but I've never known a hotter summer than that first one. I'd expect to see puddles under each of our chairs. That's when I named it 'Lois' Sweatshop.' Then, in winter it became 'Lois' Refrigerator,' because it was freezing cold. We'd call the janitor, and call the janitor. But he'd always say 'You'll have heat in five minutes.' Somehow, his master's voice was Larry. While from the beginning we observed our independence by paying rent, the janitor never acknowledged it. Larry had to plead our case."

Margaret also tells the story of how Larry idolized Bill. On one occasion, Lois came down to work at the Clearing House to find that Larry had hung a velvet rope across the doorway to Bill's "little cubicle" as if it belonged in a museum. Much embarrassed, Lois confided to Margaret that Bill would never go along with that kind of treatment, and she had the cord spirited away never to appear again.

Larry also painted portraits of Lois and Bill, Dr. Bob, and Dr. Silkworth, which he presented to the Clubhouse at its June anniversary celebrations each year.

The First AA Clubhouse in the world

. . . the old fireplaced clubroom . . .

. . . the old stairway . . .

. . . Bill's room

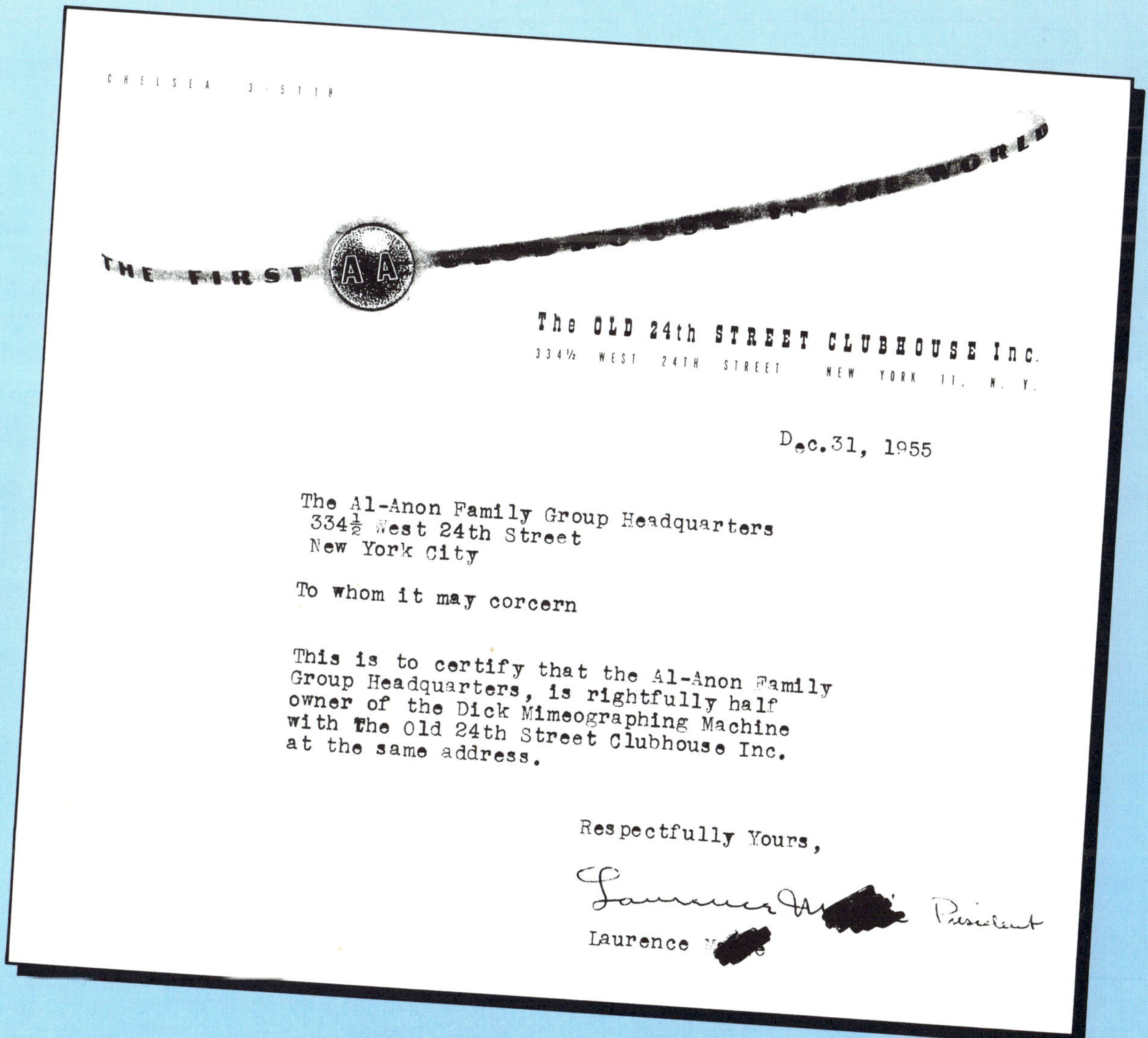

CHELSEA 3-5118

THE FIRST AA ... WORLD

The OLD 24th STREET CLUBHOUSE Inc.
334½ WEST 24TH STREET NEW YORK 11, N. Y.

Dec.31, 1955

The Al-Anon Family Group Headquarters
334½ West 24th Street
New York City

To whom it may corcern

This is to certify that the Al-Anon Family Group Headquarters, is rightfully half owner of the Dick Mimeographing Machine with The Old 24th Street Clubhouse Inc. at the same address.

Respectfully Yours,

Laurence [redacted] President

Laurence [redacted]

At an AA Round-up in Palm Springs in 1983, Anne was asked what she remembered of the transfer from Stepping Stones to the Old 24th Street Clubhouse. She said there was simply nothing to it because there was so little to take with them. She and Lois loaded a two-drawer filing cabinet, box of stationery, and little black book in which they kept the accounts into the back of the car. Anne carried Bill's trusty typewriter which she had been borrowing, and down to New York City they went.

Lois and Anne asked for volunteer help straight away. Wally S., one of Al-Anon's first male members, put up shelves at the Clearing House and drove Lois and Anne around to other groups in the metropolitan area.

January 12, 1952

Sylvia A[redacted], Secretary of Bedford Al-Anon Family Group
Agnes J[redacted], Chairman
Bernice F[redacted]

Greetings Friends,

We hope you all had happy holidays.

Do you remember when we held the meeting of the officers of the Metropolitan Family Groups here in Bedford Hills last fall, that we decided to transfer the national clearing house of the Al-Anon Family Groups to New York? Well, it looks as if the time has come when we can do this.

Your steering committee has found working space for us at the Old 24th St. A.A. Clubhouse at 33½ W. 24th St., New York City. The management there have graciously offered to let us have the use of a desk and typewriter and 2 drawers of a filing cabinet in the large room upstairs until we can get the where-with-all together to purchase equipment for ourselves.

Irma F[redacted] also graciously has offered to start the volunteer ball rolling and will be there with another volunteer of her procurement every Thursday afternoon for a month at 2:30 P.M. Anne B[redacted] and/or I will also be on hand to coach the new volunteers in the work to be done.

Do you also remember at the fall meeting, that the officers of each Metropolitan area Family Group said they would find out from their groups who would be able to volunteer to help out in this very important work? As soon as you can gather the following information together will you send it to me at Box 1475, Grand Central Annex, New York 17, N. Y.:

1. Name, address and phone number of each volunteer.
2. Those who will be free to work for this clearing house at 24th St. on Thursdays from 2:30 P.M. to about 5 P.M. on Jan. 24, 31; Feb. 7,14,21,28.
3. Also those who have other free time; kindly state day and hour.
4. Who of these volunteers can type or has had any business experience?

Voluntary contributions from a number of groups throughout the country have helped so far to defray expenses, but the time may not be too far distant when we may have to ask all the Family Groups for regular donations.

We hope to be hearing from you soon. All success to your group.

Best remembered among the first volunteers to respond to Lois and Anne's request were Margaret D., Henrietta S., Evelyn C., Sue L., Irma F., Dot L., and Mimi H. Perhaps the most articulate and colorful of this group of pioneers was Margaret D. Although three other volunteers had preceded her, she arrived on the scene early—on March 1, 1952, to be exact.

Margaret's husband, Jack, had been a member of the South Yonkers AA Group for six years when their daughter went away to college, leaving Margaret with an empty house and time on her hands. Since she had had some business training and could type, Margaret thought she would look for a full-time office job. But Nancy, the AA Group secretary, had met Lois at a retreat and had heard her plea for help at the Clearing House. She suggested to Margaret that she volunteer while looking for a salaried position, because—as Nancy confided to Margaret—the wives of AA members really needed help. This was to be the clincher for Margaret. Margaret remembers that when she telephoned Lois, she suggested Margaret start at the Clearing House right away.

"When I went there for the first time, Anne B. was there. Lois told me to walk along 24th Street until I came to a green door. She said, 'You'll have a hard time finding the bell. It's kind of high up.'

"So I walked and stood in front of that green door hunting for the bell. And you know, Jack had been in AA six years, so that I had learned to communicate with people inside AA, but apart from that I was almost completely withdrawn and afraid to meet people. If they would stay *that* far away, I was happy.

"So I stood there looking for that bell and I almost turned away to run back to Yonkers and slam the door between me and the world. I thought, 'Can I do this? Can I expose myself to people again?'

"Fortunately, I wouldn't be here if I hadn't rung that bell, and Anne came down to meet me. She took me up to a huge room, up the steepest, narrowest stairs I ever climbed, and that was the beginning. She asked me what I could do, and I said I could do anything in an office that was necessary. I could type and write letters.

"So we sat down and opened the mail. What a revelation it was! You could see the rapport that Lois and Anne had established with these people. You could also tell the ones that were writing letters for the first time from the desperation they were feeling.

"Anne gave me a set of typed questions and answers with which to write a reply. If I couldn't apply these answers, then I could interrupt her and ask for direction. I always had this safe feeling that either Lois or Anne was going to read my letters and sign them. The last thing I wanted to do was to make bad friends for Al-Anon when I was supposed to be there to help."

Although Margaret spent a good two years answering letters, she began her much better known Al-Anon work as first Editor of the *Newsletter* in June, 1954 (by September, the name had become *Family Group FORUM*). Slowly, she lost her withdrawn qualities and became known for her humor, working at her desk with a long cigarette holder held between her lips. When, in 1954 she began a full-time job with the YWCA National Board, she still continued as a member of Al-Anon's Board of Trustees. Margaret, in her own vivid words, describes how she became *FORUM* Editor, a position she would hold for 20 years.

"Today's magazine The *FORUM* began with Lois drafting our first *Newsletter* on a yellow pad at the old Clearing House. The yellow pad had to rest on her knee because there was only one desk and a table. Never a one to complain, she simply went ahead each month, writing all groups to tell them what had been accomplished or proposed.

"Lois continued writing the *Newsletter* for over two years while work increased enormously. A part-time staff member was needed to supplement our wonderful volunteers and we were fortunate enough to get Henrietta from among them. She was later to become Al-Anon's first general secretary. Henrietta took over the *Newsletter* for three issues. But as work kept increasing so rapidly, she could not finish it and write the *Newsletter* as well. I inherited the job, and am eternally grateful to her.

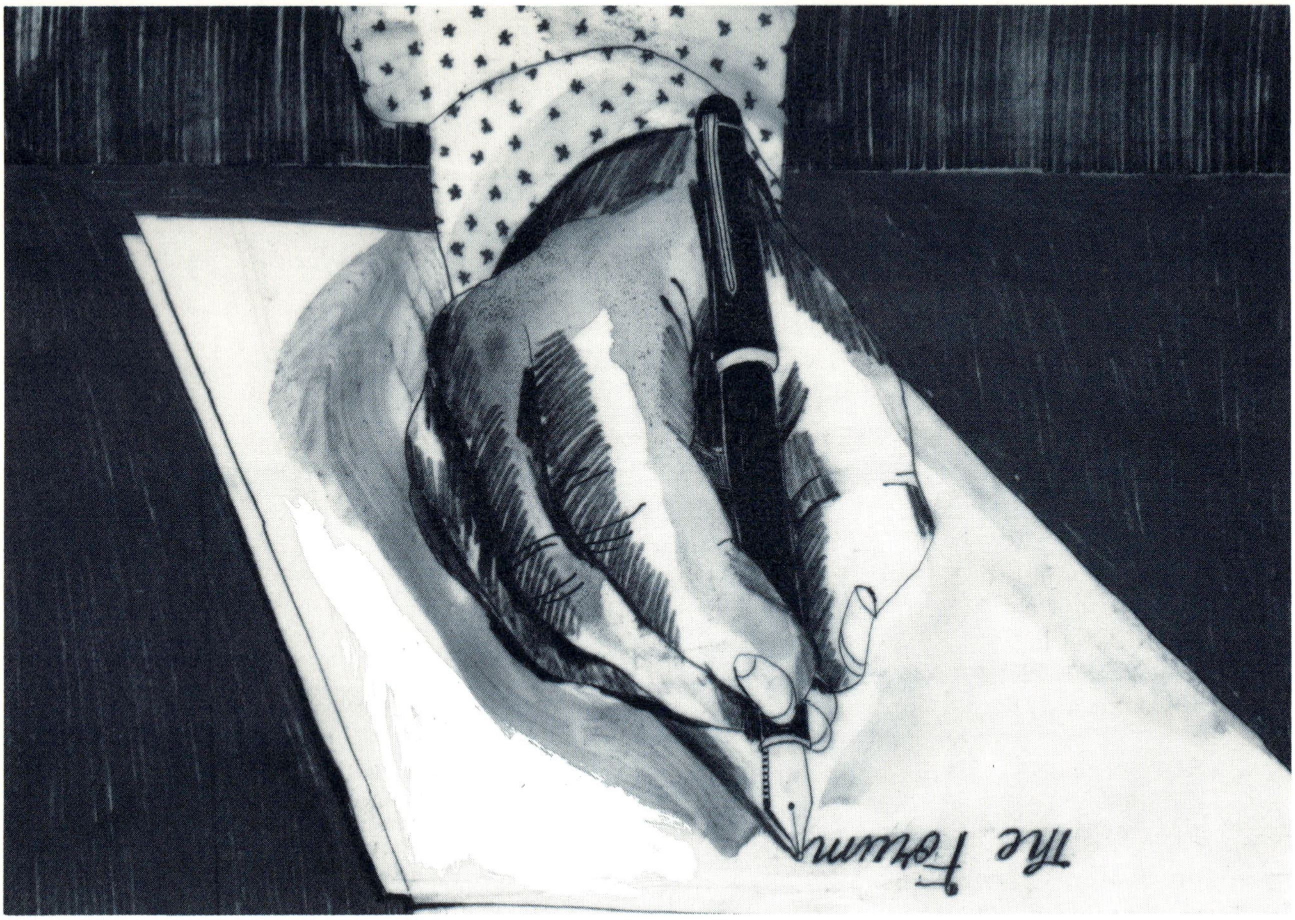

"Working on The *FORUM* as we came to call it, reading letters from all over the world, writing helpful pieces, was the greatest thing that ever happened to me. Twenty years of intense exposure to our program, deep study of the literature, and worldwide correspondence all gave me an understanding of our program I doubt I'd ever have reached without them.

"My husband didn't find sobriety for 45 years, despite AA's help. I had been so busy trying to force it on him, I hadn't given anything but lip service to our program. The *FORUM* changed that. I returned to sanity and life became worth living."

It was Lois' suggestion that no poetry be published in the *FORUM*. Henrietta gives an interesting insight into how the early *FORUM* took shape under Margaret's direction.

"The procedure was that I would gather any interesting letters that came in and Margaret would come by once a month to pick them up. After she had written her copy, it would be sent to Lois and myself for review. Very rarely did anything need changing. Then I would stencil the *FORUM* and we would try to run it off on the broken down mimeograph machine. This method lasted for two or three years before we went to offset printing."

Margaret worked in her free time at home eliminating word hangovers and recasting paragraphs. She also stapled the sheets together. The first single page mimeographed *Newsletter* expanded to two pages. Next, it became a booklet with a heading which Margaret described as looking like the world under an ice cap. The "ugly duckling" (according to Margaret) finally turned into a twelve page booklet with a two-column format for easier reading. The ice cap was abandoned, much to Margaret's satisfaction. Much later, color was added. At the end of 1955, the first full year of *FORUM* publication, 12,210 copies were mailed. That same figure was topped in one

THE A A *Grapevine* INC.

305 EAST 45TH STREET, NEW YORK, N. Y. 10017 • MURRAY HILL 6-1100

December 5, 1967

Dear Lois:

It was good to talk with you last week and I want you to know that if we can be of any possible help, it will be a very real privilege to us.

My personal thoughts are that to bring about an editorial committee or board in a natural way so that feelings and personalities are not unnecessarily bruised, a more pointed or specific interest in the Forum by present active Al-Anons is needed. As you well know the move toward suc... committee or board could not be blasted into being. E... natural desire of other members could bring ... discussions with the editor which could not ... can I see how the suggestion from an intere... committee to institute fresh ideas and form... nored. But, I've seen that happen, too.

Anyway, for what it's worth, the encl... you some thoughts in structuring a commit... the wrong track, please don't hesitate to... make an attempt for other ideas.

With best wishes and love.

Paula C...

Lois W[redacted]
P.O. Box 452
Bedford Hills, New York

PC/skh
enc.

AL-ANON FAMILY GROUP FORUM

VOL. XV, NO. 11 NOVEMBER, 1967

©AL-ANON FAMILY GROUP HEADQUARTERS, INC., 1967
P.O. BOX 182, MADISON SQUARE STATION, NEW YORK, N.Y. 10010

WHO'S TOO OLD TO LEARN?

"As you know, our new pamphlet on sponsorship is about ready. Months were spent on it; long and deep thought went into its preparation. Some unexpected ideas popped up as I concentrated on it.

"We (the Literature Committee) began with the premise that a sponsor is an old Al-Anon who holds the newcomer by the hand, takes him to meetings, tells him what to read and listens with a willing ear to his troubles. We never set a limit on how long sponsorship should last but vaguely felt it an introductory process only, to get the newcomer well established in Al-Anon. Naturally a sponsor would remain interested if further help were needed, but stress was on entering the program.

Then came the startling notion that sponsors are for everybody! No one of us is so all-fired smart in this program, or so completely and perfectly adjusted, that we are always – always, that is – able to handle all the personal problems we are close to. Sometimes we are too close to get a proper perspective, or any perspective at all.

"Having meditated on this novel idea for weeks, I asked a young woman, fairly new to our group, to be my sponsor. She looked at me in amazement and then said, "Well, you know all I'll do is to throw your own written and spoken words back at you." "That's all right," said I, "but you'll furnish the music of a new point of view to those words, and that's what I need." So she said she would.

"I cannot begin to tell you how beautifully this has worked out. After our first telephone conversation in this new relationship, I knew I had done a good thing. It seems I did know the words, all of them, all right, but I needed someone to provide the music.

"Humility, it seems to me, enters this picture. Perhaps long-established, old-time Al-Anons might not feel there is much to learn month by the December, 1969 edition. The 1970 WS Conference agreed to print the best of Margaret's editorials in a hardcover book, now published as *Al-Anon's FORUM Favorites*. In her 20 years as Editor, editing 229 *FORUMS*, Margaret never missed a deadline. Following the lead of AA, a *FORUM* Editorial Committee was formed in 1968.

In the beginning, the Clearing House mailed a copy of The *FORUM* to each of the groups. Eventually this became an impossibility. *Inside Al-Anon* was developed to keep the membership informed of WSO activities beginning in January, 1979.

Henrietta's husband was a member of the AA Bayside Group on Long Island when he heard of Lois' request for help. Henrietta describes what working at the Clearing House meant to her:

"I had no confidence in myself, although I had some skills. I could write, I could type and I had taken some accounting courses. But I felt not very much of anything, because this is what the drinking years had done to me.

"Yet the minute I walked in the door at the Clearing House I felt at home. This was early in 1953. There were approximately seven or eight volunteers working in the office at the time. I started coming regularly on Tuesdays. Much to my surprise that November, I was asked by Lois to become the first part-time paid worker. I was very pleased that they would think me capable.

"My magnificent salary was $35 for three full days a week. Even in those days, it was little more than carfare and lunch. But that wasn't the point. Working brought me out of myself. I learned to love the people with whom I was associated.

"At the Clearing House, you opened the door and walked down this long corridor. Above you there was a plaque which read 'The Last Mile.' Many times, walking into that building alone to open up, I used to look up and wonder, 'Is this really going to be my last mile?' It was quite unnerving to be there alone, but we used to manage to get two or three volunteers to come in and work with me."

Also among the early volunteers was Evelyn C., a lady who had been known to take the mail to the post office in a grocery cart.

"I had only been going to meetings for a few months when I was asked to go help Lois and Anne at the Clearing House. I had never worked in an office before, so I kept putting them off.

"Being a very shy person, I couldn't talk to anyone. The members of the Jackson Heights Family Group made me treasurer because I couldn't say no. Because I couldn't say no, and knowing that if I was asked to help I couldn't say no to Lois, the group sent me down to buy some literature.

"I was afraid to travel alone, but went on the subway from Long Island. I couldn't find 334 ½ West 24th Street. They didn't tell me it was just a door in between two houses. I walked up and down thinking I had the wrong address and [was] ready to head back to Long Island, when I met a woman on the street who was a member of my group. It was Sue L. She said, 'Evelyn, what are you doing here?' I told her. 'I know where it is,' she replied, 'I'll take you.' So that was how the Clearing House got me.

"We only worked one day a week then, but it opened a whole new world for me. I was there 24 years, the first few as a volunteer, and later as a paid staff member. Along with a lot of other jobs, I was Al-Anon's first packing and shipping department.

"I got enough courage to take a typing course, so that I could type the labels instead of printing them. Bill brought me a typewriter from Stepping Stones, and I was in business. I found out later that it belonged to Lois. One incident was very funny and gave us a laugh. When we started to use the pamphlet *Alcoholism, the Family Disease,* it was a little blue book that came from Kentucky. I had never noticed what it was packed in until one day I looked at the printing on the outside of the box, and it said 'Bourbon Whiskey.' We had some good times and a few worries when the money got low. But it always seemed to come when we needed it. So we must have been doing something right to have reached so many people."

Sue L., mentioned by Evelyn, is best known as Al-Anon's first Conference Chairman. She also helped Anne T. start Al-Anon's Intergroup in New York, and in the beginning worked full-time in a small business machine supply company. Margaret tells a well-known story about her:

"Sue would come in magically every time we had run out of mimeograph paper. She would hear one of us say 'Darn! This is the end of the mimeograph paper. What are we going to do?' Then she would disappear, and in an hour or so she would be back with a couple of packages of it. We were shameless."

Earliest of the volunteers was Irma F., who spent her mornings working in the AA Intergroup office, but who came every afternoon to the Clearing House. It was she who had to resign from the Prison

IN MEMORIAM

It is with deep sorrow that we tell you, Sue L., the first Conference Chairman, passed away October 3, 1982.

She was among the faithful volunteers at Headquarters in the early days. Her untiring efforts helped to lay the ground work for Our World Service Conference and she served as Conference Chairman from 1961-67. She was also instrumental in developing the Twelve Concepts of Service.

Over the years, her love for Al-Anon and strict adherence to the Traditions was a constant source of inspiration and encouragement to many.

Several years ago, Sue retired to Florida. Even though her health was failing, she remained an active, dedicated Al-Anon member, attending group, District and Assembly meetings.

Some of us here at the WSO had the privilege of knowing Sue and she will long be remembered for her years of devoted service to the fellowship.

We know you will join all of us in mourning the loss of this dedicated member who shall be missed.

Committee Chairmanship, due to ill health, before Anne B. took it over.

Also among the pioneers was Dot L., who put in seven years of faithful work during Al-Anon's formative years. Evidence of her willingness is described by Margaret:

"One Wednesday on which we worked that first winter fell between Christmas and New Year. There was no point to Anne and Lois coming in all the way from Chappaqua and Bedford Hills. So Dot and I decided to go in and get the mail. It was freezing cold when we got there. Dot was listing the contributions in a book, while I tried to type with gloves on. I made such a mess typing this way. When I finished one of these splotchy letters, I found I couldn't sign it because the ink in my fountain pen had frozen. Dot and I had enough sense to call it a day, and took the work home to her house to finish up."

On a recent visit to the WSO, the first in nearly 30 years, Dot L. herself remembered her years at the Clearing House:

"I joined the Clearing House as the original gal Friday. I did anything that needed doing. An Al-Anon group met on 85th Street in Manhattan in 1952. I remember Bill and Lois coming into the meeting and sitting at the back. Afterwards Lois got up and spoke about the Clearing House. She asked for volunteers, so I went up to her when she had finished and volunteered. My husband, Chauncy, was in AA, and I had no children, so I had the time.

"In those days the Clearing House was ready to take anyone who could count to nine. They were desperate for help. Everyone just got together and did what needed to be done. I wrapped packages and typed.

"Margaret D. and I were close friends. We used to help each other. When my husband died, Bill sent me so many flowers I didn't have enough vases to put them in. Shortly afterwards I moved to Florida."

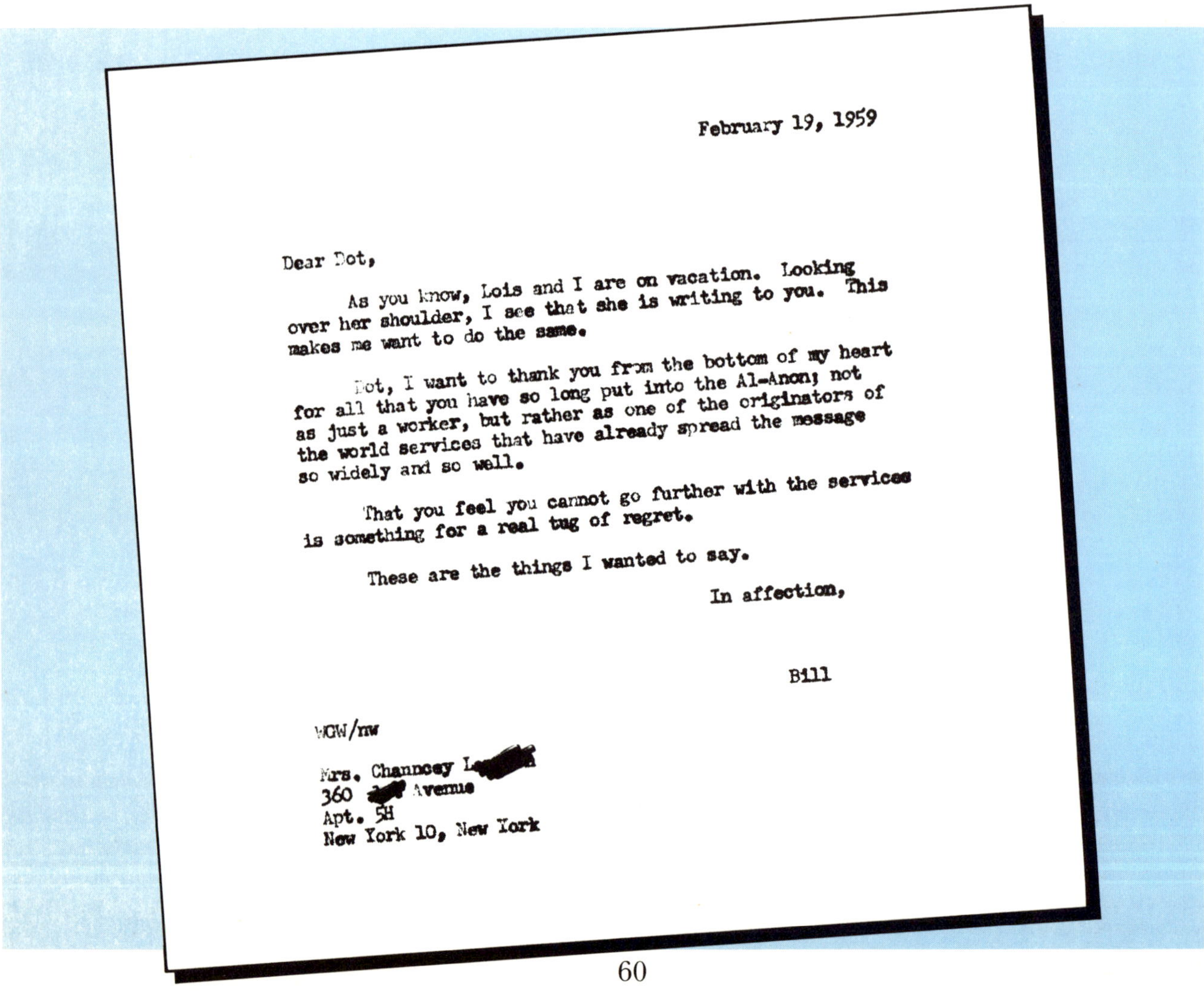

February 19, 1959

Dear Dot,

As you know, Lois and I are on vacation. Looking over her shoulder, I see that she is writing to you. This makes me want to do the same.

Dot, I want to thank you from the bottom of my heart for all that you have so long put into the Al-Anon; not as just a worker, but rather as one of the originators of the world services that have already spread the message so widely and so well.

That you feel you cannot go further with the services is something for a real tug of regret.

These are the things I wanted to say.

In affection,

Bill

WGW/nw

Mrs. Channcey L[redacted]
360 [redacted] Avenue
Apt. 5H
New York 10, New York

Among the volunteers working with Henrietta was a group in Essex County, New Jersey which sent in a weekly worker. Usually four women rotated, and if the month ran into a fifth week, a fifth volunteer arrived. Others at the Clearing House mentioned by Margaret and Henrietta are Eleanor A. who became a member of the Board of Trustees and Jean B., who chaired the Literature Review. Wanda chaired the Publicity Committee.

Talking about her days volunteering at the Clearing House, Mary K. from Scarsdale remembers working on literature:

"We started meeting in New York with Lois and three other women and myself. That's when we'd talk about different literature. We'd have these arguments about that Triple A (AA Auxiliary) Group. Lois would say 'That's not Al-Anon.' We worked together on the first book, *The Al-Anon Family Groups*—my story is in there."

Another interesting reference is made by Henrietta to the volunteer responsible for the first foreign language translations in Al-Anon:

"Among our early volunteers we had a Mimi H. She was Mexican born, but lived in New York City. She was the first Chairman of our Spanish Committee. She did all the translation of our Spanish correspondence. I would draft the letter which she would translate back in reply."

According to Margaret and Henrietta, money continued to be very scarce. From time to time, Al-Anon members would slip one or two dollars into the letters they mailed. Economy knew no bounds. Lois brought in cardboard from Bill's shirts when they were returned from the laundry. The rest of the volunteers saved wrapping paper and string with which to mail out whatever literature could be scraped together for the new and struggling groups. Index file cards of four different colors were kept in a shoebox. White cards were used to designate the first 87 groups, but everyone had long since forgotten the significance of the blue, green and yellow cards. But they were never thrown out because the entire package had cost the enormous sum of 15 cents. Margaret remembers the financial strain:

"The only thing we really couldn't finagle was postage. I called up the post office to find out what postage was and I almost fainted because a letter was three cents. We never had much money, but I think we sat in God's pocket from the very beginning, because He liked what we were doing. In time we accumulated a reserve of $200 and relaxed a bit. Whenever we considered using any part of it, something extra came in and the reserve miraculously stayed at $200, drawing interest."

Margaret describes those first days as a marvelous experience. The little group of volunteers would bring in sandwiches for lunch, and while someone went downstairs to boil water for tea or coffee in a kitchen known for its cockroaches, others would sit around for an informal Al-Anon meeting. It was fun. Margaret says she remembers when a call came in to the Clearing House, she would look up the town in an atlas and be glad if the nearest Al-Anon meeting was 400 miles away. Then she remembers when the gap closed to 200 miles, and sometimes to less than 50.

The Clearing House received not just the benefits of AA experience, but very special, enthusiastic support from Bill. He never failed to point out that Al-Anon's potential for growth was about five times that of AA because each alcoholic affected an average of about five other people. Lois, in her turn, was keenly aware of Al-Anon's debt to AA. In an interview given in 1982, Lois talking of the early days, said, "AA did the groundwork. We [Al-Anon] just came along and reaped all the benefits." As if to formalize a growing acknowledgement of two parallel movements, the AA General Service Conference of 1952 passed a resolution by standing vote, endorsing the work of Al-Anon Family Groups. This was later confirmed by written resolution at the AA General Service Conference of 1969.

From the Report of the Second General Service Conference of A. A.
April 23-27, 1952. Policy Session

FAMILY GROUPS

More time was spent in reviewing and discussing the past, present and probable future status of so-called "family groups" than was devoted to any other item on the 1952 Conference agenda. An extra full session of the Conference was convened solely for the purpose of permitting expression from all delegates who wished to be heard on this topic. Recordings of the two meetings show that nearly 30 delegates were heard--a number of them rising to speak several times.

Here is how the two sessions on this provocative topic might be summarized:

1. FAMILY GROUPS ARE NOT A NEW DEVELOPMENT. Wives of the earliest members used to get together in Akron in the first days of the Society. The first "group," Bill said, was comprised of wives who met on the second floor of the 24th Street Clubhouse in New York City.

2. FAMILY GROUPS SEEM HERE TO STAY--AND ARE INCREASING RAPIDLY. A year-and-a-half ago, there were only about 50-to-70 groups. Now Bill and Lois know of more than 250. Urged by Bill, Lois and several other volunteers have attempted to serve as a "clearing house" for the expanding movement.

3. FAMILY GROUP REPRESENTATIVES HAVE AFFIRMED THEIR DISTINCT ENTITY. The family groups are filling a distinct need, according to the evidence from areas where the idea has taken hold, and the groups are not seeking to use the "A.A." name. As a movement with local groups in all parts of this country and in Canada, the non-alcoholics have their own committees and their own program. As now set up they do not impinge on A.A. and do not seek to do so.

4. DEVELOPMENT OF FAMILY GROUPS IS VIEWED SYMPATHETICALLY IN VIRTUALLY ALL AREAS. Only two delegates out of 77 came to the 1952 Conference with instructions from area committees that might be construed as critical of the family group movement.

5. REPORTS OF FAMILY GROUP DEVELOPMENT ARE CARRIED IN THE "GRAPEVINE," WHEN NEWSWORTHY. Historically, the "Grapevine," from its first issue, has carried news of non-A.A. happenings when they relate to the interests of A.A. readers, directly or indirectly. The Conference, in a special resolution, affirmed its support of this traditional "Grapevine" policy.

6. DELEGATES TO THE 1952 CONFERENCE APPROVE UNANIMOUSLY THE WORK THAT LOIS AND BILL HAVE DONE TO ENCOURAGE AND SUPPORT THE SOUND GROWTH OF THE FAMILY GROUP MOVEMENT. This sentiment, framed in a special resolution at the close of the final policy session, was adopted by an enthusiastic standing vote of all delegates.

A RESOLUTION OF GRATITUDE

Whereas, it is the desire of this 19th General Service Conference to confirm the relationship between Alcoholics Anonymous and the Al-Anon Family Groups, and

Whereas, it is the further desire of this Conference to acknowledge A.A.'s debt of gratitude to the Al-Anon Family Groups, therefore,

BE IT RESOLVED, that Alcoholics Anonymous recognizes the special relationship which it enjoys with the Al-Anon Family Groups, a separate but similar Fellowship. And be it further resolved that Alcoholics Anonymous wishes to recognize, and hereby does recognize, the great contribution which the Al-Anon Family Groups have made, and are making, in assisting the families of alcoholics everywhere.

April 24, 1969

Chapter Five
Widening Membership

The Clearing House offered newly formed Al-Anon groups a lifeline of understanding and support which stretched across a widening membership. By 1954, the number of groups registered was over 500. The variety and number of inquiries called for larger quarters and the organization of Clearing House resources into special services. Functions were divided into literature, budget, and publicity—the names of the first Clearing House committees. To service these committees, the Clearing House was able to employ a paid professional staff. But the role of the individual volunteer Al-Anon member remained vital, both in New York or wherever the Al-Anon message was carried by pioneers across the country, and beyond.

The early members believed they had found something very special which they wanted to share with anyone affected by alcoholism, anywhere. Their belief was responsible for the rapid growth of the Al-Anon movement. Momentum was maintained by such lively members as Imogene, who, speaking at the Southern California Oldtimers Meetings said, "The first thing I do when I go to a new area is to look for Al-Anon. If there isn't a meeting there, then I'll start one."

Universally, the earliest groups seemed to have originated with AA wives meeting in each other's homes. Sometimes the smaller Al-Anon group met in a small and cramped anteroom to the much larger AA meeting. All too frequently AA members viewed the development of Al-Anon suspiciously, fearing that past alcoholic episodes would be held up to group scrutiny. This suspicion could have some odd results. Lehua W. of Hawaii tells how AA stationed a man outside the Al-Anon meeting to lie on the couch and pretend to sleep, so that he could listen-in on what the wives were talking about and report back to his group. But nervousness was not all one-sided. A New Mexico group in the early days would clockwatch, stopping their Al-Anon meeting promptly at 8:45, in order to hurry over to the AA meeting before the closing prayer at 9:00. Al-Anon wives could then claim their husbands and escort them home before these recovering alcoholics were waylaid by drinkers and lured into the neighborhood bar!

Sometimes high feelings could lead to other amusing incidents. Phyllis Q., reporting on the origins of Al-Anon in Oregon says that the fledgling North Bend group meeting room could be reached only by going through the AA meeting room. Often Al-Anon members preferred to brave the outside fire escape rather than face a roomful of rueful AA members! Yet pioneers in both programs, such as Mayme S. in Oregon and her husband Glenn, were pathfinders in developing trust between the two programs.

"We, AA and Al-Anon, finally got a room in the Old North Bend High School. It was the home economics room, which could be divided in two. AA gave us permission to use the second half of the room. In return, we were to make the coffee and furnish the cake for AA.

"In those early days in Al-Anon, we did a lot of weeping. We sat around and every time we started a meeting, some of us would just break down, but finally we got it out of ourselves. We did have a meeting format of a chairman and a subject. We tried desperately to follow it, but we did spend a lot of time on that first Step.

"Finally, the group started growing. There came a time when we had to move from the school. So we formed the Coos Bay Driftwood Groups of AA and Al-Anon. Again, Al-Anon had a little back room and still made the coffee, provided the cake and did the clean-up for AA afterwards. We said we weren't going to do this, but we still did it.

"I felt Al-Anon should be in a place where we felt more comfortable. So I approached an Episcopal minister about starting an Al-Anon meeting in his church. My husband went along with me. He decided he would start a new AA meeting on the same Wednesday night. So we both found suitable meeting rooms in the same church, one upstairs and one downstairs.

"There were many nights when I sat by myself at the Al-Anon meeting upstairs, with Glenn by himself downstairs. We had

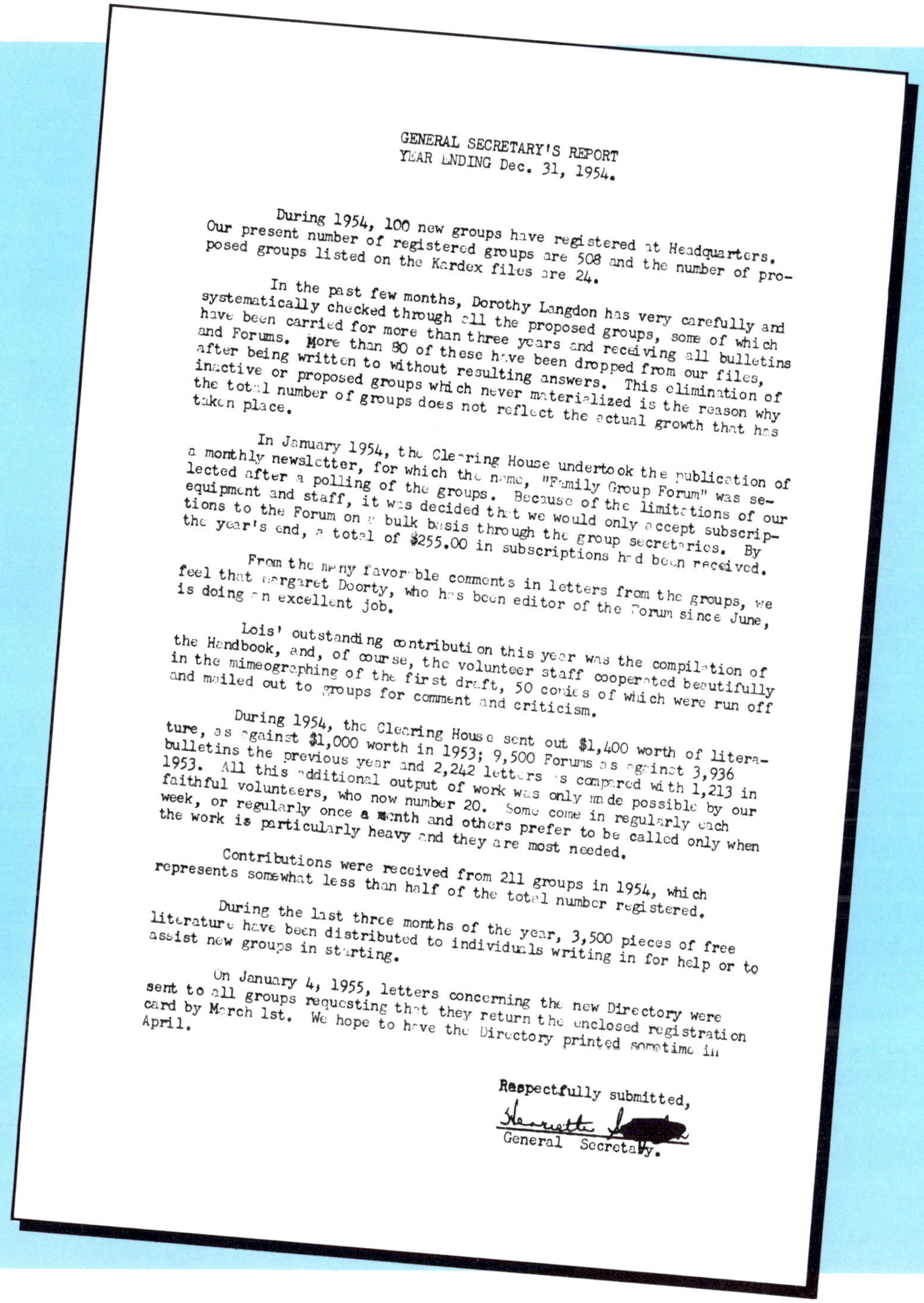

GENERAL SECRETARY'S REPORT
YEAR ENDING Dec. 31, 1954.

During 1954, 100 new groups have registered at Headquarters. Our present number of registered groups are 508 and the number of proposed groups listed on the Kardex files are 24.

In the past few months, Dorothy Langdon has very carefully and systematically checked through all the proposed groups, some of which have been carried for more than three years and receiving all bulletins and Forums. More than 80 of these have been dropped from our files, after being written to without resulting answers. This elimination of inactive or proposed groups which never materialized is the reason why the total number of groups does not reflect the actual growth that has taken place.

In January 1954, the Clearing House undertook the publication of a monthly newsletter, for which the name, "Family Group Forum" was selected after a polling of the groups. Because of the limitations of our equipment and staff, it was decided that we would only accept subscriptions to the Forum on a bulk basis through the group secretaries. By the year's end, a total of $255.00 in subscriptions had been received.

From the many favorable comments in letters from the groups, we feel that Margaret Doorty, who has been editor of the Forum since June, is doing an excellent job.

Lois' outstanding contribution this year was the compilation of the Handbook, and, of course, the volunteer staff cooperated beautifully in the mimeographing of the first draft, 50 copies of which were run off and mailed out to groups for comment and criticism.

During 1954, the Clearing House sent out $1,400 worth of literature, as against $1,000 worth in 1953; 9,500 Forums as against 3,936 bulletins the previous year and 2,242 letters as compared with 1,213 in 1953. All this additional output of work was only made possible by our faithful volunteers, who now number 20. Some come in regularly each week, or regularly once a month and others prefer to be called only when the work is particularly heavy and they are most needed.

Contributions were received from 211 groups in 1954, which represents somewhat less than half of the total number registered.

During the last three months of the year, 3,500 pieces of free literature have been distributed to individuals writing in for help or to assist new groups in starting.

On January 4, 1955, letters concerning the new Directory were sent to all groups requesting that they return the enclosed registration card by March 1st. We hope to have the Directory printed sometime in April.

Respectfully submitted,

Henrietta [redacted]
General Secretary.

a coffee pot in each place, and if no one showed up, we would dump the coffee and we'd go upstairs together. I'd take my Al-Anon book and he'd take his AA book, and we'd sit there and read to each other. It was a growing time for us both. Eventually it evolved into a wonderful AA meeting for Glenn, and a wonderful Al-Anon meeting for me."

Edna G., a member of Rosary Hall, one of the oldest groups in Cleveland, Ohio, has some significant memories of that group's beginnings:

"Rosary Hall was started on January 14, 1955, at St. Vincent Charity Hospital in Cleveland. I attended my first meeting on that date.

"The group was started by Sister Ignatia who was then the Director of Rosary Hall, the ward for alcoholic patients at St. Vincent's. Sister had worked with Dr. Bob at St. Thomas Hospital in Akron, Ohio before she came to Cleveland. Sister used to interview the wives of the alcoholics in Rosary Hall. She said that she didn't know who was more mixed-up, the alcoholic or the non-alcoholic. That was when she realized that we were sick too, and needed help.

"Before Sister Ignatia started our group, she got in touch with Lois W. Lois sent her the pamphlet *So You Love an Alcoholic,* and a little brown book called *Triple A Family Group* from Tucson, Arizona. This was what we went by, with the help of Sister Ignatia.

"When Sister started the Al-Anon group, I was very reluctant to go to meetings, but needless to say, I have fallen in love with Al-Anon, and seldom missed our group meeting. For ten years Sister was with us almost every Friday night. She guided us and inspired us. I believe that is why Cleveland has such a good, basic foundation in the program.

"My husband came to Rosary Hall in 1954, and has been sober in AA ever since. At first AA members didn't trust us. They thought we were there to roast them. Sponsors would tell the men they were sponsoring not to let their wives go to Al-Anon. Soon, however, it was shown that the families which had both programs in the home were having more success. Also, we sometimes had Open Meetings with an AA and an Al-Anon speaker, so things began to change. Soon we were getting 60 to 70 women at our meetings, sometimes standing-room-only. Sister encouraged some of the women to start groups in their neighborhoods. We now have over 100 groups in Cleveland and the surrounding area.

"When I first came to Al-Anon, I was 41 years old and the majority of the women were also around that age. In the beginning, we had all women members, most of whom had spouses who were either in Rosary Hall or had recently gone through Rosary Hall. It seems to me that the problems today are somewhat different from the early days of Al-Anon. Women today are working and are more independent. They also are younger. They are not as willing to keep the family together if the spouse continues to drink. There are many more divorces, but fortunately, some of the divorcees continue to come to Al-Anon.

"I do think that Al-Anons today talk more freely and express their feelings more openly. Such openness was very hard for me and is sometimes difficult even today. Some of the things we discuss today are things we never could have been open about thirty years ago. Also, in our area, we are getting more and more adult children of alcoholics Al-Anon Family Groups, which have had much success. I find, too, that more and more parents are coming to our meetings because their children have been to alcoholic rehabilitation centers. Some of these children have been as young as 14.

"We have an Al-Anon Information Office in the downtown Cleveland area. Every year shows a tremendous growth in telephone calls and in sending out literature orders. We now have three telephone lines and three or four people working there. Each day the office is manned by different volunteers. We have been fortunate to have a capable person to manage the office. I volunteer once a month and I find the work very rewarding."

A hazardous course could be set by an over enthusiastic early Al-Anon member

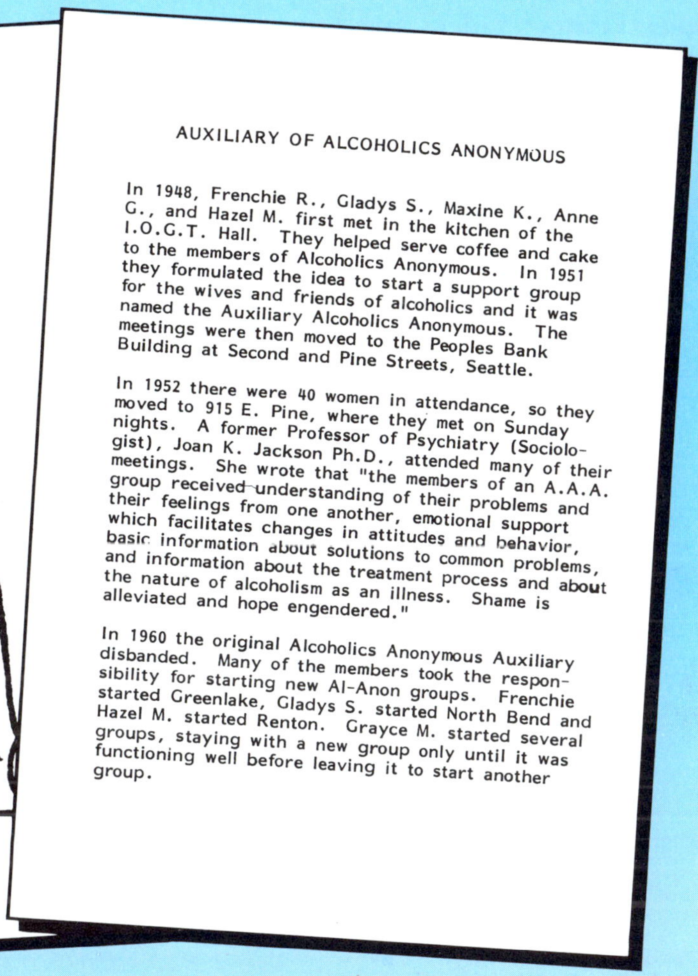
AUXILIARY OF ALCOHOLICS ANONYMOUS

In 1948, Frenchie R., Gladys S., Maxine K., Anne G., and Hazel M. first met in the kitchen of the I.O.G.T. Hall. They helped serve coffee and cake to the members of Alcoholics Anonymous. In 1951 they formulated the idea to start a support group for the wives and friends of alcoholics and it was named the Auxiliary Alcoholics Anonymous. The meetings were then moved to the Peoples Bank Building at Second and Pine Streets, Seattle.

In 1952 there were 40 women in attendance, so they moved to 915 E. Pine, where they met on Sunday nights. A former Professor of Psychiatry (Sociologist), Joan K. Jackson Ph.D., attended many of their meetings. She wrote that "the members of an A.A.A. group received understanding of their problems and their feelings from one another, emotional support which facilitates changes in attitudes and behavior, basic information about solutions to common problems, and information about the treatment process and about the nature of alcoholism as an illness. Shame is alleviated and hope engendered."

In 1960 the original Alcoholics Anonymous Auxiliary disbanded. Many of the members took the responsibility for starting new Al-Anon groups. Frenchie started Greenlake, Gladys S. started North Bend and Hazel M. started Renton. Grayce M. started several groups, staying with a new group only until it was functioning well before leaving it to start another group.

who departed too far from the growing Al-Anon experience, later to be know as a "wider group conscience." Although groups influenced by such a member flourished for a while, eventually they fell on hard times. Jo W., Archives Coordinator for Manitoba, talks of just such an occurrence:

"When I read about members meeting almost 40 years ago, right here in this province without the means to materials and structure as we have it, I feel so grateful for Al-Anon today. You see, in the beginning, the husband sought the cooperation of his wife and together they embraced the AA program. The first AA group in Winnipeg began on January 5, 1945. One year later, the wives decided to form a group and chose the name Semper Fidelis (Always Faithful). Semper Fidelis called themselves an AA Auxiliary and fulfilled that role by serving the AA group.

"There was no literature in 1946, so the AA "Big Book" was used and specifically the two chapters 'To The Wives' and 'The Family Afterwards.' Because there were no guidelines, Lelah J. as president of Semper Fidelis, wrote the Twelve Precepts and the Twelve Resolutions, using the philosophy of the AA program as her guide. They were used for many years, as well as the Creed, at the opening of each Semper Fidelis meeting. This was the way it was done when I came to Semper Fidelis in October, 1969.

"In April, 1950 Semper Fidelis approved a constitution and by-laws written by Lelah, and members accepted them as their group guidelines. Perhaps this appears awesome to us now. But with this early source of literature written by one person, it was very difficult for group members to change their thinking. Lelah died in 1964, but her influence in the group remained.

"On February 10, 1948 Lois visited

Winnipeg. The visit created a bond between Semper Fidelis and Lois so that when Al-Anon began three years later the group and individual members sent donations of support.

"My knowledge of pre-Al-Anon and the isolation of single groups helps me to understand that groups which rely on the existence of the AA group as their reason for meeting are unable to detach as a separate fellowship, unless they are involved in an Al-Anon structure—at first the Clearing House and later the District, Area, or the World Service Office."

Requests for help with Al-Anon group problems were received with increasing frequency back at the Clearing House. In 1952 alone, the Clearing House sent out 1,040 letters and 1,933 pieces of literature. Policy matters could be referred to the growing number of Al-Anon Committees, which multiplied along with the growth of Al-Anon. After Budget, Literature and Publicity, which were all founded in 1955, Public Relations was founded in 1957, from which Public Information evolved in 1973. The Alateen Committee began in 1959, followed by the Conference Committee the following year. Next came Institutions in 1967, with The *FORUM* Editor's Committee in 1968. Archives, and International Coordination were both founded in 1978, and the Regional Service Seminar in 1979. An addition in 1981, was Cooperating With The Professional Community.

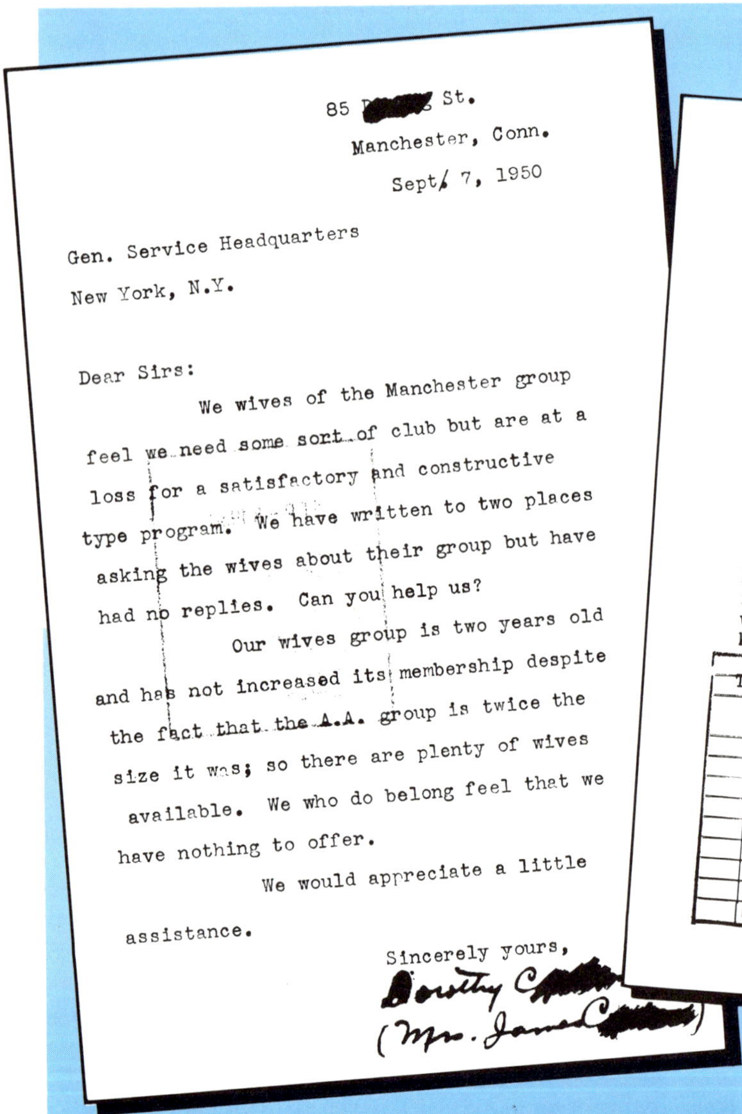

85 [redacted] St.
Manchester, Conn.
Sept. 7, 1950

Gen. Service Headquarters
New York, N.Y.

Dear Sirs:

We wives of the Manchester group feel we need some sort of club but are at a loss for a satisfactory and constructive type program. We have written to two places asking the wives about their group but have had no replies. Can you help us?

Our wives group is two years old and has not increased its membership despite the fact that the A.A. group is twice the size it was; so there are plenty of wives available. We who do belong feel that we have nothing to offer.

We would appreciate a little assistance.

Sincerely yours,
Dorothy [redacted]
(Mrs. James [redacted])

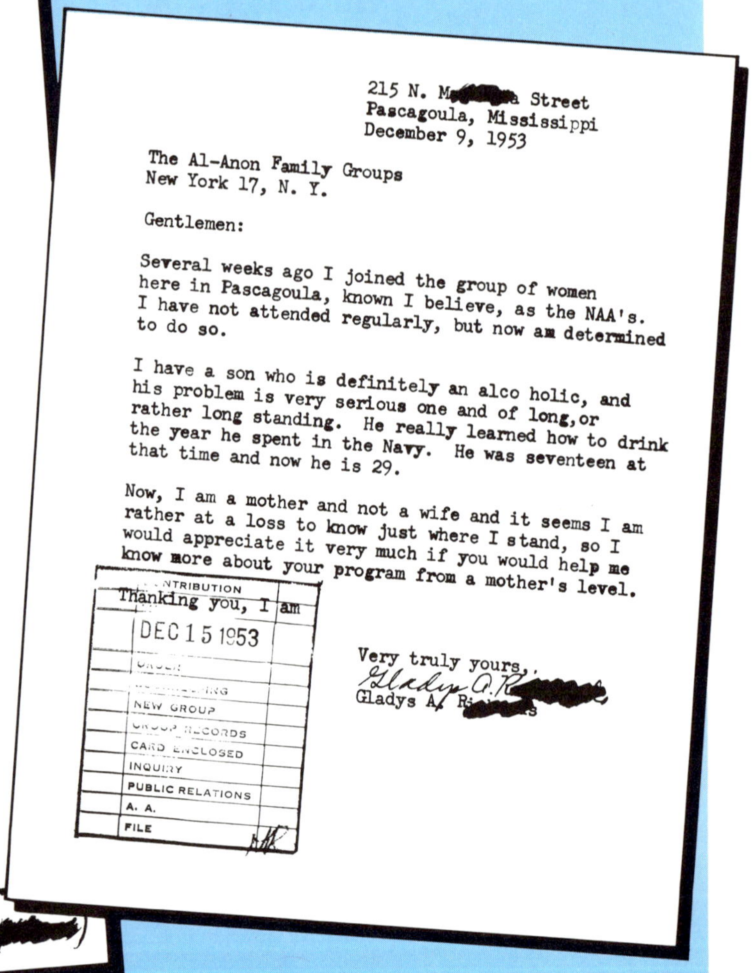

215 N. M[redacted]a Street
Pascagoula, Mississippi
December 9, 1953

The Al-Anon Family Groups
New York 17, N. Y.

Gentlemen:

Several weeks ago I joined the group of women here in Pascagoula, known I believe, as the NAA's. I have not attended regularly, but now am determined to do so.

I have a son who is definitely an alco holic, and his problem is very serious one and of long, or rather long standing. He really learned how to drink the year he spent in the Navy. He was seventeen at that time and now he is 29.

Now, I am a mother and not a wife and it seems I am rather at a loss to know just where I stand, so I would appreciate it very much if you would help me know more about your program from a mother's level. Thanking you, I am

Very truly yours,
Gladys A. R[redacted]
Gladys A. R[redacted]s

DEC 15 1953
NEW GROUP
CARD ENCLOSED
INQUIRY
PUBLIC RELATIONS
A. A.
FILE

December 3, 1952

Mr. J. V. G[redacted]
c/o G[redacted]
Bolivar Street, S[redacted]
Santurce, P. R.

JUN 22 1953

Dear Mr. G[redacted]

We are so glad to hear that you want to start a new group. We have found that the work done in a Family Group can be of great help in integrating family life.

Perhaps you would like to know something of the function of the Clearing House. Here we receive inquiries from Family Groups all over the world, asking for information on how to run meeting, requesting literature, and giving us reports on the progress of their undertakings.

The Clearing House is supported entirely by voluntaryycontrivutions, which help to defray the expense of stationery, printing, mailing, etc. However, such support is not necessary in order to receive assistance from the Clearing House, as we feel that each group will do its best when and if it is in a position to do so.

The enclosed copies of our leaflet, which contain many suggestions for running a Group, are free. Should you desire a quantity of them, we enclose a price list.

With all good wishes for your success, we are

Sincerely yours,

Volunteer

June 25, 1952

Mrs. Carol M[redacted]
4101 [redacted] Street
Corpus Christi
Texas

Dear Carol:

We are very happy to learn of the formation of your group, and have registered it with the Clearing House of the Al-Anon Family Groups. You are now on our regular mailing list and will receive all Bulletins, etc., when they are sent out.

We are interested to learn of the type of meetings you hold, and think they are very good. However, for variety, we are enclosing herewith a list of suggestions for other types of meetings. These, too, have been tried and found helpful.

With best wishes for your continued success, we are

Sincerely yours,

The Al-Anon Family Groups
Anne B[redacted] Secretary

by

idf

(Volunteer)

Mrs. S. C. Th[redacted]
C[redacted]est
Boerne, Texas

July 3, 1953.

Dear Anne B:

The secretary had me present the information which he requested I get from you some time ago, to our small group in San Antonio. It was decid that due to age + requirement etc in our group the program was not desired + therefore none was established.

Most sincerely

Edna S. Th[redacted]

JUN 17 1953

Mrs. Fred M[redacted]
1124 [redacted] Avenue
Henderson, N. C.

Dear Mrs. M[redacted]d:

Upon checking the files in the Family Group office, we find that we have inquiries from two other towns in North Carolina that may be easier for you to contact.

Perhaps you can be of service or help to these women in getting Family Groups started in your part of the state. They are: Secretary, The A. A. Aux., Alcoholics Anonymous, [redacted]t Ave., Asheboro, N. C. and Secretary, Box [redacted], Reidsville, N. C.

With all good wishes,

Most sincerely,

Anne H. B[redacted], Secretary
The Al-Anon Family Groups

Per

Volunteer

209 [redacted] Street, E.P.H.
Pensacola, Florida
November 1 5, 1952

Anne B[redacted], Secretary
The Al-Anon Family Group s
New York, N.Y.

Dear Anne:

I am enclosing card sent us which has been filled out and brought up to date. Wish we could also send our Semi-annual contribution at this time, but we will have to wait a little on that and will send it on as soon as possible.

Do you have any ideas coming in on that age-old problem - "how can we make some money"? Some in the group are opposed to anything that smacks of gambling, such as bingo or selling chances. We have no expenses in connection with a meeting place, etc. as we meet in the A.A. Club House, but would like to buy a fe w books, have extra refreshments sometimes, etc.

Just recently we had 100 copies of the enclosed leaflet p rinted
at a cost of $12.00 per 100, which we feel is a little hi...
will notice it follows quite closely the mimeographed lea...
"Purposes and Suggestions, etc." put out by the Family G...
the Clearing House, the additions being OUR FIRST PRINCI...
(which we were all thrilled at seeing in print in the cu...
Grap e Vine) and the Prayer for Peace, which we incorpor...
our meetings as we feel that it the almost-p erfect pray...
the Family Group. In fact, when we were first organizi...
different members - each unknown to the other - brought...
and it was quickly adopted by all as they felt it expre...
well and fully, just what we are trying to do for the al...
in our family, as well as for the families of other alc...
We intend to give our little leaflet to new AA members...
home to their families in order to get the family inte...
the Family Group, so they will perhaps come back with...
the next meeting.

We received all the literature we ordered, and from th...
list, are starting a little library of our own. Every...
the "Suggested Programs" and it really is a help. We...
office has done a wonderful work since organizing and...
have been up against terrific odds. Do you think, la...
you might p rint a booklet which will cover the "Purp...
Suggestions" leaflet and also include the Twelve Trad...
(Incidentally, our group approved the Traditions one...
percent) Of course, we would love to see our Prayer...
in it too - not at all because it is "ours", but bec...
it puts into beautiful words what we want to do for...
holic and for the families towhom AA hasn't yet com...
way of life.

With every good wish to you all! Most sincerely,

New Castle, Ind.
April 21, 1954

Gentlemen:

I am the wife of an A.A. of the New Castle
Groupe and also a member of our ladies
Groupe. We meet once a Month and it is
our custom to have a discussion at these
meetings. A different lady is chosen each
Month to lead and to pick the subject
matter for these open discussions.

Since I am to lead our next meeting, I
have decided to explore the subject of
children of A.A's, their part in the program,
and their rehabilitation after years in an
...holic home. We have a 9 yr. old daughter
... this subject and it's proper treatment is
... important to me and to my husband.
Is there any available material on this
...ect? How can I obtain it? Would you
... advise me as soon as possible?

Respectfully,
Mrs. Doyle K[redacted]
2114 [redacted] St.
New Castle, Ind.

CONTRIBUTION
PAYMENT
MAY 3 1954
ORDER
...OOKKEEPING
...W GROUP
...UP RECORDS
...D ENCLOSED
...RY
...RELATIONS

Mrs. George H. R[redacted],
131 C[redacted]d Ave.
Jenkintown, Penn.

July 28, 1953

Dear Kay:

It has been a long time since I have seen you. The busier we get the less we see of our old friends. When are you and George coming to New York again?

We have had a number of calls from wives in the Philadelphia area and we have no record of a Family Group there. We would like to be able to refer these inquiring wives to a Family Group. Do you know of any group that hasn't yet registered with us? I know you have your classes in spititual development that are so fine and I thought that perhaps you would not want to be bothered by these calls.

What would you suggest? Shall we try to have these gals get together and form their own Family Group? Perhaps that would be best.

We are putting out a "World Directory" and I'm afraid our card system has been mixed up and that you have not been receiving our bulletins. Under separate cover, I am sending the bulletins we have sent out during the last two years as well as some sample literature. If there is a group in your area would you ask them to fill out the enclosed card and send it to us.

The wo*k is going along wonderfully now and we have about five hundred Family Groups registered.

Bill joins me in affectionate greetings to you and George.

As ever,

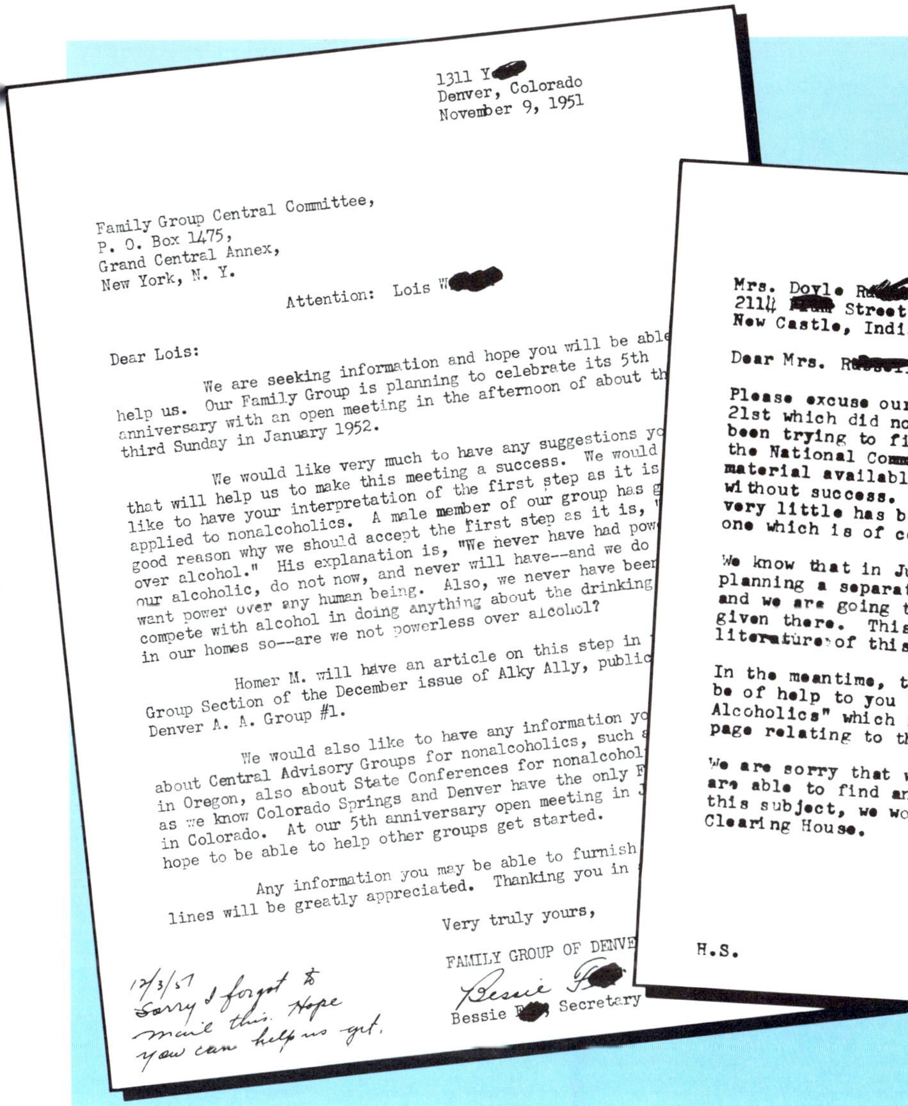

1311 Y[redacted]
Denver, Colorado
November 9, 1951

Family Group Central Committee,
P. O. Box 1475,
Grand Central Annex,
New York, N. Y.

Attention: Lois W[redacted]

Dear Lois:

We are seeking information and hope you will be able
help us. Our Family Group is planning to celebrate its 5th
anniversary with an open meeting in the afternoon of about th
third Sunday in January 1952.

We would like very much to have any suggestions yo
that will help us to make this meeting a success. We would
like to have your interpretation of the first step as it is
applied to nonalcoholics. A male member of our group has g
good reason why we should accept the first step as it is, "
over alcohol." His explanation is, "We never have had pow
our alcoholic, do not now, and never will have--and we do
want power over any human being. Also, we never have been
compete with alcohol in doing anything about the drinking
in our homes so--are we not powerless over alcohol?

Homer M. will have an article on this step in
Group Section of the December issue of Alky Ally, public
Denver A. A. Group #1.

We would also like to have any information yo
about Central Advisory Groups for nonalcoholics, such
in Oregon, also about State Conferences for nonalcohol
as we know Colorado Springs and Denver have the only F
in Colorado. At our 5th anniversary open meeting in J
hope to be able to help other groups get started.

Any information you may be able to furnish
lines will be greatly appreciated. Thanking you in

Very truly yours,

FAMILY GROUP OF DENVE

Bessie [redacted]
Bessie [redacted] Secretary

12/3/51
Sorry I forgot to
mail this. Hope
you can help us get.

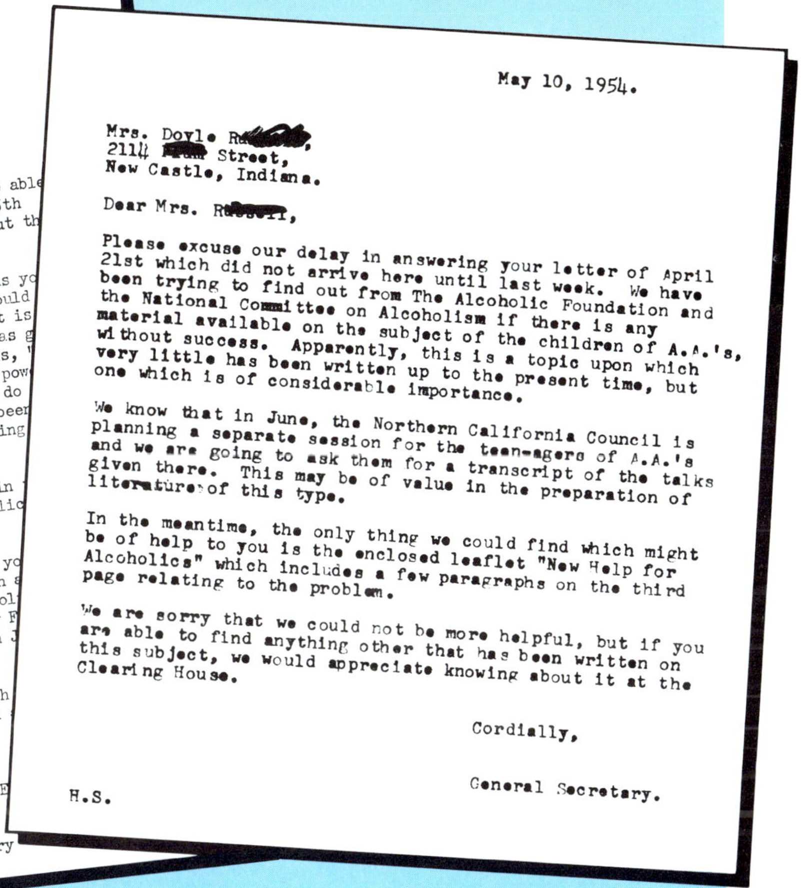

May 10, 1954.

Mrs. Doyle R[redacted],
2114 [redacted] Street,
New Castle, Indiana.

Dear Mrs. R[redacted],

Please excuse our delay in answering your letter of April 21st which did not arrive here until last week. We have been trying to find out from The Alcoholic Foundation and the National Committee on Alcoholism if there is any material available on the subject of the children of A.A.'s, without success. Apparently, this is a topic upon which very little has been written up to the present time, but one which is of considerable importance.

We know that in June, the Northern California Council is planning a separate session for the teen-agers of A.A.'s and we are going to ask them for a transcript of the talks given there. This may be of value in the preparation of literature of this type.

In the meantime, the only thing we could find which might be of help to you is the enclosed leaflet "New Help for Alcoholics" which includes a few paragraphs on the third page relating to the problem.

We are sorry that we could not be more helpful, but if you are able to find anything other that has been written on this subject, we would appreciate knowing about it at the Clearing House.

Cordially,

General Secretary.

H.S.

Inevitably, the Clearing House outgrew the space at the Old 24th Street Clubhouse. Henrietta says, "In 1957, we decided to take a big step forward and actually rent a real office. It was located at 125 East 23rd Street and when that became too small, we took a second floor with a pulley dumbwaiter going up and down. When that space became too small, we moved to 115 East 23rd Street, later taking two additional floors. Finally, in 1978, just after I retired, we moved to One Park Avenue." In 1986, another move for the WSO is being made to 1372 Broadway.

At the close of each year, Henrietta, as General Secretary, submitted her financial report. The figures reveal Al-Anon's rate of growth. An extract from the 1960 report reads:

"There was a 33% increase in cash receipts, with a parallel increase in volume of detail handled by the publications, bookkeeping and filing departments. The increase in the number of packages mailed was better than 38%, and the *FORUMS* more than 9%. Book sales have almost doubled."

It is not surprising to see that for 1960, income rose by about $10,000, but profits on literature sales alone rose by about $7,000 between 1962 and 1963. Total [Al-Anon] Family Group Headquarters' income in the same period was around $53,000, with about $51,000 paid out for salaries, insurance, telephones, office supplies and so on. It was a practical move to incorporate the Clearing House into Al-Anon Family Group Headquarters in 1954, in order to gain tax-emempt status as a nonprofit organization.

Another development was the founding of separate Al-Anon Intergroup offices. Henrietta reported: "The opening of the New York Al-Anon Intergroup has relieved Headquarters of publishing the local meeting lists and also of much of the local Twelfth-Step telephoning, formerly handled at the office. There are now six other Al-Anon Intergroups, and letters from Vancouver, B.C. and Nova Scotia, Canada and the Boston, Massachussetts area indicate that other local central Al-Anon Intergroups are on the way."

Intergroups, now known as Information Services, have grown along with the rest of Al-Anon. For example, in 1984, there were seven Information Services listed for New York, 14 for California and five for British Columbia.

The entire Al-Anon structure crystalized for the first time when Anne B. and the volunteers began the compilation of a *World Directory* in 1952. The *World Directory* was to be updated and published each successive year after that. This work required detailed and accurate updating of Al-Anon files, by obtaining information directly from the groups. Anne explains why, in a letter sent out in 1953.

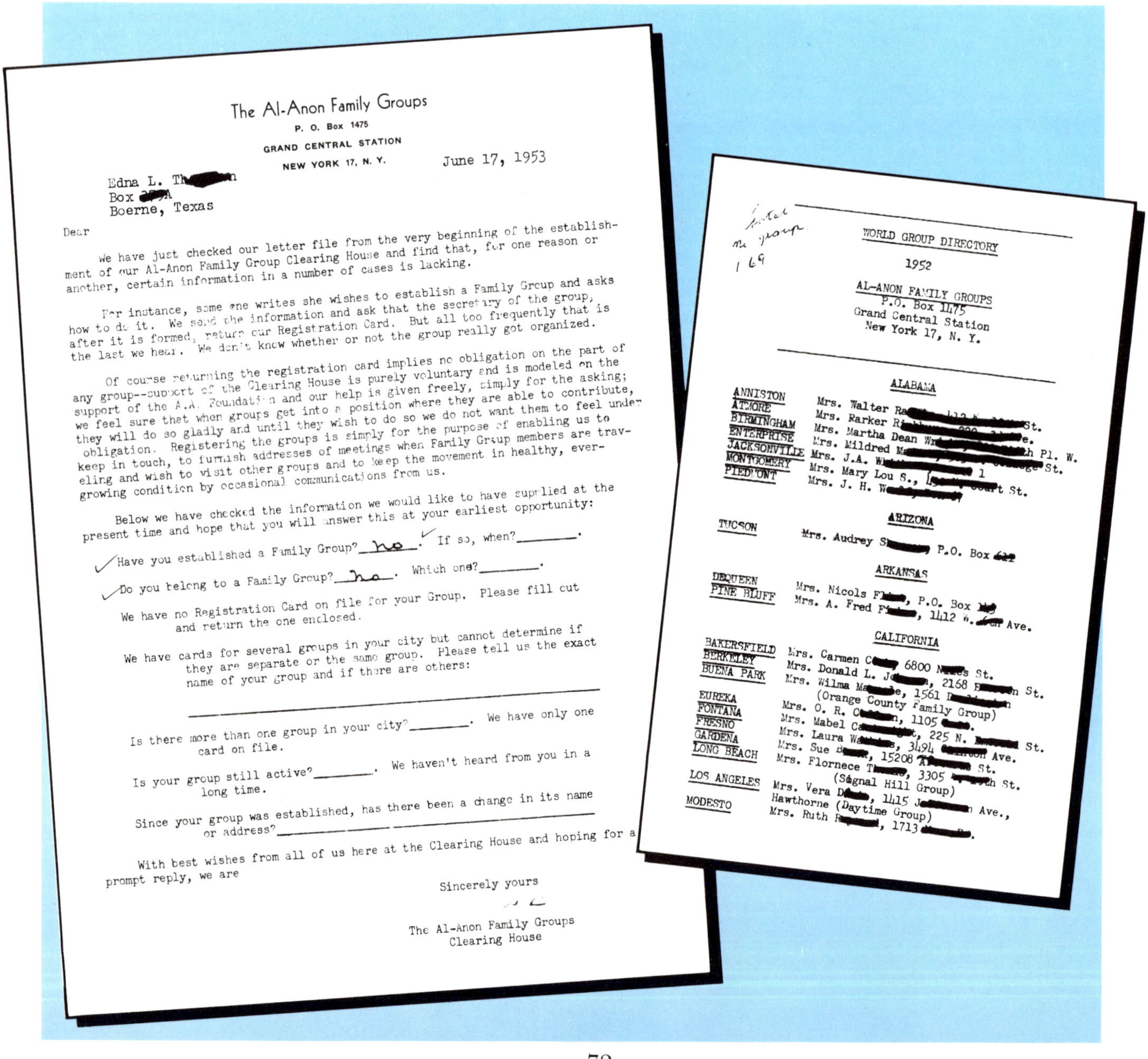

The Al-Anon Family Groups
P. O. Box 1475
GRAND CENTRAL STATION
NEW YORK 17, N. Y.

June 17, 1953

Edna L. Th[redacted]
Box [redacted]A
Boerne, Texas

Dear

We have just checked our letter file from the very beginning of the establishment of our Al-Anon Family Group Clearing House and find that, for one reason or another, certain information in a number of cases is lacking.

For instance, some one writes she wishes to establish a Family Group and asks how to do it. We send the information and ask that the secretary of the group, after it is formed, return our Registration Card. But all too frequently that is the last we hear. We don't know whether or not the group really got organized.

Of course returning the registration card implies no obligation on the part of any group--support of the Clearing House is purely voluntary and is modeled on the support of the A.A. Foundation and our help is given freely, simply for the asking; we feel sure that when groups get into a position where they are able to contribute, they will do so gladly and until they wish to do so we do not want them to feel under obligation. Registering the groups is simply for the purpose of enabling us to keep in touch, to furnish addresses of meetings when Family Group members are traveling and wish to visit other groups and to keep the movement in healthy, ever-growing condition by occasional communications from us.

Below we have checked the information we would like to have supplied at the present time and hope that you will answer this at your earliest opportunity:

✓ Have you established a Family Group? no. ✓ If so, when?________.

✓ Do you belong to a Family Group? no. Which one?________.

We have no Registration Card on file for your Group. Please fill out and return the one enclosed.

We have cards for several groups in your city but cannot determine if they are separate or the same group. Please tell us the exact name of your group and if there are others:

Is there more than one group in your city?________. We have only one card on file.

Is your group still active?________. We haven't heard from you in a long time.

Since your group was established, has there been a change in its name or address?________

With best wishes from all of us here at the Clearing House and hoping for a prompt reply, we are

Sincerely yours

The Al-Anon Family Groups
Clearing House

total no group 169

WORLD GROUP DIRECTORY

1952

AL-ANON FAMILY GROUPS
P.O. Box 1475
Grand Central Station
New York 17, N. Y.

ALABAMA

ANNISTON Mrs. Walter Ra[redacted]St.
ATMORE Mrs. Rarker Ri[redacted]e.
BIRMINGHAM Mrs. Martha Dean Wr[redacted]h Pl. W.
ENTERPRISE Mrs. Mildred M[redacted]St.
JACKSONVILLE Mrs. J.A. W[redacted] 1
MONTGOMERY Mrs. Mary Lou S., [redacted]t St.
PIEDMONT Mrs. J. H. W[redacted]

ARIZONA

TUCSON Mrs. Audrey S[redacted] P.O. Box [redacted]

ARKANSAS

DEQUEEN Mrs. Nicols F[redacted], P.O. Box [redacted]
PINE BLUFF Mrs. A. Fred F[redacted], 1412 W. [redacted] Ave.

CALIFORNIA

BAKERSFIELD Mrs. Carmen C[redacted] 6800 N[redacted]s St.
BERKELEY Mrs. Donald L. J[redacted], 2168 E[redacted]n St.
BUENA PARK Mrs. Wilma Ma[redacted]e, 1561 D[redacted]
(Orange County Family Group)
EUREKA Mrs. O. R. C[redacted], 1105 [redacted].
FONTANA Mrs. Mabel C[redacted], 225 N. [redacted] St.
FRESNO Mrs. Laura Wa[redacted], 3494 [redacted] Ave.
GARDENA Mrs. Sue B[redacted], 15208 A[redacted] St.
LONG BEACH Mrs. Flornece T[redacted], 3305 [redacted]h St.
(Signal Hill Group)
LOS ANGELES Mrs. Vera D[redacted], 1415 J[redacted] Ave.,
Hawthorne (Daytime Group)
MODESTO Mrs. Ruth R[redacted], 1713 [redacted].

2.

CALIFORNIA, Cont.

MONTEREY PENINSULAR Mrs. Jean [redacted], 151 [redacted] St.Pacific
NAPA Mrs. Ruby [redacted], 116 E. [redacted] St.
NO.HOLLYWOOD Mrs. Dorothy M. S[redacted], 10627 [redacted]
REDONDO BEACH Mrs. Chas. M. H[redacted], 110 S. [redacted]
ROSEVILLE Mr. George S[redacted], 202 [redacted]
SACRAMENTO Mrs. Emma M[redacted], 2001 [redacted]
SALINAS Mrs. Evelyn W[redacted], 1235 - [redacted]
SAN DIEGO Mrs. Earl R[redacted], 506 [redacted] Bldg
SAN FRANCISCO Mrs. Ruth [redacted], 962 [redacted] Ave.
SAN GABRIEL Mrs. Vivian H[redacted] 10439 [redacted] Rd.
SAN JOSE Mrs. Carrie [redacted] 840 [redacted] Drive
SAN LUIS OBISPO Secretary, Box 171
SAN PEDRO Mrs. Ethel M. [redacted] 26420 [redacted] Ave. Harbor City
SANTA BARBARA Mrs. Laura A. B[redacted], 27 W. [redacted] St
TORRANCE Mrs. Carolyn M. S[redacted], 1715 [redacted]
VENTURA Mrs. Emily Y[redacted] Gen.Del. P.O. Box [redacted]
WHITTIER Mrs. Bill C[redacted], 515 W. [redacted]

COLORADO

COLORADO SPRINGS Mrs. Marie B[redacted], 609 S. [redacted]
DENVER Mrs. Lelia B[redacted]t, 1311 [redacted] St.

CONNECTICUT

MANCHESTER Mrs. James C[redacted], 85 [redacted] St.
STAMFORD Mrs. Winthrop [redacted] Rd.

DISTRICT OF COLUMBIA

WASHINGTON Mrs. Bess J[redacted], 915 S. [redacted] Alexandria, Va.

FLORIDA

JACKSONVILLE Mrs. Alice F[redacted], 1288 [redacted] St
MIAMI Mrs. Frances L. S[redacted], 2140 [redacted]
Mrs. Pauline S[redacted], 146 Jefferson (Prospective Group)
ORLANDO Mrs. Ralph C. B[redacted], 406 [redacted]
PENSACOLA Mrs. Norma P[redacted]n, 209 - [redacted]

3.

GEORGIA

ALBANY Mrs. J. H. W[redacted], 1211 N.[redacted]
ATLANTA Mrs. Elma T. H[redacted], 278 - [redacted] St., (Prospective Group)
DOUGLAS Mrs. Julian W. F[redacted], D[redacted]

ILLINOIS

DANVILLE O. W. L[redacted], Box [redacted]
CHICAGO Central Office, Room 1101, 123 W. Madi
LA GRANGE Secretary, 11239 W. 71 St.
MENDOTA Arden C[redacted]l, 1218 J[redacted]
PEORIA Fern S[redacted]l, 5015 [redacted] Rd.

INDIANA

EAST CHICAGO Mrs. Neil M[redacted]d, 5030 [redacted] Ave.
ELKHART Mrs. J.H. R[redacted], 1843 [redacted] St.

IOWA

DES MOINES Mrs. Richard [redacted], 2835 [redacted] Ave.
ESTHERVILLE Mrs. W. D. K[redacted], 115 [redacted] St.
WEBSTER CITY Mrs. Kendall H[redacted], Rte [redacted]
WADENA Dawson C[redacted], [redacted]

KANSAS

ARKANSAS CITY Mrs. Herman L. F[redacted] 1312 [redacted]
BELOIT Mrs. Leon Y[redacted], 613 N. [redacted]
COFFEYVILLE Mrs. Richard M. [redacted]
COLBY Violet [redacted], 260 W. [redacted]
HUTCHINSON Mrs. Maurine A. F[redacted], 405 N. [redacted]
KANSAS CITY Mrs. Jessie [redacted], [redacted] 1925 N.
TOPEKA Mrs. Eva C[redacted], 1431 [redacted]

KENTUCKY

HARLAN Mrs. A. S[redacted], 302 B[redacted]
LOUISVILLE Mrs. James F. D[redacted], 1420 [redacted] St.

LOUISIANA

SHREVEPORT Bertha F[redacted], 3220 S[redacted] Ave.
BATON ROUGE Mrs. J. J. O'[redacted] 1564 [redacted] Dr.

4.

LOUISIANA, Cont.

NEW ORLEANS Mrs. Milo W[redacted], 1005 [redacted] Bldg.

MAINE

PORTLAND Mrs. P.H. B[redacted], Room [redacted] Congress St.
BENTON STA. Mrs. Elaine S[redacted] B[redacted]
SOUTH PORTLAND Mrs. Irene F[redacted], 33 [redacted] Ave.

MARYLAND

CUMBERLAND Mrs. Harriet O[redacted], C[redacted]

MASSACHUSETTS

BROCKTON Marie [redacted] 74 [redacted] St.
NEWTON CENTER Mrs. Roger W[redacted], 126 [redacted] St.
NORTON Mrs. Ethel M[redacted], PO Box [redacted]
LYNN Mr. Samuel K[redacted], 7 [redacted] Ave.,Salem
LONGMEADOW D.P. M[redacted], 133 P[redacted] Ave.
SPRINGFIELD Mrs. S. K[redacted], Box [redacted]
JAMAICA PLAINS Mrs. R. H. L[redacted], [redacted] Ave.
% Mrs. Martin [redacted]

MICHIGAN

BENTON HARBOR Grace S[redacted] 70 - [redacted]
ESCANABA Gladyce C[redacted], 510 - [redacted]. S
MUSKEGON Mrs. Anna M[redacted], 446 [redacted]e Blvd.
APPLETON Madlyn H[redacted], [redacted]

MISSISSIPPI

PASS CHRISTIAN Mrs. Bish M[redacted], Box [redacted]
MACOMBS Mrs. F. B. H[redacted] 331 - [redacted]
PHILADELPHIA Mrs. Joe [redacted], 533 A[redacted]

MISSOURI

INDEPENDENCE Lois S[redacted], 309 N[redacted]
JOPLIN Essie M[redacted], RFD 3, [redacted]
ST. LOUIS John F. M[redacted],6111 A[redacted]ve.

NEW JERSEY

MARGATE CITY Mrs. D. W. C[redacted], 109 S. [redacted] Ave.

5.

NEW JERSEY, Cont.

OAKLYN Mrs. John A. V[redacted], 174 K[redacted] Blvd.
VERONA Mrs. Robert V[redacted]e, 5 [redacted]es Dr.

NEW MEXICO

CARLSBAD Annie [redacted], 1007 N. [redacted]

NEW YORK

BUFFALO Jeanette L[redacted]k, 292 [redacted] St.
ELMIRA Sec., N.A.A. Helpmates, PO Box 144
NEW YORK CITY(METROPOLITAN AREA)
BAYSIDE, L.I. Doris S[redacted], 42-09 - [redacted]
BROOKLYN Helen B[redacted] 2303 [redacted]
BRONX Vera M[redacted], 689 [redacted]
85th St. Fannie L[redacted], 155 [redacted]
JACKSON HEIGHTS Irma F[redacted], 7515 [redacted]
KEW GARDENS Marge K[redacted] 63 [redacted]
NORTHERN WESTCHESTER Anne B[redacted], C[redacted], N. Y.
NORTH TONAWANDA Sybil S[redacted], Rte [redacted]
ROCHESTER Mrs. Frank B. D[redacted] 11 [redacted]
SCHENECTADY Mrs. Jessie F[redacted], Apt [redacted]
SYRACUSE Ira O[redacted], 210 N[redacted] Ave.
UTICA Agnes E[redacted] 1008 [redacted]
WATERTOWN Mrs. L. E. S[redacted], Rte [redacted]
WELLSVILLE Mrs. Geo. B. C[redacted] Jr., Bo[redacted]

NORTH CAROLINA

CHARLOTTE Melrose E[redacted], 912 [redacted] Place
FAYETTEVILLE A.F. D[redacted], [redacted]
GREENSBORO Sue P[redacted], 1909 S[redacted]
WINSTON-SALEM Sec., P.O. Box 27[redacted]

NORTH DAKOTA

BOWMAN Mrs. Eddie S[redacted] Box 3[redacted]
GRAND FORKS Mrs. L. H. G[redacted], 817 N. [redacted]

OKLAHOMA

FREDERICK Sec., P.O. Box 21
OKMULGEE Mrs. Rufus [redacted], 500 S.[redacted]

6.

SOUTH CAROLINA

CHARLESTON Elizabeth M[redacted]y, 116 S. [redacted]
GREENWOOD Mrs. L.E. C[redacted], 450 S[redacted] Ave.

SOUTH DAKOTA

YANKTON Vera S[redacted], 118 W[redacted].

TENNESSEE

GREENEVILLE Gladys B[redacted], 220 [redacted] Ave.
KNOXVILLE Mrs. Paul M[redacted], 121 [redacted] Ave
OAK RIDGE Shirley N[redacted], 112 [redacted] Rd.

TEXAS

AUSTIN Eloise C[redacted], 4101 [redacted] Rd.
COLORADO CITY Myrtle L[redacted] Box 8[redacted]
DALLAS Mrs. Lloyd C[redacted], 5740 [redacted]
HOUSTON Mrs. W. S[redacted], 7[redacted]
Mrs. Francis S[redacted], 750 [redacted]
TEXAS CITY Wylma C[redacted], PO Box [redacted]
TYLER Mrs. C. A. G[redacted], 407 [redacted]
WICHITA FALLS Mrs. Ruth K[redacted], RTe [redacted]

UTAH

GRANTSVILLE Nola [redacted], Grantsville
PRICE Wanda T[redacted], 443 [redacted]
PROVO Mrs. Thelda Y[redacted], 724 [redacted]
SALT LAKE CITY Doris H[redacted] 479 [redacted] East
E. SALT LAKE CITY Peg T[redacted], 479 [redacted] St.

VIRGINIA

ARLINGTON Mary Frances B[redacted] 2527 [redacted]
NEWPORT NEWS Jane M[redacted], 329R - [redacted].

WASHINGTON

LITTLE ROCK Mrs. W. O. [redacted], Box [redacted]
RENTON Millie M[redacted], 605 [redacted] St.
SEATTLE Dorothy G[redacted], 1733 B[redacted]
TACOMA Mrs. Weldon S[redacted]ll, 1715 [redacted] Rd

7.

WISCONSIN

GREEN BAY Mrs. Joe K[redacted] 1325 [redacted]
MADISON Phillip C. S[redacted]opf, R[redacted].Main
MILWAUKEE Dorothy S[redacted]t, 1523 [redacted]
SHEBOYGAN Evelyn P[redacted], 303 [redacted] Ave.
STEVENS POINT Mrs. Carl F. S[redacted] Route [redacted]
WAUKESHA Mabel W[redacted], 308 [redacted] Dr.

WYOMING

CHEYENNE Mrs. James H. V[redacted], 2207 [redacted] St.

CANADA

ALBERTA
EDMONTON Mrs. E.K. D[redacted], 9823 - [redacted]
CALGARY Mrs. Elsie T[redacted]t, 36 - [redacted]
BRITISH COLUMBIA
VANCOUVER Margaret [redacted] 3318 P[redacted] Ave.So[redacted]
Elsie J[redacted], 985 W. [redacted]. (Kitsilano Friendship Group)
MANITOBA
BRANDON N. T[redacted], 258 - [redacted]
ST. BONIFACE Ernestine D[redacted], 627 [redacted] St.
WINNIPEG Elizabeth L[redacted], 213 [redacted] Ave.
NEW BRUNSWICK
ST. JOHN Jack [redacted]
NOVA SCOTIA
AMHURST Mrs. Anne [redacted], 15 [redacted].
ONTARIO
TORONTO Mrs. Ann R[redacted], 169 [redacted] Ave.
Mrs. Goodwin G[redacted], 500 [redacted]
Mrs. Pearl E[redacted], 136 H[redacted] Ave. W
PORT DOVER R.B. W[redacted], 111 [redacted]
QUEBEC
SHERBROOKE Mrs. Irene S[redacted], 279 [redacted].

AUSTRALIA

GLEBE Mrs. Russell J[redacted], 13 C[redacted] Ave.

IRELAND

BELFAST Margaret C[redacted], 8 C[redacted] R. N. Ireland

SOUTH AFRICA

CAPETOWN Doris D[redacted], "Son[redacted] Claremont
EAST LONDON Miss. Margareta S. S[redacted] Fla[redacted] St.

The first *World Directory* listed 156 groups in 36 states, 14 groups in Canada and included listings in Australia, Ireland and South Africa. A second, slightly enlarged directory was prepared the following year, but the first printed booklet was published in 1955. The extraordinary growth of Al-Anon worldwide is sharply evident in this and subsequent directories. By 1956, Canadian groups totaled 93 (some of these are listed as proposed groups). The 1958 *World Directory* listed groups in Africa, Asia, Australia, Europe, Central America and South America. By 1980 the *World Directory* was published in several volumes: United States East, United States West, Canada and International. New York had 549 Al-Anon groups, and 114 Alateen groups registered, and California had 794 Al-Anon groups and 124 Alateen groups. In the Canadian directory, British Columbia had 214 Al-Anon groups and 43 Alateen groups with one Al-Anon and one Alateen group in the Yukon Territory with two lone members.

In the beginning, Lois and Anne had been able to poll each of the groups about policy decisions, such as finances, publicity, and the future of the Clearing House. Contact with all the groups was needed for financial support as well; the Clearing House had to have funding to remain operative—pay salaries, rent, and to meet literature printing costs—although some revenue could be realized from the sale of the literature itself. Anne B. pointed out many years later that she and Lois had met initial expenses out of their own pockets.

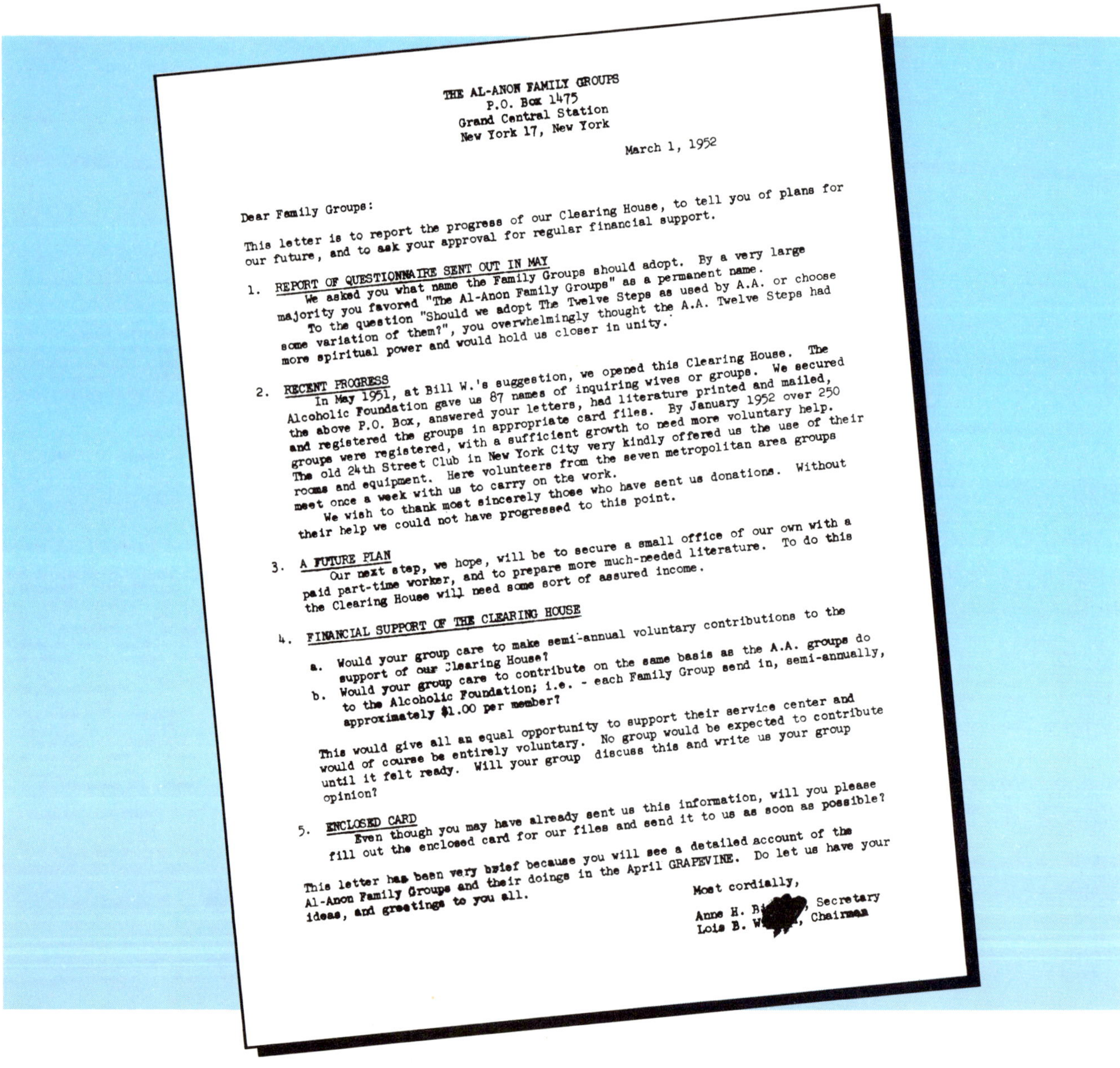

THE AL-ANON FAMILY GROUPS
P.O. Box 1475
Grand Central Station
New York 17, New York

March 1, 1952

Dear Family Groups:

This letter is to report the progress of our Clearing House, to tell you of plans for our future, and to ask your approval for regular financial support.

1. REPORT OF QUESTIONNAIRE SENT OUT IN MAY
We asked you what name the Family Groups should adopt. By a very large majority you favored "The Al-Anon Family Groups" as a permanent name.
To the question "Should we adopt The Twelve Steps as used by A.A. or choose some variation of them?", you overwhelmingly thought the A.A. Twelve Steps had more spiritual power and would hold us closer in unity.

2. RECENT PROGRESS
In May 1951, at Bill W.'s suggestion, we opened this Clearing House. The Alcoholic Foundation gave us 87 names of inquiring wives or groups. We secured the above P.O. Box, answered your letters, had literature printed and mailed, and registered the groups in appropriate card files. By January 1952 over 250 groups were registered, with a sufficient growth to need more voluntary help. The old 24th Street Club in New York City very kindly offered us the use of their rooms and equipment. Here volunteers from the seven metropolitan area groups meet once a week with us to carry on the work.
We wish to thank most sincerely those who have sent us donations. Without their help we could not have progressed to this point.

3. A FUTURE PLAN
Our next step, we hope, will be to secure a small office of our own with a paid part-time worker, and to prepare more much-needed literature. To do this the Clearing House will need some sort of assured income.

4. FINANCIAL SUPPORT OF THE CLEARING HOUSE
a. Would your group care to make semi-annual voluntary contributions to the support of our Clearing House?
b. Would your group care to contribute on the same basis as the A.A. groups do to the Alcoholic Foundation; i.e. - each Family Group send in, semi-annually, approximately $1.00 per member?

This would give all an equal opportunity to support their service center and would of course be entirely voluntary. No group would be expected to contribute until it felt ready. Will your group discuss this and write us your group opinion?

5. ENCLOSED CARD
Even though you may have already sent us this information, will you please fill out the enclosed card for our files and send it to us as soon as possible?

This letter has been very brief because you will see a detailed account of the Al-Anon Family Groups and their doings in the April GRAPEVINE. Do let us have your ideas, and greetings to you all.

Most cordially,

Anne H. B[redacted], Secretary
Lois B. W[redacted], Chairman

Following AA's lead, Lois sent out a request immediately for financial support in March, 1952. Some groups responded to this request, others did not. How to gain uniform support from all the groups remained a knotty problem. Financing the operation of the Al-Anon service structure became one of the first discussions of the Al-Anon World Service Conference nearly ten years later.

Reminiscing together, Henrietta and Lois say they are almost overwhelmed to see the extent to which their first efforts have grown. Today the WSO has a salaried staff of 67 but this nerve center for Al-Anon activity worldwide still retains much of the Clearing House flavor.

"At some level we have tried to maintain as much of the past as we possibly can," says Myrna H., General Secretary since 1978. "Although we have become more sophisticated, we try to maintain the love and caring of the early volunteers."

Myrna joined the WSO staff in 1966. Two years after Henrietta retired in 1976, she became the General Secretary, succeeding Eleanor O. when she resigned. Myrna says, "I like to think of the WSO staff as my colleagues. Over the years we have shared so many experiences together."

Myrna tells the legend of the WSO's first Office Manager, Henny Neiger, who came for an interview as a bookkeeper in 1962 wearing her son's beat-up old raincoat. Her son was six feet tall. Henny was under five feet. She really didn't want to be hired, so, according to Myrna, hoped the raincoat would deter her prospective employers. But Henrietta and Evelyn were so desperate for help at the time, they decided to take Henny, raincoat and all. Henny was to become an inspiration and a mentor to many of the WSO staff.

Henrietta, after her retirement, continued to serve Al-Anon as volunteer Treasurer of the Board of Trustees. Al-Anon has had Board chairmen over the years who have also served with an unusual degree of dedication. They are Mary S., Ted K., Stephanie O'K., Hank G. and Norma McG. Myrna points to this extraordinary dedication to Al-Anon as exemplified by the present Chairman. Norma McG. travels from Boston, where she lives and holds a full-time administrative position. At least twice a month she attends various committee meetings at the WSO. Like her predecessors, Norma is always available for phone consultations between meetings.

In addition to having volunteer Trustees and committee members, the WSO also enjoys the services of Al-Anon and Alateen volunteers who help daily with such projects as assembling packets and stuffing envelopes. Many of these volunteers, important to the whole WSO effort, join staff members at lunch time and share their sense of dedication in carrying the Al-Anon message. A party is held for the volunteers every December. "Nothing has really changed since the early days," says Myrna. "There are just more volunteers needed to help get the job done."

Myrna remembers that at 125 East 23rd Street, the WSO had a dumb-waiter. If you wanted something from the shipping department downstairs, you would ring a bell then stick your head into the shaft to talk with Gene Bennett, the shipping supervisor. She says you had to be careful to avoid getting knocked out by the ascending or descending gadget. Gene says he used a buzzer to announce that completed orders were on their way up in the dumb-waiter.

Gene began in April, 1964 as Al-Anon's first shipping clerk. He was hired by Henny to pack and ship literature and run the mimeograph machine. "After six months she began to like me," Gene says, "and Henny was like family to me."

When packages to be shipped rose from the average of 30 a day in 1962, to 130 a day in 1969, Gene's ingenuity and inventiveness grew along with Al-Anon. He first suggested to Henny that they do away with the corrugated cardboard that appeared to be inadequate protection and invest in several standard-sized cartons in which to pack the literature. Henny, according to Gene, sometimes doubted his ideas, but he says he had to come up with something because Al-Anon was growing so fast.

"Doubling and tripling within a year's time, it was hard to believe in that kind of growth," Gene says. "At first I didn't take an interest in the literature I was handling, but eventually I got curious and wanted to find out what it was all about, so I started reading. You know, those books and pamphlets really do help."

Today, the department sends out an average of 400 packages a day. *One Day At A Time* is still the most popular hardcover book, with *Merry-Go-Round Named Denial* and *Guide for the Family* leading among the pamphlets. In 1986, the shipping department will be moving to a separate location from the WSO.

Myrna's Deputy, Sandra F., started out as a secretary for P.I. Services in 1976. She became Al-Anon's first International Secretary in 1978, and Deputy General Secretary in 1981. Sandy acts as service supervisor and director of new projects.

Richard Keilly, who supervises business services, is also Al-Anon's Controller. He is assisted by an accounting staff of nine. Al-Anon will have an annual expense budget of over $5 million for 1985, processing 50,000 literature orders and handling 30,000 individual contributions.

Each of the Services, Alateen, Archives, Conference, Cooperating with the Professional Community (CPC), Institutions, International Coordination, Literature and Public Information is staffed by an administrative Staff Secretary, all of whom are Al-Anon members. The remaining positions are staffed by Al-Anon and non-Al-Anons alike, each with a sense of loyality and dedication to all that our fellowship stands for.

Myrna points out that the manual typewriter at the Clearing House was the first in a "family" of office equipment. Today, there are over 50 electric typewriters in use, word processors, and sophisticated computer systems for publications, Group Records and for the present 45,000 *FORUM* subscriptions. Should anyone feel, as did Lois and Henrietta, rather overwhelmed by the impersonal quality of this new technology, Myrna hastens to add that a telephone inquiry to the WSO is answered by any one of a number of the Staff Secretaries, all of whom are steeped in the Al-Anon Traditions and principles. A meeting of the Staff Secretaries is held weekly to discuss timely issues and to answer queries from groups or individuals, so that a WSO response relies more on the group conscience than on personal views. Many typewritten replies will contain a few handwritten lines by the sender to maintain a personal touch.

Myrna says, "In the twenty years I have served at the WSO I have been fortunate to see many firsts; the one that pleases me the most is having been a part of Al-Anon's first International Convention, held in July of 1985. We were able to work side by side with AA and still maintain our individuality."

Reminiscing further about Al-Anon's history of cooperating with AA, Myrna spoke about the occasional times that Bill would sit in the Al-Anon office with his feet up, chatting in his folksy, straightforward way, more like another Al-Anon member than the founder of AA. When Lois attended a night-time Board meeting, Bill sometimes waited, stretching out the length of an orange couch that graced the small reception area at 125 E. 23rd St., and going to sleep. After the meeting, Lois would tug at Bill's sleeve and announce, "You can take me home now." Bill would drop his long legs to the floor, and do just that.

Chapter Six
Traditions

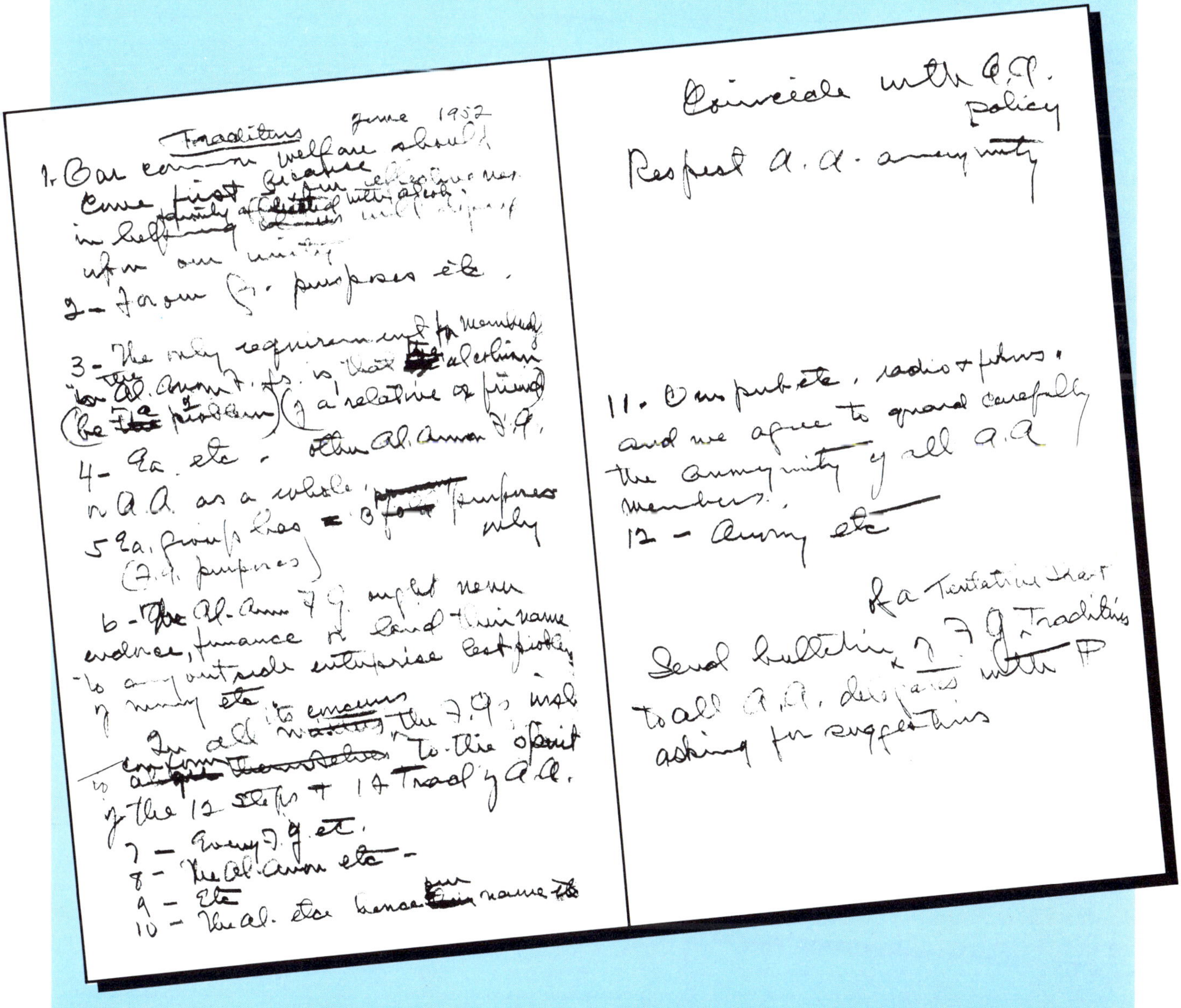

Traditions June 1952

1. Our common welfare should come first because [illegible] in helping [illegible] upon our unity

2 - For our G. purposes etc.

3 - The only requirement for membership in Al-Anon F.G. is that there be a problem of alcoholism in a relative or friend

4 - Ea. etc. other Al-Anon F.G. or A.A. as a whole

5 Ea. group has but one purpose only (F.G. purposes)

6 - The Al-Anon F.G. ought never endorse, finance or lend their name to any outside enterprise lest problems of money etc.

In all its means the F.G.s should conform to the spirit of the 12 Steps & 12 Trad of A.A.

7 - Every F.G. etc.

8 - The Al-Anon etc -

9 - Etc

10 - The Al. etc hence our name

Coincide with A.A. policy

Respect A.A. anonymity

11. Our pub etc., radio & films, and we agree to guard carefully the anonymity of all A.A members.

12 - Anony etc

Send bulletin & a Tentative chart of F.G. Traditions to all A.A. delegates with P asking for suggestions

Chapter Six/Traditions

As in AA, the Al-Anon Traditions were the framework by which the movement could keep some cohesiveness. They were written by Lois beginning in 1952. It may seem strange that a fellowship officially only one year old should begin thinking about Traditions. But the need was pressing. AA's experience had shown that guidelines for a rapidly expanding movement were necessary to provide stability. Lois' letters to the Al-Anon groups in those very early days demonstrate the relative ease with which the Clearing House could gauge a consensus. Following the AA path directly, Lois asked the membership by letter in June, 1952, "Do you give us direct authority to handle national publicity?" The question sparked a thoughtful response from the corresponding secretary in Salem, Massachusetts; he gave feedback from his group and asked for more information. Lois explained in a September letter how Al-Anon intended to follow in AA's footsteps with regard to publicity, assuring the membership of anonymity, "as you will read in the enclosed Traditions."

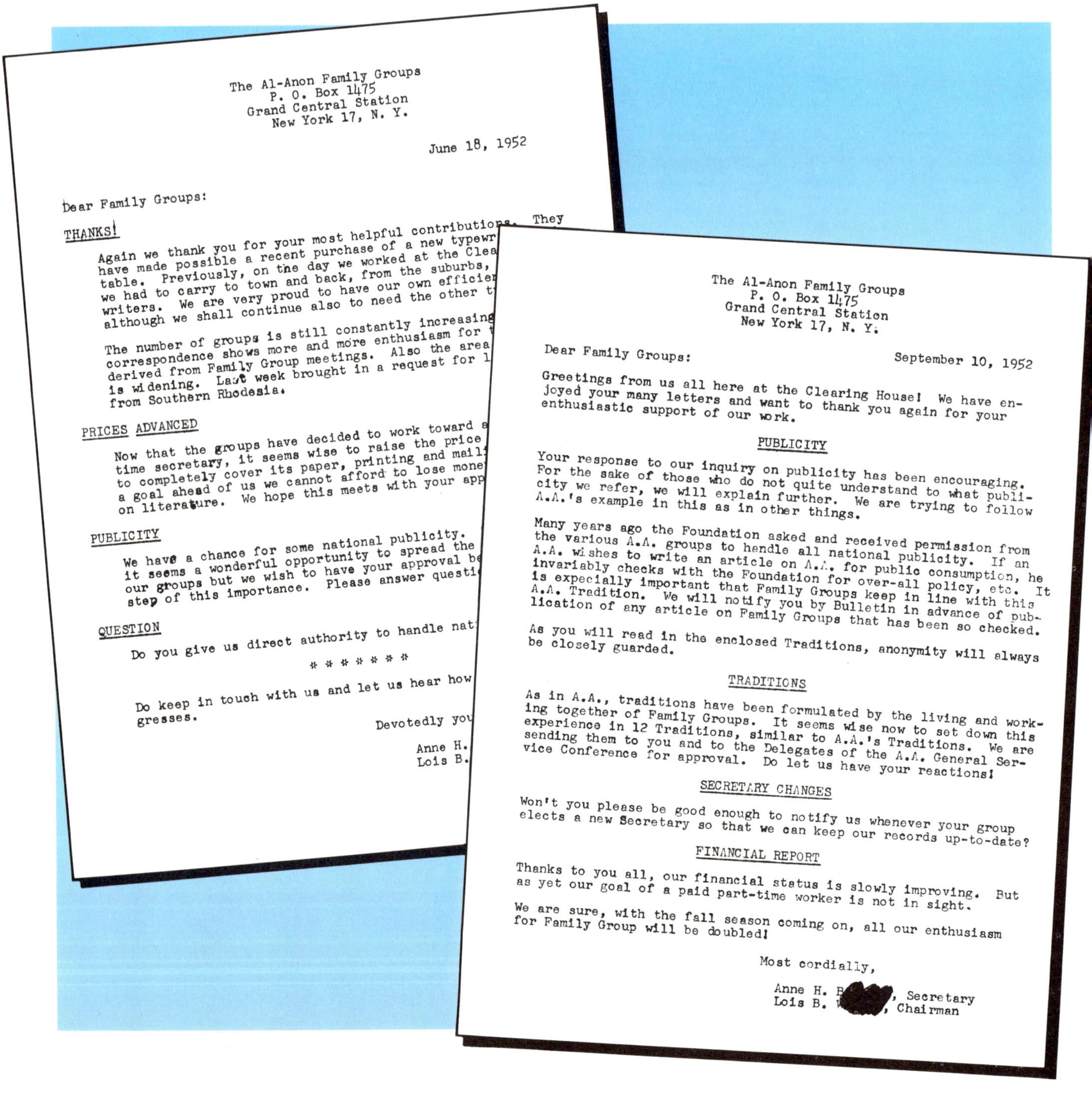

The Al-Anon Family Groups
P. O. Box 1475
Grand Central Station
New York 17, N. Y.

June 18, 1952

Dear Family Groups:

THANKS!

Again we thank you for your most helpful contributions. They have made possible a recent purchase of a new typewr table. Previously, on the day we worked at the Clea we had to carry to town and back, from the suburbs, writers. We are very proud to have our own efficie although we shall continue also to need the other t

The number of groups is still constantly increasing correspondence shows more and more enthusiasm for derived from Family Group meetings. Also the area is widening. Last week brought in a request for l from Southern Rhodesia.

PRICES ADVANCED

Now that the groups have decided to work toward a time secretary, it seems wise to raise the price to completely cover its paper, printing and maili a goal ahead of us we cannot afford to lose mone on literature. We hope this meets with your app

PUBLICITY

We have a chance for some national publicity. it seems a wonderful opportunity to spread the our groups but we wish to have your approval be step of this importance. Please answer questi

QUESTION

Do you give us direct authority to handle nat

* * * * * * *

Do keep in touch with us and let us hear how gresses.

Devotedly you

Anne H.
Lois B.

The Al-Anon Family Groups
P. O. Box 1475
Grand Central Station
New York 17, N. Y.

Dear Family Groups:

September 10, 1952

Greetings from us all here at the Clearing House! We have enjoyed your many letters and want to thank you again for your enthusiastic support of our work.

PUBLICITY

Your response to our inquiry on publicity has been encouraging. For the sake of those who do not quite understand to what publicity we refer, we will explain further. We are trying to follow A.A.'s example in this as in other things.

Many years ago the Foundation asked and received permission from the various A.A. groups to handle all national publicity. If an A.A. wishes to write an article on A.A. for public consumption, he invariably checks with the Foundation for over-all policy, etc. It is expecially important that Family Groups keep in line with this A.A. Tradition. We will notify you by Bulletin in advance of publication of any article on Family Groups that has been so checked.

As you will read in the enclosed Traditions, anonymity will always be closely guarded.

TRADITIONS

As in A.A., traditions have been formulated by the living and working together of Family Groups. It seems wise now to set down this experience in 12 Traditions, similar to A.A.'s Traditions. We are sending them to you and to the Delegates of the A.A. General Service Conference for approval. Do let us have your reactions!

SECRETARY CHANGES

Won't you please be good enough to notify us whenever your group elects a new Secretary so that we can keep our records up-to-date?

FINANCIAL REPORT

Thanks to you all, our financial status is slowly improving. But as yet our goal of a paid part-time worker is not in sight.

We are sure, with the fall season coming on, all our enthusiasm for Family Group will be doubled!

Most cordially,

Anne H. B[redacted], Secretary
Lois B. [redacted], Chairman

7 [redacted]n Avenue
Salem, Massachusetts
August 8, 1952

Mrs. Lois B. [redacted], Chairman
The Al-Anon Family Groups
P. O. Box 1475
Grand Central Station
New York 17, N. Y.

Dear Lois:

Your general letter, dated June 18th. was delayed getting into my hands and as a result it was not brought before the Lynn Family Group until this past Wednesday, Aug. 6th.

Also we are sorry for our tardiness in sending you our mid-year contribution, however, I suppose you will still appreciate receiving it. A check is enclosed in the amount of $15.00. We hope that in the future our contributions will be larger.

Your announcement that we have a chance for some national publicity comes as good news to us and we are happy to give you direct authority in handling it. If it isn't too late I would like to report to y... our feelings in this matter. Some of the questions ... would such publicity be pre-mature, do we have ... cient back-log of experience to warrant an adeq... what is the main theme of such publicity, who ... taking the writing of this publicity, is it of ... zine article type or through the medium of rad... vision, has this matter been brought before th... foundation for their approval and guidance an... what does Bill himself think of this idea and ... be given the opportunity of reading and passi... final draft? We earned the distinction at th... Conference of the General Service body of wo... ing the A. A. principles and were given a "v... Therefore, we should never jeopardize this r... one way to safeguard it is to always assume ... of importance remembering that if it wasn't ... would not have come into existence. If we ... in true humility and receive guidance from ... Power Greater than Ourselves our course sh... success and growth.

Please write and let us know mor... of publicity and also if we can be of any ... wish you continued success and progress.

Sincerely you...

Sam K...
Correspondi...

P.S. - Personal regards to you and Bill from Emily,

August 13, 1952

Mr. Sam K[redacted]
7 M[redacted]on Avenue
Salem, Massachusetts

Dear Sam:

Thank you so much for the contribution of fifteen dollars which we received today. As you thought, it is most welcome and is deeply appreciated. Please extend our thanks to all the group.

The Bulletin of June 18th was late in reaching you because the mimeographing machine broke down; it was sent for repair and they were very late in returning it. Had we known how long it would take to repair it we would have had it done commercially.

We are glad you give us permission to handle publicity. As for the questions about it: we feel we have enough of a back-log now so that publicity would be helpful in reaching a number of people who have never heard of this movement. The theme of the article (magazine) is simply an exposition of the Family Group idea, how it works, what it does, etc. Bill has read and approved the article and it was at his suggestion that we asked our groups for their authority to handle publicity. The article was written by a Family Group member and a worker at the Clearing House--that is, by a Family Group-er who does volunteer work here. It has not yet been submitted so that it may never see the light of day but since the number of groups which have authorized us to handle publicity is now large enough, it will be sent soon and all of us at the Clearing House hope it will be accepted.

With best wishes and again thanks

Cordially yours

Anne H. B[redacted], Secretary
The Al-Anon Family Groups

mmd

Per
Volunteer

Several drafts of the Al-Anon Traditions exist which speak of the struggle to try to clarify the relationship with AA:

"Our common welfare should come first, because our effectiveness in helping families afflicted with alcoholism will depend on our unity."

"Our common welfare and that of Alcoholics Anonymous should come first; although a separate organization, our effectiveness in helping families afflicted with alcoholism depends on our cooperation with AA."

"The unity of Al-Anon Family Groups depends on our adherence to these Traditions. Although a separate entity, we should cooperate in every way with Alcoholics Anonymous."

Lois decided to send a draft of the Al-Anon Traditions to the AA General Service Delegates as early as July, 1952. She asked the Delegates, "Do they [the Traditions] align themselves with the spirit of the Twelve Steps and Twelve Traditions of AA?"

THE AL-ANON FAMILY GROUP TRADITIONS

Our group experience suggésts that:

1. Our common welfare should come first, becuse our effectiveness in helping families afflicted with alcoholism will depend upon our unity.
2. For our group purposes there is but one authority - a loving God as he may express Himself in our group conscience. Our leaders are but trusted servants - they do not govern.
3. T The only requirement for membership in the Al-Anon Family Groups is that the alcoholism of a relative or friend be a problem.
4. Each group should be autonomous, except in matters affecting other Al-Anon Family Groups or A. A. as a whole.
5. Each group has three purposes only:
   a. To live by the 12 Steps of A.A.
   b. To give encouragement and understanding to the A.A. at home.
   c. To welcome and give comfort to the families of A.A.s.
6. The Al-Anon Family Groups ought never endorse, finance or lend ~~their~~ name to any outside enterprise lest problems of money, property and prestige divert us from our primary spiritual aim. In all its concerns the Family Groups wish to conform to the spirit of the 12 Steps and 12 Traditions of Alcoholics Anonymous.
7. Every Family Group ought to be fully self supporting, declining outside co...ibutions.

...n Family Groups should remain forever non-professional, ... centers may employ special workers.

... Family Groups, as such, ought never be organized; ...e service boards or committees directly responsible ...ve.

...amily Groups have no opinion on outside issues; ...ht never be drawn into public controversy.

...ations policy is based on attraction rather than ...always maintain personal anonymity at the level ... films. We agree to guard carefully the anonymity

...e spiritual foundation of all our Traditions, ...place principles above personalities.

TRADITIONS OF THE AL-ANON FAMILY GROUPS

Our group experience suggests that:

1. The unity of the Al-Anon Family Groups depends upon our adherance to these traditions. ~~Although a separate entity, we should cooperate in every way with Alcoholics Anonymous.~~
2. For our group purposes there is but one authority - a loving God as He may express Himself in our group conscience. Our leaders are but trusted servants - they do not govern.
3. The only requirement for membership is that there be a problem of alcoholism in a relative or friend. Relatives of alcoholics gathered together for mutual aid may call themselves an Al-Anon Family Group, provided that, as a group, they have no other affiliation.
4. Each group should be autonomous, except in matters affecting other Al-Anon Family Groups, ~~any A.A. Group,~~ or A. A. as a whole.
5. Each Al-Anon Family Group has but one purpose:- to help families of alcoholics. We do this by practicing the 12 Steps of A. A. OURSELVES, by encouraging and understanding our alcoholic relatives, and by welcoming and giving comfort to families of alcoholics.
6. Our Family Groups ought never to endorse, finance or lend our name to any outside enterprise, lest problems of money, property and prestige divert us from our primary spiritual aim.
7. Every group ought to be fully self-supporting, declining outside contributions.
8. 12 Step work ~~We~~ should remain forever non-professional, but our service centers may employ special workers.
9. Our groups, as such, ought never be organized; but we may create service boards or committees directly responsible to those they serve.
10. The Al-Anon Family Groups have no opinion on outside issues; hence our name ought never be drawn into public controversy.
11. Our public relations policy is based on attraction rather than promotion; we need always maintain personal anonymity at the level of press, radio and films. ~~Particularly~~ we need guard ~~carefully~~ the anonymity of all A. A. members.
12. ~~As in A. A.~~, anonymity is the spiritual foundation of all our Traditions, ever reminding us to place principles above personalities.

Most of the Delegates were wise enough to leave well enough alone and responded positively by offering Al-Anon Family Groups support and encouragement. Al-Anon groups themselves were a little slower in answering. So Lois wrote to them again in January, 1953, saying, "We have heard from so few of you about the suggested Traditions we sent you that as yet we do not know whether you approve of them as written. Kindly send us your thoughts on the matter if you haven't yet done so." The comments trickled back with some changes suggested.

The Al-Anon Family Groups
P. O. Box 1475
GRAND CENTRAL STATION
NEW YORK 17, N. Y.

July 1952

LETTER TO AA GENERAL SERVICE TRUSTEES

We here at the Clearing House would like your personal advice. Many Family Groups have asked us to formulate suggested Traditions.

This step seems wise because of the necessity which has arisen of defining the exact relation of Family Groups to A. A., as well as forming a framework within which Family Groups may operate in unison.

We would greatly appreciate your personal opinion of the enclosed suggested Traditions. Do they align themselves with the spirit of the 12 Steps and 12 Traditions of A. A.? How can they be improved? Have you any other sugge…

Thanks so much for your consideration … matter.

Sincerely,

The Al-Anon F…

Lois B. W…

TRADITIONS OF THE AL-ANON FAMILY GROUPS

Our group experience suggests that:

1. The unity of the Al-Anon Family Groups depends upon our adherance to these traditions. Although a separate entity, we should cooperate in every way with Alcoholics Anonymous.

2. For our group purposes there is but one authority - a loving God as He may express Himself in our group conscience. Our leaders are but trusted servants - they do not govern.

3. The only requirement for membership is that there be a problem of alcoholism in a relative or friend. Relatives of alcoholics gathered together for mutual aid may call themselves an Al-Anon Family Group provided that, as a group, they have no other affiliation.

4. Each group should be autonomous, except in matters affecting other Al-Anon Family Groups, any A.A. Group, or A. A. as a whole.

5. Each Al-Anon Family Group has but one purpose:- to help families of alcoholics. We do this by practicing the 12 Steps of A. A. OURSELVES, by encouraging and understanding our alcoholic relatives, and by welcoming and giving comfort to families of alcoholics.

6. Our Family Groups ought never to endorse, finance or lend our name to any outside enterprise, lest problems of money, property and prestige divert us from our primary spiritual aim.

7. Every group ought to be fully self-supporting, declining outside contributions.

8. We should remain forever non-professional, but our service centers may employ special workers.

9. Our groups, as such, ought never be organized; but we may create service boards or committees directly responsible to those they serve.

10. The Al-Anon Family Groups have no opinion on outside issues; hence our name ought never be drawn into public controversy.

11. Our public relations policy is based on attraction rather than promotion; we need always maintain personal anonymity at the level of press, radio and films. Particularly we need guard carefully the anonymity of all A. A. members.

12. As in A. A., anonymity is the spiritual foundation of all our Traditions, ever reminding us to place principles above personalities.

The Al-Anon Family Groups
P. O. Box 1475
GRAND CENTRAL STATION
NEW YORK 17, N. Y.

September 3, 1952

Mr. Walter B[redacted]
[redacted] Road
Morristown, New Jersey

Dear Walter:

We here at the Clearing House would like your personal advice. Many Family Groups have asked us to formulate suggested Traditions.

This step seems wise because of the necessity which has arisen of defining the exact relation of Family Groups to A. A., as well as forming a framework within which Family Groups may operate in unison.

We would greatly appreciate your personal opinion of the enclosed suggested Traditions. Do they align themselves with the spirit of the 12 Steps and 12 Traditions of A. A.? How can they be improved? Have you any other suggestions?

Thanks so much for your considerati matter.

Sincerely,

The Al-Ano

Lois

Lois B.

Dear Lois -
This looks fine
will see you in
October. Mrs E B

Delegates & Trustees
who made suggestions

Cliff W[redacted] 3 1
1 Leonard S[redacted] 2
Cecil B[redacted] 6
Leo R[redacted] 5
Al Ki[redacted] 4
Adam Co[redacted] 7
Daryl W. C[redacted] 8
George St[redacted] 10
Jim H[redacted] 9
Tom [redacted]

The Al-Anon Family Groups
P. O. Box 1475
GRAND CENTRAL STATION
NEW YORK 17, N. Y.

Thank you so much for your cordial approval of our suggested Traditions of the Al-Anon Family Groups.

It might seem a little early for so new an organization to presume to have Traditions but we felt it would be valuable, particularly at this time when our Groups are multiplying so rapidly, to have these Traditions as a pattern; they will help tremendously in keeping all the groups working in unison and should prevent mistakes in policy.

We think you'll be interested and glad to hear that our Groups now number 386, including groups in England, Ireland, Australia, New Zealand and four in South Africa.

Thanks again for your courtesy in answering.

Cordially,

/mmd

Lois B. W[redacted], Chairman
The Al-Anon Family Groups

Groups Acceptance of Traditions

85th St Family Group
Brooklyn
Portland, Oregon
Essex Co. New Jersey
Muskegon, Mich. Center of Utica N.Y.
[illegible]
[illegible]
[illegible]
[illegible]
[illegible]
Hollywood Beach [illegible] Calif.
Manhattan Beach Calif (So. Bay [illegible])
Mansfield, Mass.
Orem, Utah (Provo [illegible])
Big Spring, Texas
Group #7 of Denver, Col.
Utica, N.Y.
Waterville, N.Y.
San Jose, Calif
Brinkley, Arkansas
[illegible] Canada
[illegible] Col. 2/7/53

Suggested Changes in traditions:

Trustee Leonard St[redacted]
" Cecil B[redacted]
" Cliff. W[redacted]
" [illegible] [redacted]
" Al K[redacted]
" [illegible] R[redacted]
" Daryl W. C[redacted]
" George St[redacted]
" Tom Sh[redacted]
" Jim Ha[redacted]
~~Hilliard T. B[redacted]~~

Greensboro, NC
Kamloops, B.C. Canada
Sterling, Colo.
Tulsa, Okla
Marysville Nakoma Club, Marysville Cal. 3/31/53
Jamestown, N.Y. 3/31/53
San Pedro, Calif.
Minneapolis Minn 4/7/53
Sacramento Calif 4/14/53
Arlington Va. 4/14/53
6/2/53

Traditions Accepted as written:

Delegate Kenneth G[redacted]
" Jack W[redacted]
" "Mike" E[redacted]
Trustee Frank G[redacted]
" A. LeRoy C[redacted]
" Bernard B. S[redacted]
" Jack A[redacted]
Delegate Gerald M[redacted]
" R. W. S[redacted]
" Charles G. A[redacted]
" George B. M[redacted]
" Charles F. St[redacted]
" Mrs. John C. D[redacted]
" Z. Miles N[redacted]
Ray H[redacted]
" R. Fay B[redacted]
" Charlie B[redacted]
" Walter B[redacted]
Trustee John W. J[redacted]
" Frank B. A[redacted]
Dr. John L. N[redacted]
Delegate - Lois A[redacted]
" A.R. B[redacted]
" M. W. N[redacted]
" A. J. P[redacted]
" Clifford H. C[redacted]
" George C[redacted]
" Rowland B. I[redacted]
" Curt H[redacted]
" Fisk M[redacted] (approved verbally)
" Wm. F. C[redacted]
Ray M[redacted] (Nebraska)

IMPORTANT

9-23-52

Lois B. [redacted]
Box 1475
Grand Central Station
New York 17, N.Y.

Dear Lois:
I received your letter and the copy of the traditions of the Al-Anon Family Groups. I think they are very fine, and can neither critize nor add anything to them. My best regards to you & Bill.

Sincerely,
Reg [redacted]

---

ups

n

October 15, 1952

groups who so desire
. Your wonderful sup-
typewriter, a cabinet
ns showing the location
terature printed and
hough regular income
In your responses to
approved of following
lly on the basis of
dstick and would not
ding us more, or that

volunteers in this
contributions and
groups now regis-

Cards

We are enclosing new cards as we shall do again in the spring. Will you please fill in any changes since your last card and send it on?

Traditions

We have received the approval of most of the A.A. delegates concerning our suggested Traditions. Do let us have your ideas about them.

We know you all are starting the fall with enthusiasm and happiness in your Family Groups after the summer vacations are over. All good wishes for a useful and fruitful year.

Cordially,

Anne H. B[redacted]n, Secretary
Lois B. W[redacted]n, Chairman

The Al-Anon Family Groups
P. O. Box 1475
GRAND CENTRAL STATION
NEW YORK 17, N. Y.

January 28, 1953

the feeling of accomplishment that we feel here at the
r the record of our past year's work.

d this office in the Old 24th Street Club House where
As Tuesday is the day, if you have an important com-
so that it will be delivered Monday or Tuesday.
nearly a week.
er 400 groups including groups in England, Ireland,
frica.

The Clearing House has sent out 1,040 letters and 1,933 bulletins, including much literature, a great deal of which was sent free to new groups.
We have put out one World Directory and are working on the second. Because of constant growth and change in secretaries, etc., this is a long complicated job.
You have sent us enough money
To buy: Two new typewriters with tables-
A metal cabinet for supplies-
A large wall map to show locations of groups-
To share equally with the Club House here in the cost of reconditioning a mimeograph machine-
To pay the Club House rent-
To have printed $505 worth of literature-
To have paid $300 for stationery and postage, and
To have a growing bank account to be used eventually for the salary of a part-time paid worker. Our volunteers have been most faithful, some of them coming from as far as New Jersey and Connecticut. They are working out so well and the cost of even a part-time worker would be such a constant drain that we are postponing this expense at present.

We feel we now have enough material and we hope we'll have time this Spring to get out a large pamphlet with anonymous stories of family recoveries and group experiences.

Your Decisions: During the past year you have decided several important questions:
You have chosen a name--The Al-Anon Family Groups.
You have decided to support this Clearing House by sending voluntary contributions approximating $1 per head per group twice a year.
You have thought it wise for this Clearing House to handle all national publicity.

But we have heard from so few of you about the suggested Traditions we sent you that as yet we do not know whether you approve of them as written. Kindly send us your thoughts on the matter if you haven't yet done so.

A.A.'s Thanks: In April, 1951, the General Service Conference of A.A. passed a resolution giving thanks to those who helped foster Family Groups.

Our Thanks: We all want to thank you so much for your cooperation and encouragement last year and hope in this present one we shall be able to help even more families with their alcoholic problems.

Cordially

Anne H. B[redacted]n, Secretary
Lois B. W[redacted]n, Chairman

The Al-Anon Traditions were ratified by the AA General Service Conference of 1955, and again at Al-Anon's first trial Conference in 1961. In her own book, Lois has this to say about them:

"These Traditions were sent not only to the Al-Anon groups but also to many AA groups. We wanted AA's approval of the guiding principles of our fellowship. We received even more encouragement from AA than we did from our own groups. Maybe most Al-Anon groups were too young in experience to think much about group problems. However, the Al-Anon Traditions would now be there when groups needed them."

Just why the Al-Anon fellowship did not respond more readily to the advent of the Traditions is a puzzle. A testimonial on the need for the Traditions comes from a longtime member, Mabel S., then living in Virginia:

"In 1950, AA had the first International Convention in Cleveland. This became the time for our group here in Virginia to take a group inventory. We did not know those words, then, but that is what happened. Many of us went to Cleveland, and while there we attended a wives' meeting. We, including AA members, heard talks by Lois and members of a Toronto group sharing their experience, strength and hope with us. These were wives who had used the Twelve Steps and found serenity!

"We came back, and out of our group inventory we all became more united in our purpose. You may be interested to know that we had a very large group about this time. I have a list of members and there are over 40 names on it. A surprising number of them stayed in Al-Anon for years.

"As you can see, these were the days before the Traditions. We had many personality clashes and strange things sometimes went on in the group. There were two ladies who wanted to be president, or group leader and there was a constant battle going on between them. Anonymous letters floated about. No one as far as I know, ever knew who the writer was. We had some very interesting meetings in those days!"

Organization into what would become known in Al-Anon as a "wider group conscience" was only just beginning in 1952. The Traditions themselves would foster that unity at the local, national, and international level at which acceptance of group principles could first take root, but a structure for communicating them had not been developed. The Steps, on the other hand, could be incorporated and practiced by the individual member or group anywhere, at any time.

The *FORUM*, as the voice of the fellowship, was two years away from publication. A careful survey of the *AA Grapevine* shows that contributions from nonalcoholics still were predominantly expressing gratitude for the presence of AA in their lives, and did not show a development of Al-Anon consciousness until 1955. Al-Anon did not follow AA all the way this time. According to the November, 1950 *AA Grapevine*, an AA Tradition issue, Bill organized a Tradition Week when it was suggested all the AA groups devote time to studying the AA Traditions. But AA had held its first International Conference at Cleveland in July of that year. That was the difference.

To make a distinction between the AA experience and the Al-Anon experience, several Family Groups had set about organizing their own local structures long before the Clearing House had gotten its start. As early as 1941, the Chicago Family Groups had just such a strong, local fellowship. The correspondence shows that by August, 1951 eight Family Groups in the Chicago area were registered with AA Intergroup and were directing all mailings from the Clearing House through this central channel—a practice the Clearing House agreed to. Then, when Lois sent her April, 1952 letter to all groups outlining Clearing House plans and requesting financial support, the Chicago Family Groups declined to go along. Their structure was already sufficient, according to their local leadership.

Mrs. L. E. T[redacted]
[redacted] Ave
Evanston, Ill.
Aug. 11 - 1951

Dear Mrs B[redacted] -

The "Family Groups of Chicago" have decided to have any correspondance in the future coming from N.Y. - sent to the fo
address - "Family Gro
Room 1101 - 123 W. M
Chicago -
Sending correspondanc
individuals, as you
doing, is rather c
& does not help t
of our groups.

Sincerely,

Kathar

P.S. We registered at the
office before you had a
number eight groups - sam

Chicago Family Group
123 W. Madison St.
Chicago, Illinois

COPY

April 23, 1952

Mrs. Lois W[redacted]
P.O. Box 1475
Grand Central Station
New York 17, New York

Dear Lois:

We have received your letter telling the Chicago Family Group of your plans for the pressnt and future. We felt it necessary for the representative Family Groups committee to meet for discussion of the plan and it was then presented to the A.A. committees. The following decision was reached by both groups in a joint meeting.

As you know, we started our Family Group in Chicago some eleven years ago and feel we have functioned in rather a good manner for fulfillment of our needs, using the Family Group for self-improvement, helpfulness to new wives, as well as standing ready to serve in A.A. when called upon by the members. We have no officers, dues or money transactions. Our idea has always been and is to go along quietly and simply, without promotion or organization, therefore, we have been whole heartedly accepted by the A.A. members. The concensus of opinion of both the Family Group and A.A. committee groups of Chicago was that it would be better in our situation to continue in this manner and preserve our unity as we now enjoy it.

If in the future conditions change, we will be happy to contribute to your plans. We hope you understand our situation. We do not wish to disassociate ourselves from the National Family Group, but want you to know we are always ready and anxious to help other groups and be of service whenever and wherever possible. However, at this time we feel we had better pursue our present course.

Sincerely,

Chicago Family Group

The situation was complicated by the fact that the Clearing House received letters from individuals in the Chicago area. Tension was created between Chicago and the Clearing House in a difference of opinion about who was doing what best. But Lois could be counted upon to pour oil on troubled waters with her personal touch. At any rate, due to their strong leadership and its early beginnings, many Chicago Family Groups did not join the Al-Anon fellowship until 1962.

Chapter Seven
Literature

The development of the Al-Anon literature shaped both the movement itself, and Al-Anon's relations to others—notably AA and the professional community. Written first by Lois and Anne B. as a tool for individual recovery and group functioning, the literature was to serve other purposes as well, including keeping groups within the mainstream of Al-Anon experience. It has been revised over the years to reflect an evolution in Al-Anon ideas, especially as new understandings of the disease of alcoholism have come to light, and help for family members has become available from professional and community sources.

By placing principles above personalities, a spiritual goal has worked for groups who have consulted the written as well as the spoken word to see what others in Al-Anon have done before them. Just as a "wider group conscience" was an idea born of a certain amount of trial and error, the literature reflecting that conscience became important to the uniform development of Al-Anon as a whole.

In the beginning, Al-Anon literature helped to fill the constant demand for reading material by the membership. But there was a scarcity of appropriate written material. Often this meant borrowing from other sources. Clearing House letters recommended study of such authors as Dale Carnegie and Norman Vincent Peale.

The first Al-Anon price list distributed in September, 1952, shows that Al-Anon sold the AA "Big Book" and *AA Grapevine* subscriptions, besides the pamphlets already referred to. Also included were publications by Marty Mann, founder of the National Council on Alcoholism, and the important pamphlet *Freedom from Despair,* developed by the San Diego Family Group. This is the first piece of Al-Anon literature written outside of New York to be adopted by the fellowship as a whole. Others would follow.

Henrietta mentions that two more part-time staff members were taken on at the Clearing House in 1954 in order to help with mimeography, mailing of The *FORUM*, increasing literature orders and to process the manuscript of Al-Anon's own book. This had started out in 1952 as a handbook written by Lois. By 1955, it had developed into a full blown hardcover. In her own words, Lois describes what happened:

"Meanwhile we had struggled to prepare our first book, *The Al-Anon Family Groups.* With Bill's help I wrote the first draft of what we thought was going to be a pamphlet. Margaret then made a connected manuscript out of it. Bill and I went over it again and added some material. Ralph B., an AA writer, edited it, and we sent mimeographed copies to groups selected at random. Many of their suggestions and stories were so good that the pamphlet grew into a book. Finally, at the 1955 AA International Convention in St. Louis (where Al-Anon participated in five workshops), the multi-authored book made its appearance and sold quite well." (In 1960, this book was revised and retitled *Living With An Alcoholic.* In 1984, the book reverted to its original title.)

By 1954, the Al-Anon literature list had expanded again. It included a subscription to the *FORUM*, some new AA publications and reprints on alcoholism from such publications as the *Christian Herald*. But local Intergroups were also happily printing away. The 1954 price list makes reference to publications by Toronto, Ontario. At the same time, Southern California had put out such a long literature list that it had been subdivided into sections. There was even a section for Spanish translations! The list includes a book called *Just One More* by James Lamb Free, and a single printed sheet called "The Twelve Steps of AA and Their Biblical Comparisons." Clearly some overall policy needed to be developed about writings by people who were not Al-Anon members. Further, decisions had to be made about the variety of literature being developed by different groups across the country, and beyond.

The history of the Al-Anon literature as a whole is, indeed, a complex one. Many groups at the local level were saddened when a particular, much loved pamphlet failed to gain acceptance by New York—or Conference after 1961. With a strong local following, such pieces continued to circulate. The Detroit Family Groups went on printing their own literature until 1982. Reasons for the adoption of the Conference approval concept are outlined in the 1961 Conference Summary.

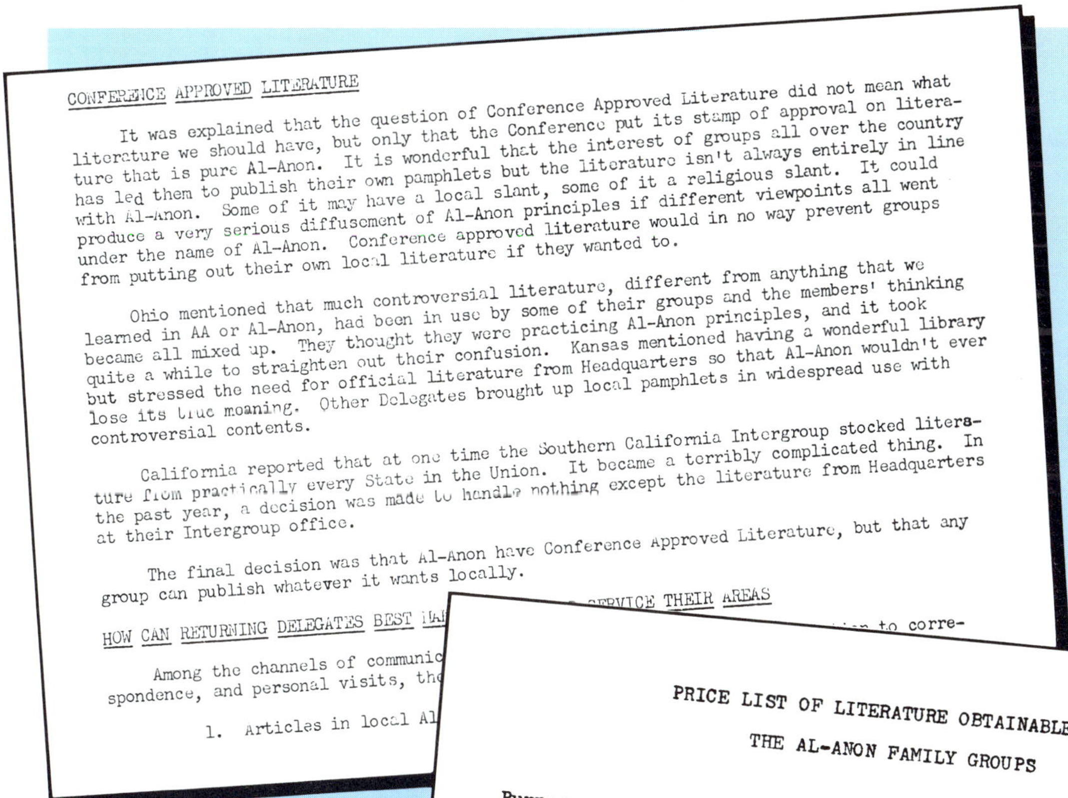

CONFERENCE APPROVED LITERATURE

It was explained that the question of Conference Approved Literature did not mean what literature we should have, but only that the Conference put its stamp of approval on literature that is pure Al-Anon. It is wonderful that the interest of groups all over the country has led them to publish their own pamphlets but the literature isn't always entirely in line with Al-Anon. Some of it may have a local slant, some of it a religious slant. It could produce a very serious diffusement of Al-Anon principles if different viewpoints all went under the name of Al-Anon. Conference approved literature would in no way prevent groups from putting out their own local literature if they wanted to.

Ohio mentioned that much controversial literature, different from anything that we learned in AA or Al-Anon, had been in use by some of their groups and the members' thinking became all mixed up. They thought they were practicing Al-Anon principles, and it took quite a while to straighten out their confusion. Kansas mentioned having a wonderful library but stressed the need for official literature from Headquarters so that Al-Anon wouldn't ever lose its true meaning. Other Delegates brought up local pamphlets in widespread use with controversial contents.

California reported that at one time the Southern California Intergroup stocked literature from practically every State in the Union. It became a terribly complicated thing. In the past year, a decision was made to handle nothing except the literature from Headquarters at their Intergroup office.

The final decision was that Al-Anon have Conference Approved Literature, but that any group can publish whatever it wants locally.

HOW CAN RETURNING DELEGATES BEST ... SERVICE THEIR AREAS

Among the channels of communic... ...n to corre-
spondence, and personal visits, th...

1. Articles in local Al...

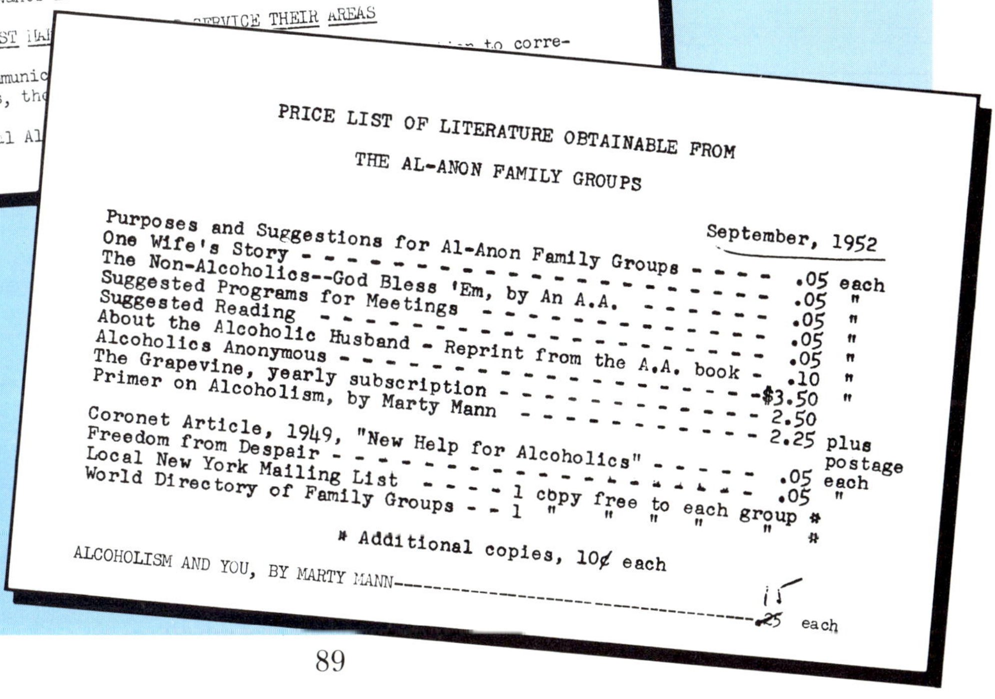

PRICE LIST OF LITERATURE OBTAINABLE FROM

THE AL-ANON FAMILY GROUPS

September, 1952

Purposes and Suggestions for Al-Anon Family Groups	.05	each
One Wife's Story	.05	"
The Non-Alcoholics--God Bless 'Em, by An A.A.	.05	"
Suggested Programs for Meetings	.05	"
Suggested Reading	.05	"
About the Alcoholic Husband - Reprint from the A.A. book	.10	"
Alcoholics Anonymous	$3.50	
The Grapevine, yearly subscription	2.50	
Primer on Alcoholism, by Marty Mann	2.25	plus postage
Coronet Article, 1949, "New Help for Alcoholics"	.05	each
Freedom from Despair	.05	"
Local New York Mailing List	1 copy free to each group #	
World Directory of Family Groups	1 " " " " " #	

Additional copies, 10¢ each

ALCOHOLISM AND YOU, BY MARTY MANN -------- ~~.25~~ 15 each

PRICE LIST OF LITERATURE

Al-Anon Family Group Headquarters,
P.O. Box 1475, Grand Central Annex, New York 17, N.Y.
****

GROUP NAME ____________________

Mail order to (PLEASE PRINT) ____________________

PLEASE INCLUDE REMITTANCE WITH ALL ORDERS.***(For discount, see below)

ITEM	Unit price	Quan-tity	Amount
Family Group Forum (Newsletter) Yearly Subscription* (No charge for one copy sent to each group monthly)	1.25		
Just for Today - Cards (25 for $1.00)	.05		
Purposes and Suggestions	.05		
Suggested Programs	.05		
How to Start a Group Group Structure	.05		
Suggested Reading	.05		
Family Group Traditions	.05		
Suggested Welcome and Preamble to the Twelve Steps	.05		
One Wife's Story	.05		
How One A.A. Wife Lives the Twelve Steps	.05		
New Help for Alcoholics (reprint from Coronet, 1949)	.05		
Freedom from Despair	.05		
The Non-Alcoholics, God Bless 'Em (reprint from Grapevine)	.05		
About the Alcoholic Husband (A.A. Publication)	.15		
About the Alcoholic Wife (A.A. Publication)	.15		
Alcoholism and You (reprint from Pageant)	.15		
Alcoholism, the Family Disease	.25		
You Can Help an Alcoholic (reprint from Christian Herald)	.10		
World Directory (one free to each group)	.35		
Primer on Alcoholism by Marty Mann**	2.25		
TOTAL			

LITERATURE OBTAINABLE FROM OTHER SOURCES

Alcoholics Anonymous Alcoholic Foundation Box 459, Grand Central Annex New York 17, New York		3.50
Grapevine, yearly subscription The A.A. Grapevine Inc. P.O. Box 85, Knickerbocker Station New York 2, New York	in Canada	2.50 3.00
Family Groups of A.A. Family Groups Station Q, P. O. Box 24 Toronto, Ontario, Canada		.25

*All subscriptions sent to secretary of group with group's free copy.

**Please add $.16 for postage when ordering the Primer.

***A 10% discount will be allowed to groups on any items ordered in lots of 10* or more.

10/7/54 - hfs.

Conference approval for the literature was further redefined in the Summary the following year. "At Sue's request, Lois explained that last year the Conference voted to have Conference-Approved Literature. This year it was to consider its approval of the present Headquarters literature. The four Delegates who offered their services were to check this literature with the Headquarters Committee and report at a subsequent session... A motion was made that we do not permit [outside] institutions to reprint Al-Anon literature."

In 1963, a motion was passed to adopt Conference-Approved Literature only. The review of new literature by a committee is described in the Conference Summary. The chairman, Ruth M., stated, "We are finding our Delegate 'Members-At-Large' very helpful. They read the manuscripts carefully, make excellent comments and suggestions, and are prompt about returning them. We have a fine working committee here at home base, made up of Amy B., Joan L., Alice B., and myself. We meet on a weekly basis, often consult each other in between meetings and work together in harmony."

And again, at this Conference, some gentle persuasion was used by the Literature Chairman to select only Conference-Approved Literature (CAL). "The Literature Committee Report was enlarged by its Chairman, the benefits of Conference-Approved Literature emphasized. It was explained why certain pieces suggested by the groups were considered unsuitable for Conference approval."

By 1965, the Conference was ready to stand firm on the Conference-Approval concept. Alice B., by now Literature Chairman, explains why in a statement attached to the 1964 Conference Summary.

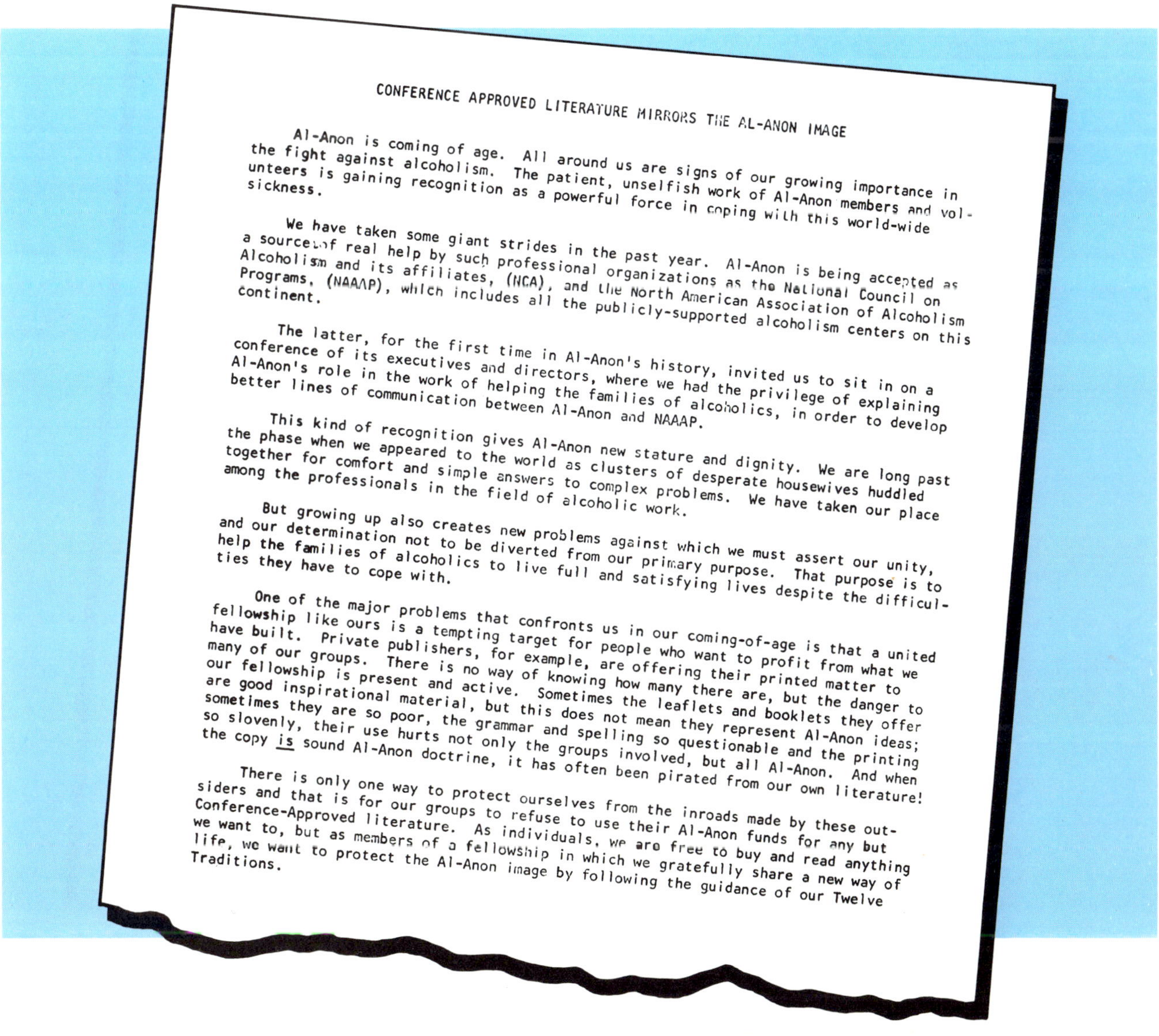

CONFERENCE APPROVED LITERATURE MIRRORS THE AL-ANON IMAGE

Al-Anon is coming of age. All around us are signs of our growing importance in the fight against alcoholism. The patient, unselfish work of Al-Anon members and volunteers is gaining recognition as a powerful force in coping with this world-wide sickness.

We have taken some giant strides in the past year. Al-Anon is being accepted as a source of real help by such professional organizations as the National Council on Alcoholism and its affiliates, (NCA), and the North American Association of Alcoholism Programs, (NAAAP), which includes all the publicly-supported alcoholism centers on this continent.

The latter, for the first time in Al-Anon's history, invited us to sit in on a conference of its executives and directors, where we had the privilege of explaining Al-Anon's role in the work of helping the families of alcoholics, in order to develop better lines of communication between Al-Anon and NAAAP.

This kind of recognition gives Al-Anon new stature and dignity. We are long past the phase when we appeared to the world as clusters of desperate housewives huddled together for comfort and simple answers to complex problems. We have taken our place among the professionals in the field of alcoholic work.

But growing up also creates new problems against which we must assert our unity, and our determination not to be diverted from our primary purpose. That purpose is to help the families of alcoholics to live full and satisfying lives despite the difficulties they have to cope with.

One of the major problems that confronts us in our coming-of-age is that a united fellowship like ours is a tempting target for people who want to profit from what we have built. Private publishers, for example, are offering their printed matter to many of our groups. There is no way of knowing how many there are, but the danger to our fellowship is present and active. Sometimes the leaflets and booklets they offer are good inspirational material, but this does not mean they represent Al-Anon ideas; sometimes they are so poor, the grammar and spelling so questionable and the printing so slovenly, their use hurts not only the groups involved, but all Al-Anon. And when the copy _is_ sound Al-Anon doctrine, it has often been pirated from our own literature!

There is only one way to protect ourselves from the inroads made by these outsiders and that is for our groups to refuse to use their Al-Anon funds for any but Conference-Approved literature. As individuals, we are free to buy and read anything we want to, but as members of a fellowship in which we gratefully share a new way of life, we want to protect the Al-Anon image by following the guidance of our Twelve Traditions.

The First Tradition says: "Our common welfare should come first; personal progress for the greatest number depends on unity."

Living up to this Tradition means delivering the Al-Anon message without distortion or dilution, by using only the literature which has been carefully prepared and screened to reflect Al-Anon as a whole.

Our Second Tradition says: "Our leaders are but trusted servants; they do not govern." Among those who serve are the members of the Literature Committee, ten in number, and the staff and volunteers at HQ. They are dedicated to the task of making our literature correct in approach and content, as well as in the language used to express Al-Anon ideas. These servants are worthy of confidence.

Our Fourth Tradition says: "Each group should be autonomous, except in matters affecting another group, or Al-Anon and AA as a whole." It is true that we are autonomous, but that does not give us the right to use the Al-Anon name in ways that could affect the fellowship adversely. When one part of Al-Anon publishes literature which is not Conference-Approved, it is a serious threat to Al-Anon unity. There are even now thousands of pieces of literature being distributed in the name of Al-Anon which are marred by misspellings, grammatical errors, inappropriate material, distortions of Al-Anon principles and even gross corruptions of the Twelve Steps, which we are privileged to use through the generosity of AA. We thus hurt not only our own fellowship, but AA, to whom we owe so much.

This is not to say that some of the literature is not excellent. It is! But if Group X prints a good piece of literature, Group Z is just as free to publish one that may hurt the Al-Anon image.

Two years ago, the WSC, in the persons of our own elected delegates, voted to use only Conference-Approved literature. Our continued unity and growth depend upon our living up to this decision.

The Literature Committee receives most gratefully, and often uses, ideas suggested by groups and intergroups. This is a vital part of the information that enables us to do the job for the benefit of all Al-Anon. Working as a central clearing house, we are able to maintain a balanced list of literature to meet the varied needs of our far-flung groups and to get the most mileage out of every Al-Anon dollar spent. Duplication would waste money that could be used to print much-needed new material for the whole fellowship.

The members of the Literature Committee are well-fitted to write and edit Al-Anon literature. The quality of our booklets and leaflets is evidence of this, and all of them play an active and constructive role in every writing project. Every word is weighed and measured, not only for its pertinence to a particular problem, but in its relation to the other literature on our list.

Our booklets are in demand by many of the public services in the field of alcoholism who use them in working with the families of alcoholics. A recent order for over $200 worth of Al-Anon literature was accompanied by this statement: "This literature is being made available to our officers in order that they may interest their clients whom we meet in Juvenile and Family Court. We have found that Al-Anon has had better than average success in helping the partner or the child of an alcoholic."

We have the inestimable blessing of the counsel of Lois and a group of early volunteers. The total of their experience covers many years of struggle with Al-Anon's problems, growth and aspirations. They know, and can save us from, many unsuspected pitfalls we might blunder into, often through solutions early worked out by trial and error in AA. Their wise help in the preparation of Al-Anon literature keeps it in character, unfailingly representing the ideas by which all of us are striving to live in Al-Anon.

HQ serves as a clearing house for Al-Anon world-wide. Thousands of new situations, problems and answers are revealed by the letters received. This gives the Literature Committee a broad base of information for its guidance in selecting subjects to be covered, and in preparing the copy for them, making Conference-Approved literature valid for all Al-Anon. In addition, new information on alcoholism research is continually being funneled into HQ, often suggesting ideas that keep our literature in step with modern advances.

For all these reasons it is vital that we make full use of our Conference-Approved literature, which truly reflects our wonderful, growing fellowship. All of us are but leaves on a single, flourishing tree; offshoots can only weaken it!

Adoption of local literature by the fellowship as a whole happened from time to time. If requests for a certain regionally-developed pamphlet were constant, as shown by repeat orders at the Clearing House, then the Conference acknowledged the pamphlet's wide appeal and deemed it appropriate for Conference approval. In instances such as these, a "wider group conscience" in operation could be identified.

As of 1985, such Conference-approved pamphlets (with Al-Anon revisions) of local origin that have withstood the test of time are: *So You Love An Alcoholic*, developed by the Texas Commission on Alcoholism, *Alcoholism the Family Disease,* compiled by Harold B. and printed by Al-Anon Family Groups of Prestonburg, Kentucky, and *Alcoholism the Merry-Go-Round Named Denial* and *A Guide for the Family of Alcoholics* both written by the Reverend Joseph L. Kellermann, former director of the Charlotte, (North Carolina) Council on Alcoholism, and San Diego's *Freedom From Despair. It's a Teenaged Affair* was originally a reprint from a 1957 *Grapevine* article, and *To the Mother and Father* (formerly *Parents) of an Alcoholic* was first written by Mary G., a member from New Zealand.

Outstanding pieces of Conference-Approved Literature which have since been dropped from the lists are *Bill's Talk at the First World Service Conference, 1961, Allies for Al-Anon in Helping the Family,* a talk by the Reverend Yvelin Gardner at the 1966 Conference, and *Do's and Don'ts for the Relatives and Friends* published by Southern California. (Many ideas from this last pamphlet have been incorporated into other current Conference-Approved Literature.) Toronto's *Little Brown Book,* which contains a number of the Al-Anon slogans, has also been integrated into other literature as have "One Wife's Story" and "How One Wife Lives the Twelve Steps". The latter two stories can be found in *Lois' Story.*

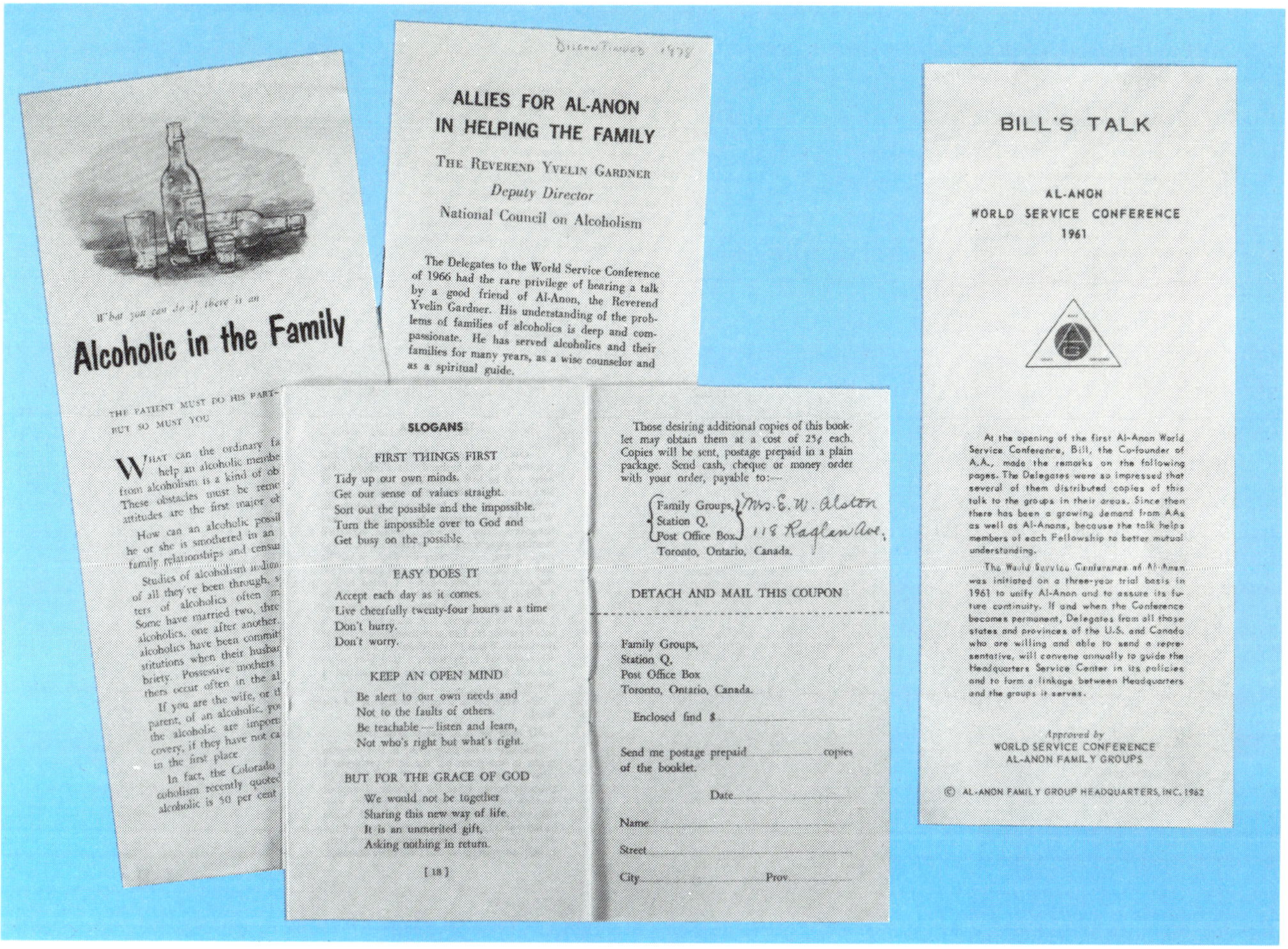

Al-Anon literature of the 1960's refers to Al-Anon's growing relationship with professionals in the alcoholism field. At this time, professionals such as Gardner were invited to address Al-Anon members at the Conference level. The 1960 edition of *Living With an Alcoholic* was reviewed by Marty Mann, as well as by a judge, a psychiatrist, and a minister. The Reverend Joseph Kellermann gave Al-Anon permission to print and distribute *The Merry-Go-Round Named Denial* after it was so enthusiastically received at an Al-Anon workshop in Milford, Connecticut.

In truth, Al-Anon welcomed the contributions of professionals at this time, when any recognition by outsiders of the problems involved in living with alcoholism was looked upon as a giant step forward. Non-Al-Anon contributions were not common, nor were generally considered by a grassroots membership to be detrimental to the Al-Anon movement. On the other hand, the new professionalism in the field of alcoholism tended to speak with more of a single voice than they do today. In the words of Mary S., 1965 Chairman of the Al-Anon Board of Trustees:

"Many of us come into Al-Anon to find out what we can do to get our alcoholic sober, not to find out what we can do to get ourselves emotionally sober. Because we don't know we are not sober. There are agencies working in the field of alcoholism who are our welcome allies. And, while Al-Anon is sufficient for most of us, we do recognize that there are instances where we are not equipped to help. Rather, we help these members when we assist them to find what they need from these professional agencies."

Recognition of the professional contribution to Al-Anon was included in a second hardcover book, *Al-Anon Faces Alcoholism* first published in 1965. A second, updated edition was released in 1984. It contains a section written by leading professionals in the alcoholism field about the value of the Al-Anon program in their work. The section is called "Those Who Work with the

Problem." Al-Anon's policy of friendly cooperation with professionals is open ended. A special committee, Cooperation with the Professional Community, formed from the original Public Information Committee in September, 1980, has formalized this relationship.

No history of the literature would be complete without a special reference to the writing of literature by Al-Anon members who were sharing their experience, strength and hope. There are now twelve books, and over 50 pamphlets and leaflets containing recovery and service messages from one member to another. Much of this material has been reprinted for many years. *One Day At a Time in Al-Anon (ODAT),* first printed in 1968, is now in its 18th printing, with sales over the two million mark. It has been translated into Finnish, French, Flemish, German, Italian, Japanese, Norwegian, Portuguese, and Spanish.

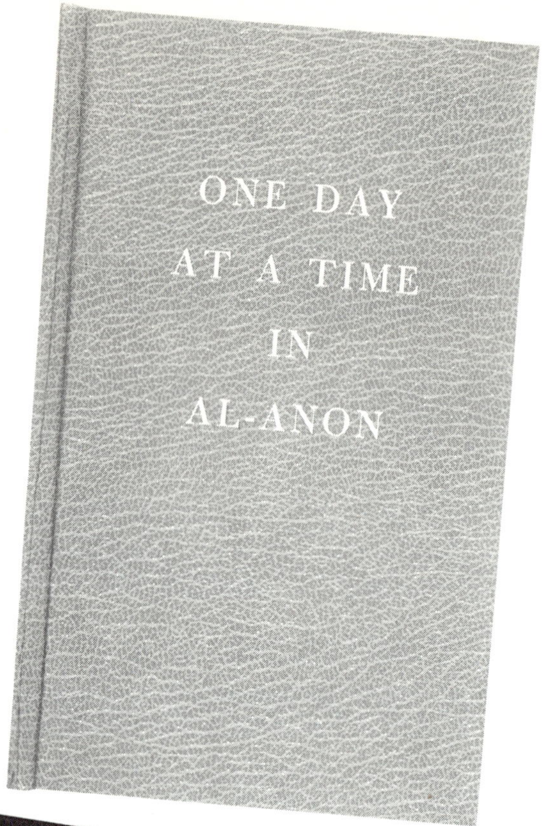

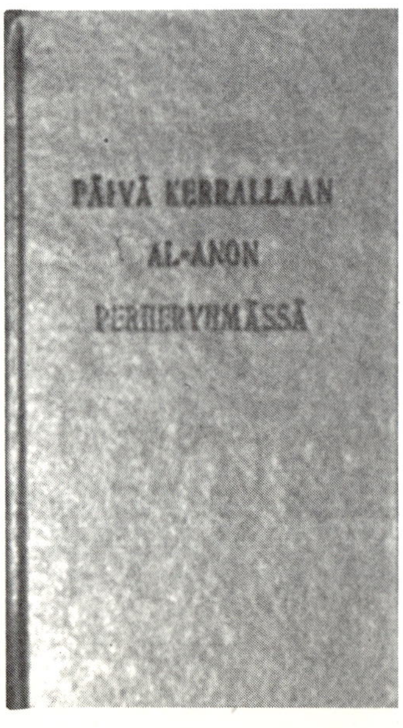

The *ODAT* was written by Alice B., Chairman of the Literature Committee from 1964 to 1971. After she resigned as Literature Chairman, Alice then went on to become a member of the Executive Committee, and until 1981, a member of the Board of Trustees. As to authorship of the *ODAT,* Lois wrote an inscription in the 1972 edition, "To Alice, the transcriber (for I know a Power greater than ourselves is the author) of this book with all gratitude and love, Lois."

As a transcriber of inspirational writings, which have been a daily tool for recovery and a blessing to millions, Alice B. was an extraordinary person. *Inside Al-Anon,* at the time of her death in 1984, read, "Alice had a love for all of mankind. Similarly, everyone who knew Alice loved her. She was never too busy to listen and she always made you feel important. Her warm smile and twinkling eyes will be sorely missed, but not forgotten. The legacy she left, through the printed word, will benefit future generations of Al-Anon." Alice also wrote *The Dilemma of the Alcoholic Marriage,* published in 1967, and provided the groundwork for *Al-Anon's Twelve Steps and Twelve Traditions,* published in 1981.

Alice B. was born to a family of modest means in upper Manhattan. To her, receiving an orange on Christmas morning was a big event, and she remembered it all her life. Hers was a life of some personal hardship and hard work. Yet she possessed a sense of fun and experienced fully the joy of the moment. Alice was a self-taught writer who contributed professionally to *Ladies Home Journal* and other Hearst publications. Although she put her own life experiences into a series of short stories, such as "Wannamaker Ladies Wore Hats," none were ever successfully published. It was only when Alice's talent and life experience were combined with the Al-Anon program that she poured herself, at the age of 72, into her lifework, the *ODAT.* Her son, Kelly Campbell wrote a compassionate eulogy of his mother in 1984:

"Just take this as a letter from a person who has lost a friend. An exceptionally important friend, that is, one who had known me shortly before I knew her. My mother, Alice B. has slipped out of this life and into something more comfortable.

"I can't say that she went willingly. I'm not even sure that she understood anything beyond life at the present moment. The problem before her was the problem to solve. In an active business career which spanned most of 60 years, she was used to writing to order and on deadline. From her pen and typewriter flowed untold reams of copy, crisp, original, persuasive. She was a professional to her fingertips.

"As a member of the Al-Anon Literature Committee, she set to work editing and revising books on alcoholism published by Al-Anon. There was a need felt among those in the Al-Anon leadership for a book that could inspire, comfort, and sustain the men and women who were living the experience of alcoholism. Alice B. was asked to try her hand at it. She told us later that she had no idea how she would do it but she saw it as an opportunity to make a very special contribution.

"She was at it for more than a year, sitting hour after hour at the typewriter in her little cubbyhole at the top of the stairs in the house. It was her passion, her total preoccupation for that year. No one could have imagined, Alice least of all, the success of the *ODAT.* When, at the AA International Convention twelve years later she was handed the leather-bound millionth copy, she stood at the microphone, looked down at the sea of faces, and said, 'People ask me how I wrote the *ODAT*. I tell them that I just sat down at my typewriter and waited for it to come.'

"That's all she would ever say. She would not suggest that it was divinely inspired, but I think she believed it. When she left us on May 4 last, *ODAT* was well on its way to the second million. Needless to say, her life was not just *ODAT*. *ODAT* was, however, the final product of Alice's years with the problem of alcoholism. It was her last gift to people in trouble."

The Al-Anon membership joins with Lois in a quote from the inscription to a first edition copy, "What a monument to your devotion to, and understanding of Al-Anon is this book! Thank you," said from the heart of Al-Anon, with love.

ABBEY OF GETHSEMANI TRAPPIST KENTUCKY 40073

June 8 1966

Dear Mrs B[redacted]

Certainly you may quote those books. As a matter of form you need to clear this with the publishers.

As to my books of verse, they are all published by New Directions.

Many books are sent to me & I do not have time to read most of them, but no doubt your two books would find a good place in our library.

With best wishes –

Most cordially

fr Louis Merton

CHARLES SCRIBNER'S SONS

PUBLISHERS

597 FIFTH AVENUE NEW YORK, N. Y. 10017

February 19, 1968

Miss Alice E. B[redacted], Chairman
Literature Committee
Al-Anon Family Groups
P. O. Box 182, Madison Square Station
New York, New York 10010

Dear Miss B[redacted]

Thank you very much for your letter of February 10th requesting permission to include a quotation from a poem by George Meredith in a book of readings being prepared for members of the Al-Anon Family Groups. We appreciate your having written for permission; it shows a very thoughtful recognition of the importance of observing copyright protection.

We are pleased to grant you permission to use, without fee, the requested quotation in the manner described in your letter, our only requirement being that you cite the work from which the excerpt is taken, its author and ourselves as publishers.

Sincerely yours,

Kathleen A. Mann
Kathleen A. Mann
Rights and Permissions

ROBERT K. GREENLEAF
27 WOODCREST AVENUE
SHORT HILLS, NEW JERSEY 07078

Dear Mrs B[redacted]

Thank you for your letter of Nov 20. Indeed you may use anything of mine in Al-Anon publications.

I have another paper coming from the printer in a few weeks and will try to remember to send it along. I'm pleased to have these things used for a good cause.

Sincerely

Robert Greenleaf

Chapter Eight
Alateen

In 1957, Al-Anon added its Alateen branch for the teenaged children of alcoholics. Although Alateens conduct their own group meetings, sponsors, who are members of Al-Anon, can be consulted on matters of group functioning.

Interest in Alateen began when an article appeared in the August, 1957 edition of the *AA Grapevine* about a teenager from California called Bob, who had a father in AA and a mother in Al-Anon. Bob was in trouble in his own life. His parents urged him to try the principles of their own programs. Bob met with five other young people, and the first Alateen group was formed in Pasadena, California. From the start, Lois was in contact with Bill M., an AA member and prime mover in the establishment of Alateen. She urged the California groups to adopt the Steps and Traditions of Al-Anon.

"I have always loved the children of AA members. In the early days young teenagers often attended the meetings with the other members of the family. The AA program fulfilled the idealism of youth. It

943 [redacted]n Avenue
La Puente, California
July 12, 1957

Mrs. William Gl W[redacted]
Stepping Stones
Bedford Hills, New York

Dear Lois,

I am most grateful for your personal interest in the Alateen movement, as are
the members of the Pasadena Alateen Group. Incidentally, the Pasadena Group is
still the largest and is maintaining an attendance of 20 to 30 each week with an
average if 2 new [illegible], The other Groups out here look to them as the
"Mother Group" and so we are sure that the decisions made on the 12 steps and 12
Traditions will be adopted by all existing Southern California Groups.

This is truly a tremendous thing, and I do so wish it were possible for you
and Bill to sit in on one of their meetings. They are very sincere in their efforts
to understand the family problem, as well as to place their own lives "on the
program." Their patience, understanding and instructive help to the teen-age be-
ginner is a spiritual experience akin to Bill's and Dr. Bob's meeting.

The Group in Monrovia, California has been forced to de-activate, and I will
explain it a little to you as there is a message in it for all Alateen Groups yet
to be formed.

As Ala-Anon experienced in the start (and still does in some areas) there is
much opposition to Alateen from some AA members. The only reason I can ascertain for
this (and I don't want to be taking other's inventories) is that there is a slight
tendency on the part of AA members to be selfish with regards to sharing AA's lime-
light. The strange part of it is that the members who are more strongly opposed to
Ala-Teen are actually some of our best 12th Step workers. Perhaps, then, the real
reason for the opposition is best explained in Herbert S[redacted]'s quotation at the top
of page 380 in the "old" book.

The Monrovia Group, in sincerity of purpose, requested one male and one female
AA member to act as host and hostess and sort of advisory council to their meetings.
Each of these alcoholic's had children in the Group. Things were going well until
the parents began assuming the role of governing board and began to establish rules
and policies. This led to petty jealousies and resentments among the teen-agers,
and gradually those really seeking fellowship, strength and hope drifted away to
the Pasadena Group. Some of the former Monrovia members are now seeking to start
another Group in that area, and as we know - "If it be GOD's Will -----".

I feel that in preparing literature for the Alateen, that some diplomatic
statements concerning such an occurence should be included. AA and Ala-Non members
are welcome and invited to the Pasadena Group, but realize from the start that they
are merely there out of propriety. The kids are quick to seek their advice when a
situation calls for it, but most of us have discovered that it is seldom they need
to use this recourse. There is a perceptiveness and depth of understanding in the
child of an alcoholic who is active in Alateen, that amazes even such people as
Chuck C. and Jim B., both of whom have talked to the Pasadena Group, I am most
humble that I have been led into this work in the same manner and through the
same Power that led me into AA.

not only helped children to understand their alcoholic parents, but also enabled them to apply the principles to themselves, although not always consciously.

"At the Clearing House we began to recognize the special need of these young people and planned a session for them at the AA International Convention in St. Louis in 1955. This was a great success. There was a heavy demand for copies of these teenage St. Louis talks which were distributed by the Clearing House. In 1957 we prepared a pamphlet called *Youth and the Alcoholic Parent,* copies of which were sent with every Al-Anon order to alert our membership about Alateen."

Clearing House Advisory Committee minutes record the growth of Alateen, beginning in November, 1957. "In all there have been 40 inquiries to date about starting Alateen groups. So far, only four have registered as groups, and one (Vancouver, B.C.), not registered, has sent in a contribution. In the last bulletin received from Southern California Intergroup, the Santa Ana and Santa Monica Teen groups were mentioned, and also a second California Stag Discussion Group. After getting

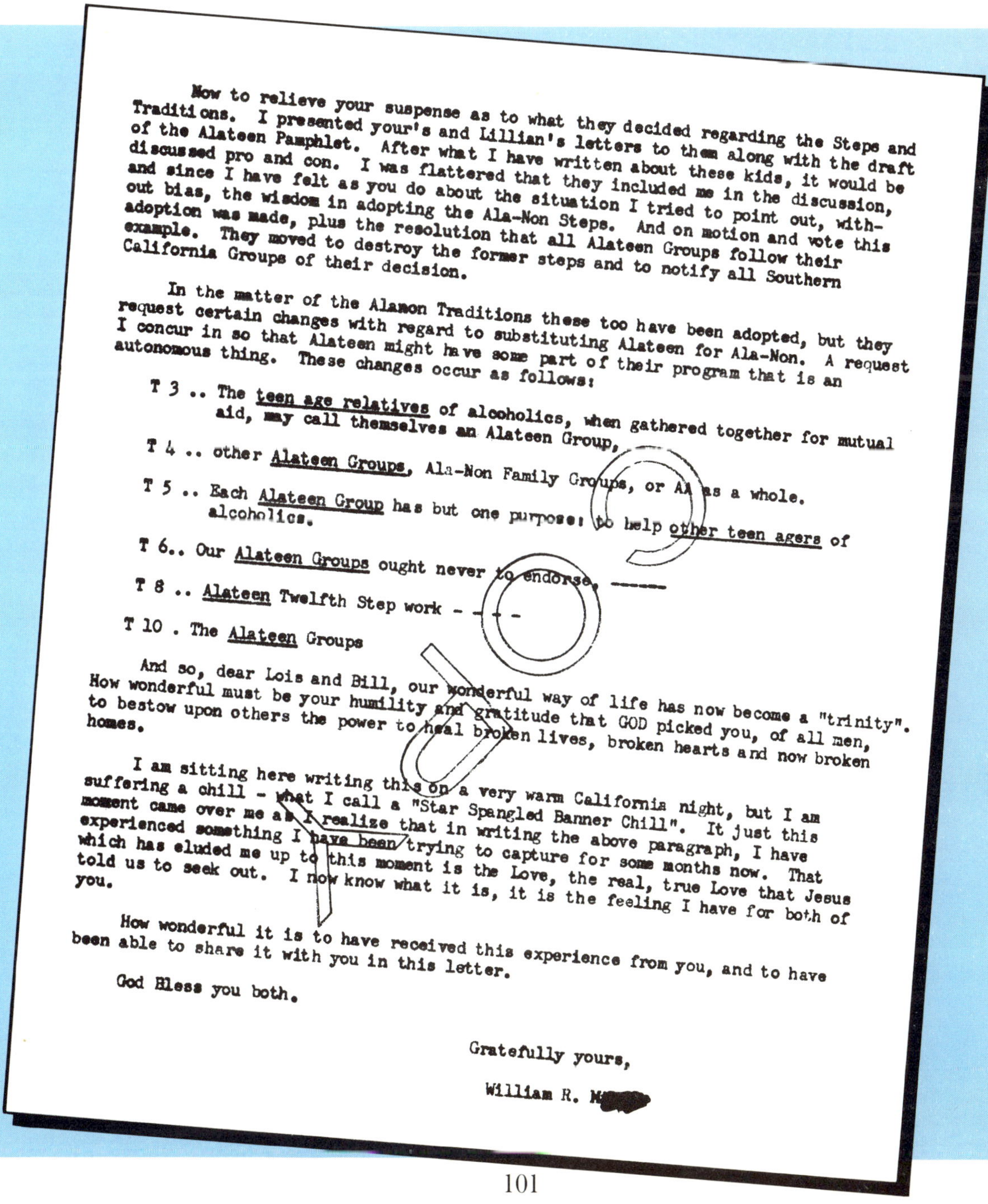

Now to relieve your suspense as to what they decided regarding the Steps and Traditions. I presented your's and Lillian's letters to them along with the draft of the Alateen Pamphlet. After what I have written about these kids, it would be discussed pro and con. I was flattered that they included me in the discussion, and since I have felt as you do about the situation I tried to point out, without bias, the wisdom in adopting the Ala-Non Steps. And on motion and vote this adoption was made, plus the resolution that all Alateen Groups follow their example. They moved to destroy the former steps and to notify all Southern California Groups of their decision.

In the matter of the Alanon Traditions these too have been adopted, but they request certain changes with regard to substituting Alateen for Ala-Non. A request I concur in so that Alateen might have some part of their program that is an autonomous thing. These changes occur as follows:

T 3 .. The teen age relatives of alcoholics, when gathered together for mutual aid, may call themselves an Alateen Group,

T 4 .. other Alateen Groups, Ala-Non Family Groups, or AA as a whole.

T 5 .. Each Alateen Group has but one purpose: to help other teen agers of alcoholics.

T 6.. Our Alateen Groups ought never to endorse, -----

T 8 .. Alateen Twelfth Step work - - - -

T 10 . The Alateen Groups

And so, dear Lois and Bill, our wonderful way of life has now become a "trinity". How wonderful must be your humility and gratitude that GOD picked you, of all men, to bestow upon others the power to heal broken lives, broken hearts and now broken homes.

I am sitting here writing this on a very warm California night, but I am suffering a chill - what I call a "Star Spangled Banner Chill". It just this moment came over me as I realize that in writing the above paragraph, I have experienced something I have been trying to capture for some months now. That which has eluded me up to this moment is the Love, the real, true Love that Jesus told us to seek out. I now know what it is, it is the feeling I have for both of you.

How wonderful it is to have received this experience from you, and to have been able to share it with you in this letter.

God Bless you both.

Gratefully yours,

William R. M[redacted]

their addresses from Lee C., secretary of Southern California Intergroup, all three were written letters to which no reply has been received, as yet. Lee also wrote that some of the youth groups folded over the summer ...."

Then, on August 12, 1958, the minutes read: "Hugh S., Advisory Committee member, asked for suggestions to help the Alateen group in Westchester. The following were made: sponsors should talk of Alateens to their own groups. Each member should be notified of the meetings by telephone instead of written notices for a while. Get speakers from AA and Al-Anon. Ask ministers to announce meetings to their young people's groups."

On February 17, 1959, "Henrietta asked that a committee be formed to write to the existing Alateen groups and to find out exactly what they do at their meetings, so that the office may be better informed when they answer proposed group letters. Hugh agreed to chair this and Wanda to help him." Wanda was to become Alateen Chairman for a number of years.

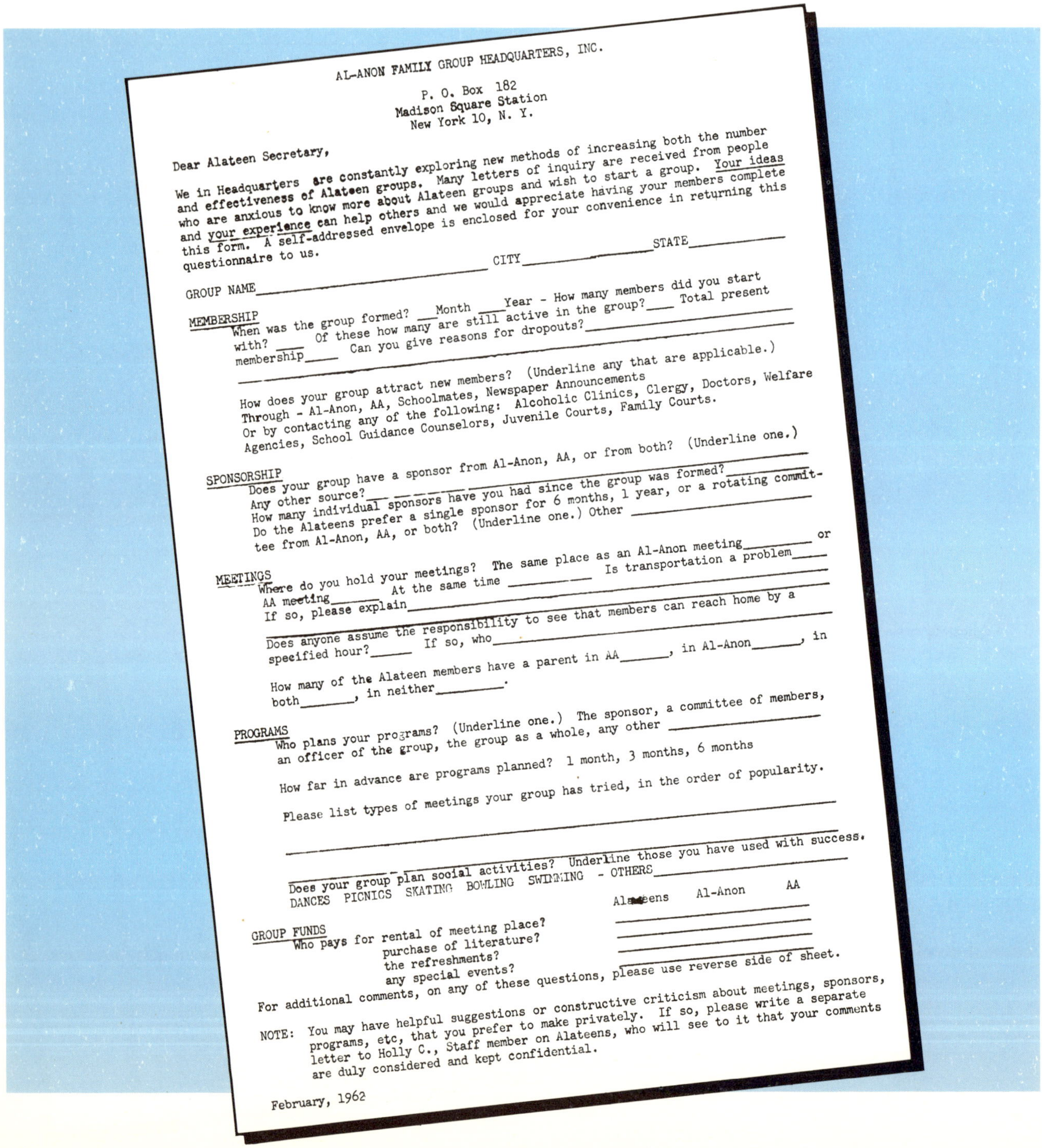

AL-ANON FAMILY GROUP HEADQUARTERS, INC.

P. O. Box 182
Madison Square Station
New York 10, N. Y.

Dear Alateen Secretary,

We in Headquarters are constantly exploring new methods of increasing both the number and effectiveness of Alateen groups. Many letters of inquiry are received from people who are anxious to know more about Alateen groups and wish to start a group. Your ideas and your experience can help others and we would appreciate having your members complete this form. A self-addressed envelope is enclosed for your convenience in returning this questionnaire to us.

GROUP NAME ________________ CITY ____________ STATE ____________

MEMBERSHIP
When was the group formed? ___Month ___Year - How many members did you start with? ___ Of these how many are still active in the group? ___ Total present membership ___ Can you give reasons for dropouts? ________________

How does your group attract new members? (Underline any that are applicable.)
Through - Al-Anon, AA, Schoolmates, Newspaper Announcements
Or by contacting any of the following: Alcoholic Clinics, Clergy, Doctors, Welfare Agencies, School Guidance Counselors, Juvenile Courts, Family Courts.

SPONSORSHIP
Does your group have a sponsor from Al-Anon, AA, or from both? (Underline one.)
Any other source? ___________
How many individual sponsors have you had since the group was formed? ________
Do the Alateens prefer a single sponsor for 6 months, 1 year, or a rotating committee from Al-Anon, AA, or both? (Underline one.) Other ____________

MEETINGS
Where do you hold your meetings? The same place as an Al-Anon meeting______ or AA meeting______ At the same time ________ Is transportation a problem_____
If so, please explain ________________

Does anyone assume the responsibility to see that members can reach home by a specified hour?______ If so, who ________________

How many of the Alateen members have a parent in AA______, in Al-Anon______, in both______, in neither________.

PROGRAMS
Who plans your programs? (Underline one.) The sponsor, a committee of members, an officer of the group, the group as a whole, any other ____________

How far in advance are programs planned? 1 month, 3 months, 6 months

Please list types of meetings your group has tried, in the order of popularity.
____

Does your group plan social activities? Underline those you have used with success.
DANCES PICNICS SKATING BOWLING SWIMMING - OTHERS ____________

	Alateens	Al-Anon	AA
GROUP FUNDS Who pays for rental of meeting place?			
purchase of literature?			
the refreshments?			
any special events?			

For additional comments, on any of these questions, please use reverse side of sheet.

NOTE: You may have helpful suggestions or constructive criticism about meetings, sponsors, programs, etc, that you prefer to make privately. If so, please write a separate letter to Holly C., Staff member on Alateens, who will see to it that your comments are duly considered and kept confidential.

February, 1962

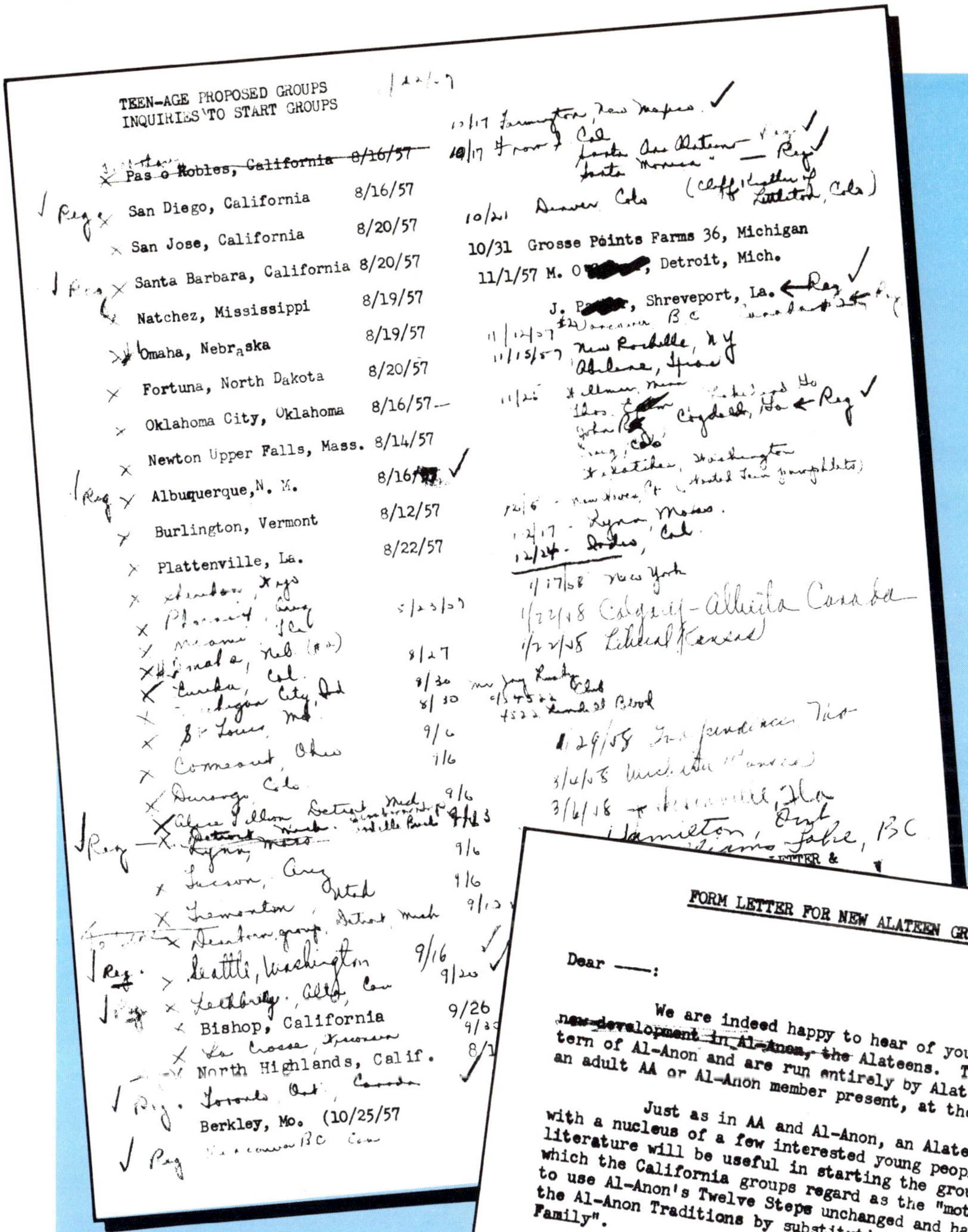

TEEN-AGE PROPOSED GROUPS
INQUIRIES TO START GROUPS

~~Pas o Robles, California~~	~~8/16/57~~	10/17	Farmington, New Mexico
San Diego, California	8/16/57	10/21	Denver, Colo
San Jose, California	8/20/57	10/31	Grosse Pointe Farms 36, Michigan
Santa Barbara, California	8/20/57	11/1/57	M. O[redacted], Detroit, Mich.
Natchez, Mississippi	8/19/57		J. P[redacted], Shreveport, La.
Omaha, Nebraska	8/19/57	11/15/57	New Rochelle, N.Y.
Fortuna, North Dakota	8/20/57		Abilene, Texas
Oklahoma City, Oklahoma	8/16/57		
Newton Upper Falls, Mass.	8/14/57		
Albuquerque, N. M.	8/16/57		
Burlington, Vermont	8/12/57	12/17	Lynn, Mass.
Plattenville, La.	8/22/57	1/17/58	New York
		1/22/58	Calgary - Alberta Canada
		1/22/58	Liberal Kansas
Conneaut, Ohio			
Seattle, Washington	9/16		
Bishop, California	9/26		
North Highlands, Calif.			
Toronto, Ont., Canada			
Berkley, Mo.	(10/25/57		

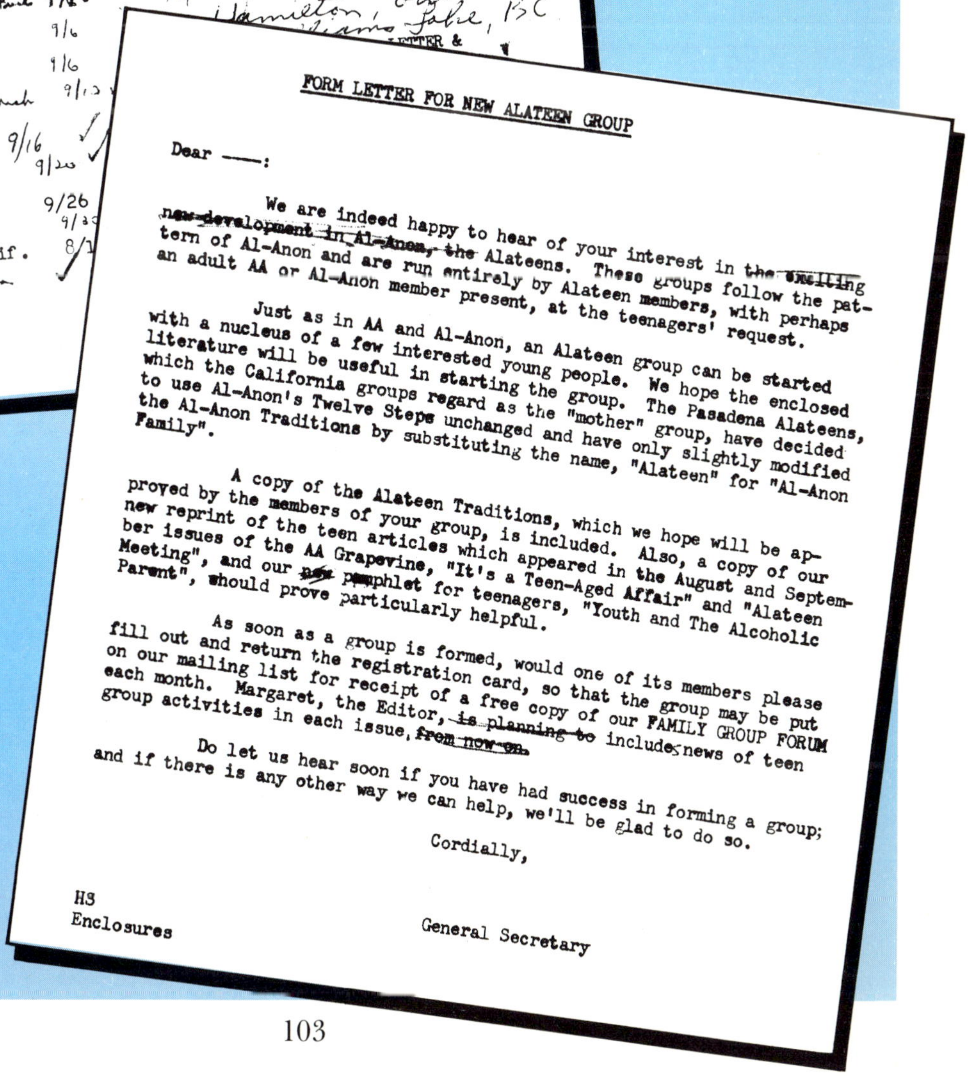

FORM LETTER FOR NEW ALATEEN GROUP

Dear ----:

We are indeed happy to hear of your interest in ~~the exciting new development in Al-Anon, the~~ Alateens. These groups follow the pattern of Al-Anon and are run entirely by Alateen members, with perhaps an adult AA or Al-Anon member present, at the teenagers' request.

Just as in AA and Al-Anon, an Alateen group can be started with a nucleus of a few interested young people. We hope the enclosed literature will be useful in starting the group. The Pasadena Alateens, which the California groups regard as the "mother" group, have decided to use Al-Anon's Twelve Steps unchanged and have only slightly modified the Al-Anon Traditions by substituting the name, "Alateen" for "Al-Anon Family".

A copy of the Alateen Traditions, which we hope will be approved by the members of your group, is included. Also, a copy of our new reprint of the teen articles which appeared in the August and September issues of the AA Grapevine, "It's a Teen-Aged Affair" and "Alateen Meeting", and our ~~new~~ pamphlet for teenagers, "Youth and The Alcoholic Parent", should prove particularly helpful.

As soon as a group is formed, would one of its members please fill out and return the registration card, so that the group may be put on our mailing list for receipt of a free copy of our FAMILY GROUP FORUM each month. Margaret, the Editor, ~~is planning to~~ includes news of teen group activities in each issue, ~~from now on.~~

Do let us hear soon if you have had success in forming a group; and if there is any other way we can help, we'll be glad to do so.

Cordially,

HS
Enclosures

General Secretary

PLEASE SEE THAT YOUR SPONSORS HAVE AN OPPORTUNITY TO READ THIS REPORT

May 1962

Dear Alateens:

Last March, Headquarters & Alateen Committee sent a questionnaire to all the
approximately 160 registered Alateen Groups. We are herewith reporting to you
a summary of thex questionnaires returned to date. Also, in the March Forum
we asked sponsors to write us about their groups. Those we have heard from wrote
with great pride about the way our teen-agers are responding to their program.
Their letters ~~should~~ would be an inspiration to others to sponsor Alateen groups.

MEMBERSHIP

The returns from the questionnaire have been most enlightening. Most
of the groups that replied are comparatively new and have anywhere from 2 to 62
members, with quite a number of original members still active. The following
reasons for drop-outs are given in the order of their frequency: Growing up
and participating in adult activities such as working, getting married and
going into the service or to college; parents neither understanding nor sym-
pathizing with their children's need of an Alateen program; teenager's own
lack of interest in applying the program to themselves, usually because of
confusion at home due to parent's drinking; and moving away. Only a few drop
out for such reasons as: Not enough social activity; meetings held too late;
no privacy; and age differences. The latter was rectified in some instances
(usually in the larger groups) by the formation of two groups, 12-15 yrs. and
16-20 yrs., and there are even a few Alatot groups.

Most new members hear about Alateens through Al-Anon and AA, although school
mates and School Guidance Counsellers also play an important part in informing
teenagers about Alateens. Unfortunately, only a few groups use newspaper
announcements, alcoholic clinics, Juvenile or Family Courts to contact new
members. Also, few clergymen or doctors referred children to the groups.
One group mentioned radio and another the School Nurse as a xxxxx source of
new members. It is apparent that sponsors could do a lot more to utilize public
agencies and professional people. If your group is not doing this, it might help
not only other teen-agers but alsoyourselves to inform such people about your group.

The recent formation of Alateen groups in two juvenile correctional institu-
tions; one in Paso Robles, California and the other across the country in Provi-
dence, Rhode Island, is a most hopeful new development. The sponsors of these
groups report excellent acceptance of their groups and the authorities are grateful
for this new technique in helping solve juvenile problems. There is unlimited
opportunity to help others find a new way of life by living the 12 Steps and we
cannot stress too much the importance of our program for teenagers at this crucial
time of their lives.

SPONSORSHIP

The question of sponsorship is becoming increasingly important for it appears
that the strongest, most progressive groups usually have dedicated, responsible
sponsors, x These sponsors are usually Al-Anon members with perhaps an interested
AA member acting in an advisory capacity. Only one or two groups reported no
sponsor at all, but a number have had difficulty in finding devoted sponsors with
no teenagers of their own in the group. While some groups prefer a sponsor com-

mittee, composed of both Al-Anon and AA members, which rotates every six months to a year, most seem to want ~~x~~ constant sponsors ~~whom~~ they will get to know and trust and who will know and understand them. The advantages of this are apparent. Alateens seem to want privacy in their affairs and to run their meetings themselves, but they need good sponsors to take the initiative and preserve the unanimity of the group. Because of the very nature of youth, membership constantly changes as the members mature, and good sponsors will see that the leadership of the group is not jeopardized by being dependent upon one or two teenagers and then find the group falters when they move on to ~~the~~ adult activities.

MEETINGS

It was surprising to note how frequently Alateens meet at times and places other than those of Al-Anon and AA, although sometimes at the same place but at a different time. It would seem that frequently different hours are more suitable and convenient for young people to meet. The only problem this presents, as one group put it, is what to do with the parents! Another group suggests parents drop the teenagers off, then later pick them up. Regardless of the time and place of meetings, transportation is a problem in many groups. Teenagers that drive can pick up other members. In most groups the sponsor sees that the members reach home by a specified time. Getting home early was not a problem especially with two groups who said they were so proud of their fellowship that they would do nothing to harm its reputuation. Because the alcoholic does not attend meetings, or the parents are not sympathetic of the needs of the teenager and because we have too few Alateen groups and the distance is often too great, ~~we~~ ~~are depriving~~ many children of alcoholics of attending Alateen meetings.

The number of Alateens who have parents in neither AA nor Al-Anon is surprisingly low. This is an area in which more information and education is needed. Again, these teenagers can best be informed through school functions, public agencies and professional people such as clergymen and doctors.

PROGRAMS.

Programs generally are planned from 1 week to 3 months in advance by the groups as a whole or by the chairman, who may be rotated each week or month. Outside speakers are the most popular type of meeting, especially speakers from other Alateens or AA. Talks b[illegible] Al-Anon members and professionals in the field of alcoholism were next in popularity. Meetings on the 12 Steps and 12 Traditions as well as discussion meetings on inventory, attitudes, self-revelation and personal problems are well liked. Tape recordings and movies, when [illegible], are very popular. Closed meetings without sponsors were also mentioned. Neither business meetings nor social activities are very frequent, although some groups hold occasional dances [illegible] a few run skating and swimming parties. Other activities mentioned were a very successful beatnik [illegible] to the mountains, Christmas party, open house, movies, field tri[illegible], [illegible]. Exchange meetings and attendance at AA and Al-Anon Conventions are extremely popular. Many groups, however, find socializing incompatible with the program and feel that they are more successful when they stick to it.

- 3 -

GROUP FUNDS

An outstanding bit of information noted from these questionnaires, is that most Alateen groups are self-supporting. Of course, it must be remembered that those groups which responded show a certain amount of responsibility and maturity, which might not be the case with the other groups. The reporting groups usually had a free place to meet, or paid for one themselves. Practically always, they provided their own literature and refreshments and took care of special events. Occasionally, groups were helped out by donations from AA and Al-Anon. However, most sponsors and Alateens are proud of the way they are maintaining themselves, and absorbing and explaining the program.

RECOMMENDATIONS

Among the suggested improvements is the need of more literature on their own age level and more varied types of meetings to keep up the interest. At our recent World Service Conference it was suggested that our Literature Committee prepare a new Alateen pamphlet and we hope to have more items on Alateens in the Forum. Perhaps this report will give you new ideas as to type of meetings that you can try. It was also suggested that perhaps Alateen mail from Headquarters might be addressed to the sponsors. However, we feel that it is up to the individual group to make this decision, although we recommend that whenever possible mail be sent to a P. O. box.

Because of the problem of finding good sponsors, we are endeavoring in future communications and publications to clarify the quualifications and duties of a sponsor through our Conference Alateen Committee and this matter is to be further pursued at our 1963 World Service Conference. Meanwhile, we want to stress the responsibility of Al-Anon groups to do all they can to assist and support the Alateen groups by sponsorship and understanding.

It is quite evident that Alateens are experiencing the same misunderstanding that Al-Anon did at first. A good suggestion is that Alateens speak whenever possible at open Al-Anon and AA meetings so that parents and the public can learn what a terrific job these teenagers are doing in applying the 12 Steps to themselves.

By continuing the ~~terrific~~ job you are doing of applying the Alateen program to yourselves, ~~our~~ Alateens will bring about greater understanding and sympathy for y ur groups. Thus we hope, others will be inspired to start new Alat en groups and we will be better able to help and give comfort to the children of alcoholics. We hope the foregoing report will enable you to know what other Alateens aredoing and give you some ideas for improving your group. We are always grateful for any suggestions or recommendations that you or your sponsors think would be helpful. Please let our Alateen Committee at Headquarters know how you are doing and what we can do to help you.

THE ALATEEN COMMITTEE

Sponsors of Alateen groups in areas where there are more than one group might find it helpful to get together periodically for the purpose of discussing problems and sharing ideas.

The first report of the Alateen Committee was made on May 12, 1959. "Hugh said there had been a very definite response to the questionnaire. It looks like the basis of something we can take down and digest and pass back to the teens. They seem to know what they want, and they seem to be getting it in their own way."

Henrietta had been given the additional responsibility of handling Alateen inquiries in 1958 until 1959 when Holly C. joined the staff and took over this responsibility. Holly was later to become the first Conference Secretary. A chapter on Alateen was included in the 1960 edition of *Living With An Alcoholic.* At the AA International Convention at Long Beach, California in 1960, workshops were held by and for Alateens. Lois says, "Both AA and Al-Anon members who attended were thrilled by these sessions and reported that the young people grasped the program better and with more understanding than they themselves had. Alateen, then numbering about 100 groups, had sprung into being in the five years since the St. Louis Convention.

The phenomenon of Alateen was and is, as Lois points out, the readiness with which young people grasp the principles and apply them to their own lives. Two anony-

Copied from enclosure in letter of Mrs. Chester B[redacted], 217-[redacted] St.,
Sherrill, New York 12/11/59

WHAT I GET OUT OF AL-ATEEN
(Unsigned from our Al-Ateen)

girl 12 yrs

Al-teen has helped me at home in most ways. It helps me get along with my parents, by doing what they ask and not giving a reason for not doing it first.

Al-teen has helped me at school in Science when we studied about alcohol, and also getting along with fellow students, and teachers. It helped me push myself along as to get into school activities and extra clubs like Youth Fellowship which is a church activity and Science Club and also Citizenship Clubs put on by the School Board and T achers.

Al-teen has helped me to push myself along and get to church on Sunday and not going because my parents tell me I have to, by going of my own free will.

---

girl 12 yrs

Before I started to come to Al-teen I felt very sorry for myself. I thought my parent was always wrong and I was the only one who had this problem. Now I feel completely different. I know that I had the wrong attitude myself and there are many others with the same problem.

---

girl 15

Before Alateen I used to beef about my father's drinking, stamp out of the house and make a big fuss about it. Now I understand why my father drank. I realize that my father was sick and that it will take a long time to get well.

Also it has helped me in school, and my social life. Also family life. I have learned to take my father's moods a lot better... I enjoy coming to Al-Ateen very much.

---

boy 13

Out of Al-Ateen I get a true understanding of why my parents or relatives drink. I find that this helps me in my school work and other outside activities, knowing that it isn't entirely their fault, and that if they are going to be cured or even helped it will take time and understanding.

Before I knew why my father drank I thought of him as a little off because of the way he acted and I thought that he drank just because he wanted to annoy people. After attending a few meetings of Al-Ateen I now know the true reason why my father drank.

---

girl 16

Al-Ateen has helped me in many ways in my family life as well as my outside life.

I have learned how to get along with people and not take their habits too seriously even though they may annoy me.

In my family life I have learned to understand my father better and understand that a power which he cannot control makes him want to drink. Al-Ateen has helped me understand that alcoholism is a sickness which cannot be overcome unless the alcoholic is willing to help himself.

Through Al-Ateen I have learned to understand my teachers and classmates better. I have more patience with people and can realize why people act as they do.

mous Alateens talk about what their program means to them:

"I escaped from problems at home by staying in my room, watching TV and listening to the stereo. But I had missed out on the ability to share. When I went to my first Alateen meeting, that was what was happening—sharing. Kids my own age were talking about their problems, and that shocked me, because I had never heard of this. After the meeting, kids came up to me. I felt they cared. So I kept coming back. The more I came back, the more caring I got. Eventually I was able to share something of what I had received. The big change that's come about in my family is that we have learned to communicate better. We are more trusting and willing to share. The biggest change that's come about with me has been a change in attitude. I've come to see that many of the problems I brought about myself. If I wanted to, I could change any situation by taking the First Step."

"When I came in, I thought I would have to talk about my parents, and I didn't really want to do that. The friendship was what I really liked at first. They didn't care about the kind of clothes you wore. They didn't care about any of that ... that kept me coming around. I started to listen, and I started to get interested. The way the group is structured, we talk about ourselves. I found that very hard at first, because I didn't really know myself, but I found I could learn to deal with me. There were no teachers and no counselors. That was something I was afraid of because I was having trouble at school. I thought they were going to try to teach me. It's really funny but the way we help each other in Alateen is to tell our own experiences. That really works for me because I don't feel I am being forced into

A) Coordinators Report

A year ago July, four Alateens and one sponsor from Massachusetts attended the first Alateen Conference, which was held in College Park, Maryland. A saturday afternoon meeting was held to decide what area could hold next year's conference; and it was during the course of this meeting, that the delegation from Massachusetts said it would try to hold the conference in 1963.

When we returned, and enthusiastically told the people of our committment, they said that we simply couldn't do it. Alateen simply could not undertake the project.

Sample Argument: we wanted to send out a letter to ask how many groups would attend, but we couldn't do that, because we couldn't guarantee that we wouldn't go into the red after it was all over.

On the last Sunday of November, we held a meeting to discuss plans for the conference with three of the Alateen groups in the area and a delegate from the Alanon Council in Boston. At this meeting, three things were decided:

1) We would try - not sit and say it couldn't be done.
2) We would form a working committee.
3) This committee would send out a letter and a questionaire to all Alateen groups within a four hundred mile radius of Boston.

The structure of the committee evolved durning the first two months of existence. No one gave it much thought at the time; we just wanted a conference. There were two major structures: the Committee and the Coordinators. The conference committee was made
up of the officers and sponsors of the Mass
groups plus a delegate from the council in
to come up with a basic plan and to rule o
coordinators submitted. The coordinators w
into a reality.

The basic plan was made after t
the replies from the first questionaires
about the first of the year. (It takes a
to write, send and receive the replies f
deadline should be set for returns abou
the questionaires are sent out - many n
was to hold a conference on one on the
June. The basic structure of the meeti
would be kept, but more emphasis place
upon the discussion of the program. T
ence was not to exceed twenty dollars

The largest problem we face
system of accommodations for the con
hall, suitable for meetings and meal
or dormitory in the same area, sinc
place to place takes too much time.
finding a hotel and a hall in the s
college or a private school would
facilities to us. After almost a m
based around a hotel in Cambridge
caterer would serve meals in the
up with the system that we used.
should go to Doctor Robert Mille
College, who made all the arrang
sure that the 1963 Conference wa
his efforts.

The following is a table of the proposed cost for both plans:

	Tufts College	Hotel Continental
Room	$ 4.00	$ 8.00
Linen	2.75	.00
Meals	6.50	6.40
Extra	1.75	2.60
Total	$15.00	$17.00

About the first week in May, we ordered our literature from New York. It included five books and a large assortment of Alateen phamplets plus a few Alanon("Just for Today", "Moral Inventory Sheets", etc.). A mistake was made in packing in New York, but since we had done this early, we were able to send the order back and receive all our literature in plenty of time.

The last few weeks before the conference were busy ones. We had to clean up many unfinished jobs. A checking account had to be opened and the money from registrations deposited. Speakers from AA and Alanon had to be asked for the Friday night open meeting. Refreshments, paper cups, etc. had to be picked up.

There were two big problems which couldn't or didn't work themselves out until Friday afternoon. First, we had planned to have all the rooms assigned before the groups started to arrive. Unfortunately, we didn't get this done in time, so registrations were slowed a little at first. Second, we didn't begin to think about tape recorders until it was almost too late. As a result of this, we didn't get Friday night's meeting on tape, and we didn't have enough recorders to cover as many of the Saterday meetings as we had hoped.

We arrived at Houston Hall, our dormitory, shortly before 3:00 p.m. and began to prepare for registrations. After forming a room plan, we gave each member of a group their room number, key, and linen. The groups then paid the entire group amount. They were each given a schedule of events, a copy of the house rules and a map of the campus. About 9:00 p.m., we formed a new list of rooms assigned to members according to groups. This was most helpful during check-out.

Saterday was given over to attending the various meetings. A small miracle was performed Saturday morning. We had planned a sight-seeing trip around Boston, but it fell through. Around 10:00 p.m., we thought that we could rent some busses and since we were in good shape financially, we contacted the Grey Line Bus Company in Boston. They were able to set up a tour for us that lasted for two and one half hours.

In passing, we paid all of our bills by check, in order to keep records. Also, we kept only about $ 200.00 on hand. The remainder was placed in the night deposit at the bank.

Sunday, we had to be out of the dormitory by 2:00 p.m., due to the summer school at the college. The group members cleaned their rooms and stripped their beds. Later, they returned their keys and linen, group by group.

By next week, we had paid all of the bills. The remainder($ 150.00) was divided into donations for New York, Boston and Syracuse.

Running an Alateen Conference is a big, but truly important job and working at it a day at a time, cut it down to size. All things considered, the conference was a success, and we were to be a part of it. We hope that New York will put us to shame in '64.

Sincerely,

Mickey & Jim

doing something. What works for one may not work for another. The Twelve Steps help me with my daily ups and downs. So do the slogans."

Alateen groups seem to work best with a diligent and loving sponsor. As one Alateen put it, "Three people is all you need for a meeting—two Alateens and a sponsor. When I walked in, the last person I wanted was an adult. But a sponsor is someone who wants to be there for you. They are not going to judge you. They can give guidance on how the meeting should be run. After a while, I just look upon sponsors not as adults, but as friends, people. The Alateen program would not be the same without the Al-Anon sponsors."

The drawbacks to Alateen are that teenagers eventually grow up. Fluctuations in membership are greater than in Al-Anon. Summer vacations and competing interests also make steady inroads into attendance at meetings. Alateens have gained much themselves through regional conferences to give them a sense of wider Alateen membership. Due to the vision and hard work of the same Bill M. who started the first groups in California, Alateen sponsored its first conference in 1962 in College Park, Maryland.

The second conference, held at Tufts University in Medford, Massachusetts, the following year, was a combination of Alateen meetings and fun, at minimal cost. The coordinators, Mickey and Jim reported, "Running an Alateen conference is a big, but truly important job and working at it a day at a time, cut it down to size. All things considered, the conference was a success, and we were glad to be a part of it. We hope that New York will put us to shame in 1964."

An Alateen Eastern Seaboard Conference was held in Syracuse, New York the following year, and another in Philadelphia in 1965. By 1971, Alateen conferences numbered ten across the country. Alateens also participated in AA and Al-Anon Conferences. Wanda R, Alateen Chairman at Headquarters, with the help of a newly appointed Alateen Staff Secretary, Timmy W., corresponded with the groups and initiated a quarterly newsletter, *Alateen Talk.*

Publicity in national magazines sparked hundreds of letters of inquiry, and groups were started at an increasing rate. Twenty-four new groups registered in 1966. By comparison, the number of groups totaled 800 in 1971. Alateen's own literature was developed, and a hardcover book, *Alateen—Hope For Children of Alcoholics* was first published in 1973. Alateens continue to add their own brand of enthusiasm, honesty, and imagination to the Al-Anon experience. The Al-Anon membership has always held these young people in high regard.

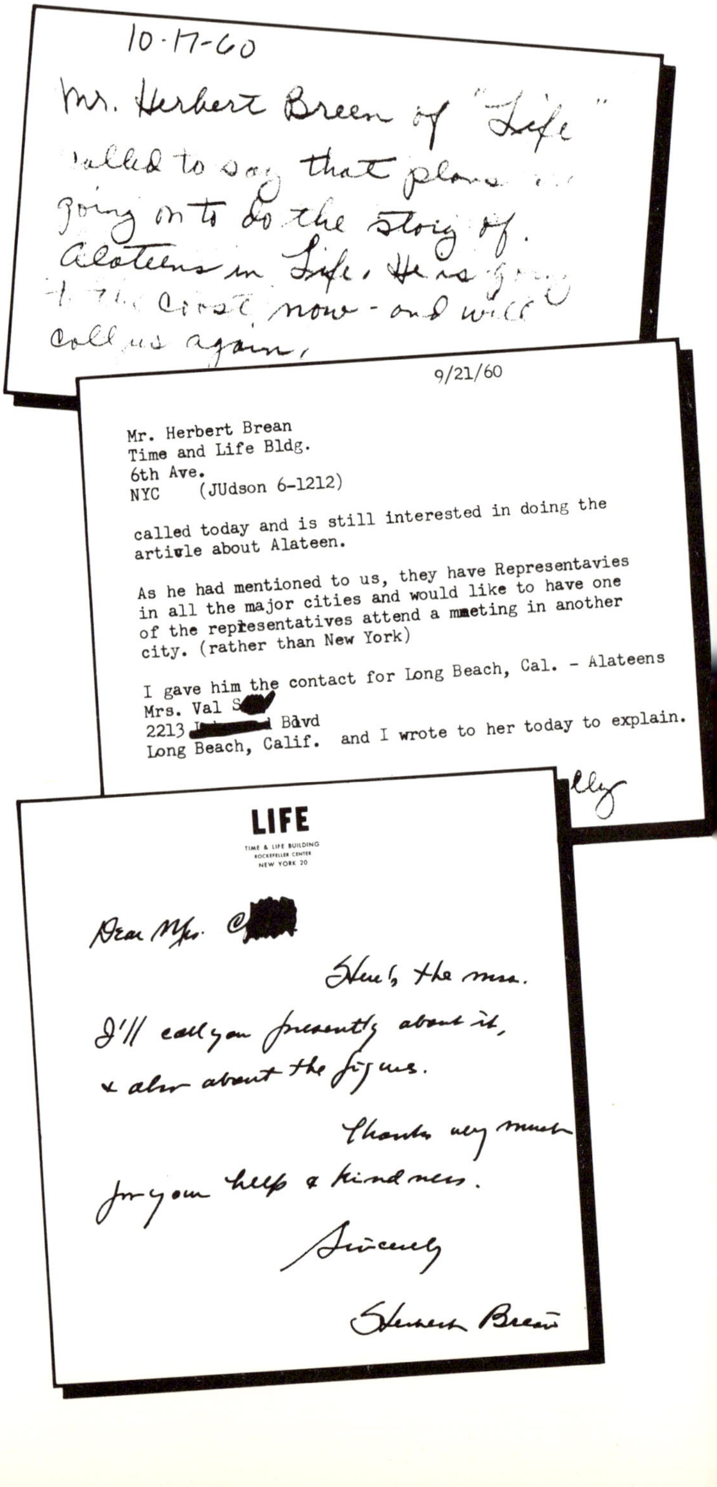

10-17-60

Mr. Herbert Breen of "Life" called to say that plans ... going on to do the story of Alateens in Life. He ... coast now - and will call us again.

9/21/60

Mr. Herbert Brean
Time and Life Bldg.
6th Ave.
NYC (JUdson 6-1212)

called today and is still interested in doing the artivle about Alateen.

As he had mentioned to us, they have Representavies in all the major cities and would like to have one of the representatives attend a mmeting in another city. (rather than New York)

I gave him the contact for Long Beach, Cal. - Alateens
Mrs. Val S[redacted]
2213 [redacted] Bdvd
Long Beach, Calif. and I wrote to her today to explain.

LIFE
TIME & LIFE BUILDING
ROCKEFELLER CENTER
NEW YORK 20

Dear Mrs. C[redacted]

Here's the ms.

I'll call you presently about it, & also about the figures.

Thanks very much for your help & kindness.

Sincerely

Herbert Brean

Chapter Nine
Worldwide Fellowship

Al-Anon became a truly international movement when, following in the footsteps of AA, lone members established outposts for Al-Anon in other countries. In time, these overseas pioneers created a network of groups, organized translations of the literature, and in some instances, initiated a separate national conference. Energy and dedication were the hallmarks of these people. None of this could have happened but for the presence of a regenerating force, called by Al-Anon members spirituality, and a link with a "wider group conscience" for which the Conference was to be the focus. Lois describes it when she talks of AA, Al-Anon and Alateen as the "A's" in her book:

"True to my sentimental, optimistic self, I believe there is a great future for our fellowships. It seems to me the world is on a not-so-dry bender and is ready for a regenerating force that can bring the kind of faith, security and happiness that the "A's" have found. But the survival of our "A's" depends on growth—growth in spirit more than in numbers."

Yet Al-Anon's growth in the spirit has never been uniform, despite its increase in numbers. Wives, as partners of AA members and still-drinking alcoholics first came into the Al-Anon fellowship to form the backbone of the movement. Women still make up about three quarters of our membership. But men, as husbands and fathers have been a very important minority from the beginning. As their numbers have increased, the need for stag, or exclusive men's meetings has declined. This may be true of other specialized groups such as gays, parents, and adult children. Even now, many of these Al-Anon members feel quite comfortable in the mainstream, and regard the specialized group as a halfway step into the program.

Equally important has been the outreach of Al-Anon worldwide. Reading the early correspondence between the Clearing House and the overseas membership, staff members and volunteers experienced Al-Anon growth as awe inspiring. When the airmail letters came slipping back to New York to report the beginnings of Family Groups around the world, they generated replies that show a sense of wonder. As the Clearing House sent off its packages of literature and letters of encouragement, the scribbled pencil at the edge of the page, which reads "Send six of everything" seems to capture the thrill that came with the knowledge that Al-Anon was happening everywhere.

The present format for Al-Anon meetings was in use by 1961. The manual states that, "meetings conducted by the chairman, or other designated leaders like those of AA, open with a moment of silence and close with a prayer acceptable to the group. Many groups include the reading of the Suggested Welcome, the Preamble, the Twelve Steps and Twelve Traditions." All meetings are restricted to Al-Anon members, with the exception of those designated "Open" which may be attended by non-members.

Choosing the group name is considered important. To quote from the manual again, "a name which includes the town, or section of the town, meeting day, or a phrase from our program would be inviting to all. A group's name should not imply any affiliation with any commercial venture, agency, religious group, rehabilitation facility, or other outside enterprise." The WSO will register any group provided it agrees to call itself an Al-Anon group, abide by the Traditions and remain open to all Al-Anon members."

GROUP STRUCTURE

The organization of an Al-Anon Family Group is very simple, but it has to have enough form to avoid confusion. Even a small group needs a program chairman and secretary. The secretary can act as treasurer as well, until the group is large enough to need a separate treasurer. As the group grows, a Service or Advisory Committee is useful. Some groups also have a refreshment chairman. All officers and committees are on a rotating basis, elected at a business meeting held every three or six months, and usually called before or aft r a regular meeting.

THE PROGRAM CHAIRMAN of a group plans the meetings in advance and obtains speakers. She either leads the meeting herself or appoints a leader.

For the various types of meetings which may be held, see the leaflet entitled "Suggested Programs for Family Group Meetings".

Where there are enough Al-Anon groups in an area to warrant an Intergroup Association, (some places call this a Central Office or United Council) the Program Chairman meets regularly with other Program Chairmen of the area and arranges "Exchange Meetings", where a team from one group conducts the meetings for a neighboring group. In this way, the scope of the group is broadened and a schedule of meeting programs can be planned well in advance.

THE SECRETARY is the link between Al-Anon Family Group Headquarters and the group. She receives all Headquarters bulletins as well as the Monthly Forum and sees that every member has a chance to read them.

She keeps an up-to-date list of names, addresses and telephone numbers of all members and sees that they are notified about meetings.

She orders sufficient Al-Anon literature not only for the group's use but enough to hand out to guests, to ministers, doctors and welfare workers.

She sees to it that the literature is on display at meetings.

During the intermission, at the time the contribution basket is being passed at the meeting, she makes whatever announcements there may be.

THE TREASURER of course, has the cus... of whatever money there is. Family groups do not need much, but ...ment, and perhaps light and heat of the meeting; spring... Family Group Headquarters help carry on Al-A... literature. There may be a few miscellaneous... nouncement in the paper or a P.O. Box. Many... after each meeting. In areas where there is... bute towards its operating cost.

The Treasurer, keeps a record of a... complete report of the Group's financial s...

Budgeting your expenses will simp... of the funds needed by the group. A contri... ings during the intermission. Some groups... older members who desire to make them.

Most groups find that having mo... necessary burden and even sometimes caus...

A SERVICE or ADVISORY COMMITTE... several older members, is useful to han... lations, intergroup relations and any i...

June 1961

SUGGESTED PROGRAMS FOR AL-ANON FAMILY GROUP MEETINGS

Meetings, conducted by the chairman or other designated leader, like those of AA, open with a moment of silence and close with the Lord's Prayer. Many groups include the reading of the Welcome, the Preamble, Twelve Steps and Twelve Traditions.

PERSONAL STORY MEETING

One or more speakers tell how they came to believe that the Al-Anon program was a way of life for them.

TWELVE STEPS MEETING

The group takes up one or more of the Twelve Steps, and the members discuss the application to themselves and their own problems.

PANEL DISCUSSION

Group members write anonymous questions which are then answered by a panel of several members.

AA SPEAKER MEETING

An occasional talk by an AA member clarifies the need for adjustments and cooperation in the home.

FAMILY ADJUSTMENT MEETING

Husband and wife teams - one an alcoholic, the other a non-alcoholic - discuss the problems of home life.

EXCHANGE MEETING

An individual or a team of speakers from another group is stimulating.

OUTSIDE SPEAKER MEETING

Physicians, members of the clergy, court workers, social workers, psychiatrists, psychologists, and others may be asked to address a meeting.

LITERATURE MEETING

At the discretion of the leader, a suitable chapter from the Bible or any other helpful book, magazine or newspaper article may be read. A discussion of the value of the Serenity Prayer and of the slogans is also helpful.

OPEN MEETING

Many groups hold an open meeting once a month at which alcoholics and other guests are invited to attend so that they may learn just what work is done by Al-Anon. Emphasis is placed on the cooperation of the Al-Anon member with the alcoholic at home. (This type of meeting is especially suitable for the celebration of anniversaries.)

The list of possible meetings could well nigh be endless. These self-explanatory titles may be suggestive:

TWELVE TRADITIONS
A CHAPTER FROM THE AL-ANON BOOK
FILMS OR TAPE RECORDINGS
THE PROBLEMS OF NEWCOMERS
DISCUSSION BY YOUNG PEOPLE

August, 1961
From- MANUAL for Al-Anon Family Groups

Exclusivity was not a part of early Al-Anon, because the membership was too small. Men, sometimes in one's or two's, joined groups made up of women. As already mentioned, Wally S., one of the pioneers, had an alcoholic son. It was Bill who suggested to Wally that he should encourage his son, by then a young adult to become independent. Wally took Bill's advice. He put his son on a bus headed north with a few dollars in his pocket. After many near disasters, the son joined AA. Many parents of young alcoholics who are members of Al-Anon will relate to Wally's dilemma as a parent.

The fact that Al-Anon's first voluntary contribution came from a man, Sam K. of Lynn, Massachusetts has already been mentioned. Ray C. of San Jose, California talks about the history of men in Al-Anon:

"I heard of Family Groups first in 1951. I met with three or four wives in Salinas, California. In those days we thought we would do the Steps, so we sat down and looked at 'em. Well—the First Step didn't apply to us, so we went on to the Second. We got to the Eleventh Step in one hour, and that was the end of our Step meeting and my stay in Al-Anon—temporarily.

"I came back to Al-Anon in 1956. There were about two or three other guys by that time. We would get off in a corner and all hang together, just like real sticky glue. It was very disturbing to have to meet with a bunch of women, but I was getting the help I needed from the group. I knew that. So I did what I could to try to fit in.

"I was very uncomfortable in... Al-Anon. I nearly chickened out. Even now, I don't know that I like the number of women to be that big. But things were getting better at home, so I got active in the program.

"This stag issue was a very thorny one at that time—not for the women, but for the men. At the 1970 Convention at Miami, one of the questions was, 'Where have all the men gone? Why don't men stay in Al-Anon?' At an impromptu meeting, it was decided that men's pride was the biggest thing that got in the way. At that Miami meeting I thought something must be wrong with me to be meeting with a bunch of women.

"Then I went on a retreat where I had to walk through an AA meeting to get to the Al-Anon meeting. I wondered what the AA men thought of me. My own self image was not too good, and these AAs forced me to look at it. I still have some character defects—they can really stick out all over.

"Two others guys and I started a men's group in San Jose. It went on for about ten years, and then it faded. I guess we found it wasn't necessary any more. In San Jose today we have lots of young fellows. The group is about equal—one man for one woman. It's just worked out beautifully."

Meeting the men's point of view in Al-Anon is reflected in the literature. The 1961 Conference spoke of "the need for literature specifically written for men." The following year a pamphlet, *The Stag Line* was developed. This was later dropped, and another, *What's Next? Asks the Husband of an Alcoholic* was written by a stag group member from New Jersey. Other pamphlets, *My Wife is an Alcoholic* and *Al-Anon IS For Men* were added a few years later. Stories by men have been included in all of Al-Anon's hardcover books.

Beginning in the 1960's, growing professionalism in the alcoholism field led eager recovering people in AA and Al-Anon to seek professional qualifications. Those "wearing two hats," as these counselors were called, created discussion on how their status should be viewed within the Al-Anon program. Their point of view was also expressed in separate literature.

Awareness of another group within Al-Anon gained recognition in the 1970's—those who were also members of AA and other Twelve Step programs. A pamphlet was developed in 1977, called *Double Winners.* The name was later changed to *The Al-Anon Focus* but in 1978, 80,000 copies of the pamphlet were sold. The effects on the rest of the Al-Anon membership caused by highlighting a special population is addressed by Margaret K. of Conoga, Pennsylvania:

"I used to resent the double winners. But I finally got the idea that they need Al-Anon too. I always felt they should practice their own program. Then I gradually realized that they were just as confused as we were about facing the other alcoholics in their lives. We don't advise them to come into Al-Anon right away, but after a time they should join us."

Another recent addition has been the phenomenal growth of the adult children movement within Al-Anon. The 1984 World Service Conference approved a statement about adult children. Parts of the statement follow:

"Although there have always been adult children in our fellowship, recently Al-Anon has been recognized as a resource for those whose lives had been affected, perhaps years ago, by the alcoholism of a parent. Many of these members felt that they benefited most when they shared at meetings with other adult children of alcoholics. To attract those with similar experiences, they called their Al-Anon meetings, 'Adult Children of Alcoholics,' 'Children of Alcoholics,' and 'Sons and Daughters of Alcoholics.' The formation of these groups seems to be a response to a need expressed within the fellowship.

"Growth in the registration of adult children Al-Anon membership in Al-Anon's World Service Office has rapidly increased... With an increased awareness of the adult children membership in Al-Anon, the need to include their stories in Conference-Approved Literature (CAL) became evident... Our membership offers a wide variety of experience, most of it indicating that the disease of alcoholism isolated each of us in one way or another. In the recovery process we come to realize that joining together in a spirit of unity insures that Al-Anon will be preserved and passed on to others. As we see the results of our commitment to the program, our common bond is enriched, and we realize that our progress toward recovery is more important than how we came into Al-Anon or whose alcoholism may have affected us. It is therefore, our hope that adult children will also attend other Al-Anon meetings where the background of its members is more widely varied."

The same holds true of other special groups. Al-Anon today tends to regard the feelings of isolation as part of the family disease of alcoholism, and not a social or emotional difference that should separate members from one another.

"Ar[redacted]",
[redacted]ad,
[redacted] Bay,
Cape Town. S.A.
1st November, 1949.

Dear Ann,

Allow me to introduce myself. My name is Irene. Pat, the Secretary of the Cape Town Group of Alcoholics Anonymous has given me your address.

My intention is to start a Non-Alcoholics Group in Cape Town. For the past few weeks we have been having small gatherings on the same nights as the Alcoholics have their closed meetings. So far these meetings have been of an informal nature without a Chairman etc., where we have just discussed our problems and tried to explain the movement to wives etc. of new members of the A.A.

I am wondering if you would be kind enough to let me know how the Non-Alcoholic Group operates over in the States. Also if you have any literature on the subject which you could let me have I would be very grateful.

Hoping to hear from you soon.

Yours sincerely,
Irene D[redacted]

waiting
N/C

Go Ma[redacted] Office.
Bloemfontein.
Union of SOUTH AFRICA.
12th June 1952.

New Gr

Dear Sir,
Or is it madam? – anyhow I soon hope to know, as we are in need of information!

I have had a letter from Ann (foreign secretary to AA.) and she gave me your address.

Our AA group has been going nicely for the last 6 months, but we feel the urgent need for the formation of "Family Groups". Can you please supply us with information – and pamphlets – on what you regard as the best way of going about in the formation of such a family group? I can assure you that any literature will be most welcome.

2.

No doubt, you also have the problem of ~~a~~ receiving many letters from anxious wives & other relatives of the Alcoholic – and this is our problem too! We also feel that many of these people are so frustrated that they expect something more than the advice we can offer them! Many have reached that stage where the wish to rid themselves of their "baby"!

Thank you ever so much for the assistance.

Kindest regards
from
Tommy (T.D. van S[redacted])

Kind regards to Ann M[redacted] if you should see or phone her!!

ans 3/25/51

13 [redacted] Glebe
Sydney, N S W
Australia. 10th January 1951.

Dear Lois.

Bill's letter to Russ arrived today, and gave
us a warm feeling. Jack H[redacted] from the Marshall Islands
sent a snapshot taken at the Cleveland Conference, so
now we know what you both look like. It brings you
nearer to us. Sydney's A.A. Christmas was a wonderful
one. We had a big, combined party, and everyone had a
wonderful evening. A member who is a nightclub entertainer
pd brought along two of his pals who certainly brought the
house down with their acts.

But the best of all was that wonderful
is the spirit of A.A. Radiant smiles, instead
fixed smiles.

Many were dubious of the success of such a
we have never before had a party which was al
a social affair, but we opened with the
by an address by a very sincere member, w
established the fact that this was A.A.
relaxation, and everyone, as usual was i
AA fellowship, which made each one presen
eager to please. Wonderful is the only w
the feeling of friendship that was there.

Someday our dreams may come true,
be able to see AA members in America
it will not matter, because distance d

anything when we are all striving
help others. I feel that I can never
repay the love & friendship that has been given to me in just
five years, so it seems that as time goes on my debt to AA
will become like the national one, but perhaps I can pay
the interest, with God's help. It means a great deal to me
to have a letter from you sometimes. Will you tell me of some
of your personal problems and how you dealt with them?

One of my biggest tasks was to talk to a person under the
influence without the horror of past events overwhelming me. I
found that the 11th step was the one to carry me through it.
We are leaving on our holidays soon for three weeks and will
visit two other states. I am hoping to make new friends among
the AAs there. Please write soon.

Affectionately Dorothy [redacted]

---

281 G[redacted] Street,
Dunedin,
New Zealand.
28/2/55.

Henrietta S[redacted],
General Secretary,
Family Groups Headquarters,
New York.

Dear Henrietta,

I enclose reference card with the information you request for inclusion in the Family Group Directory and trust it will reach you in time.

We wives in Dunedin are very grateful to you, and the many helpers in A.A., for the literature you have sent and I am sure we will be able to make good use of it. When we started the "Wives Meeting" last June our intentions were to help the wives of new members of A.A. as well as ourselves, to a better understanding of alcoholism, and perhaps in a year or two be able to include other members of the family. Meantime our progress is slow, but I feel sure we are laying a foundation that will stand in good stead in the years ahead.

It would help us if you could give us some idea of the best way to send money to you. Would it be alright for us to send it along with monies from the A.A. Group?

Yours faithfully,

Caroline K. S[redacted]

MAR 14 1955
ORDER
CLIPPINGS
NEW GROUP
GROUP RECORDS
CARD ENCLOSED
INQUIRY
PUBLIC RELATIONS
A. A.
FILE

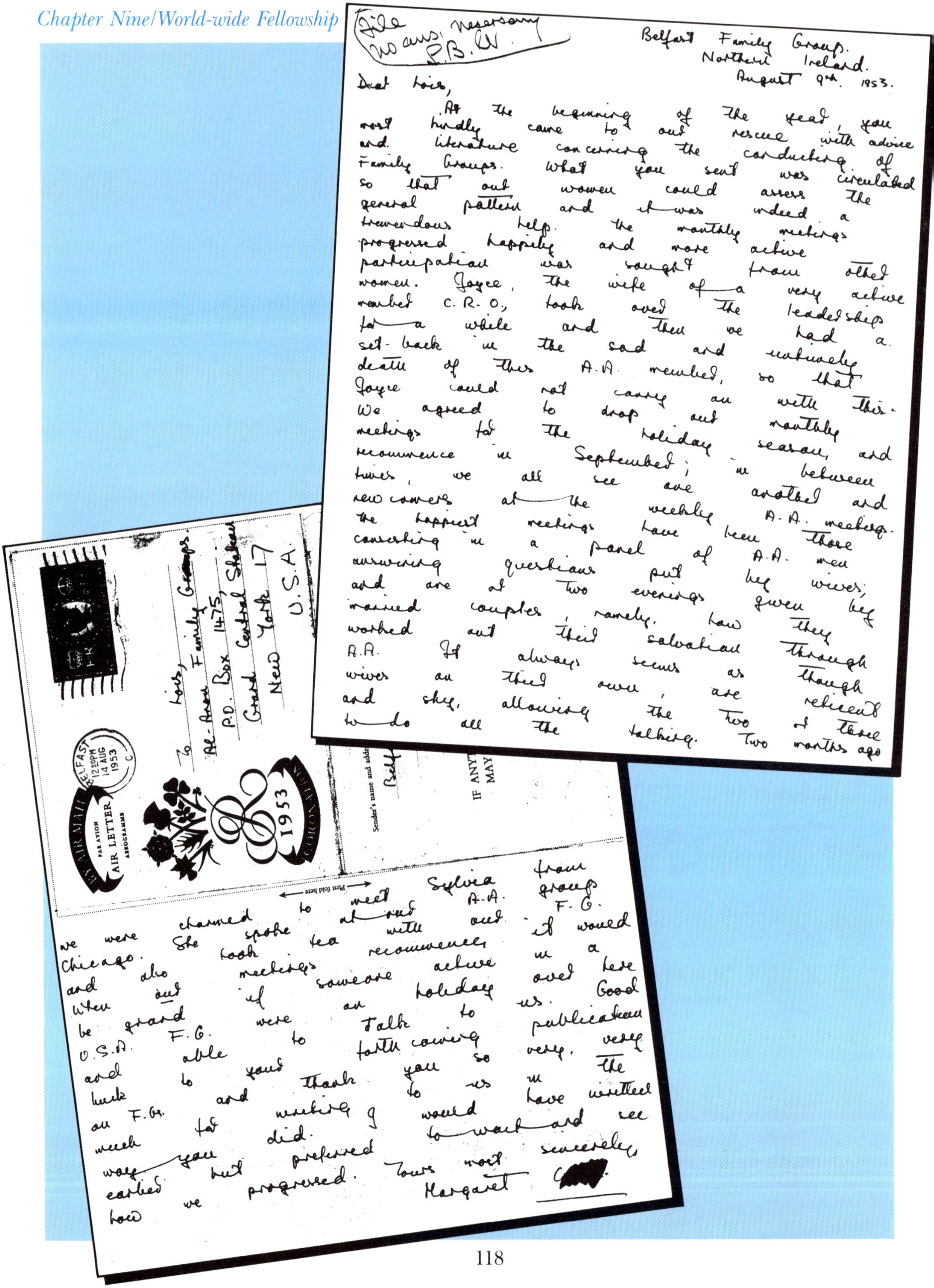

Belfast Family Group.
Northern Ireland.
August 9th. 1953.

Dear Lois,

At the beginning of the year, you most kindly came to our rescue with advice and literature concerning the conducting of Family Groups. What you sent was circulated so that our women could assess the general pattern and it was indeed a tremendous help. The monthly meetings progressed happily and more active participation was sought from other women. Joyce, the wife of a very active member C.R.O., took over the leadership for a while and then we had a set-back in the sad and untimely death of this A.A. member, so that Joyce could not carry on with this. We agreed to drop our monthly meetings for the holiday season, and recommence in September; in between times, we all see one another and new comers at the weekly A.A. meetings. The happiest meetings have been those consisting in a panel of A.A. men answering questions put by wives; and one of two evenings given by married couples namely, how they worked out their salvation through A.A. It always seems as though wives on their own, are reticent and shy, allowing the two of three to do all the talking. Two months ago we were charmed to meet Sylvia from Chicago. She spoke at our A.A. group and also took tea with our F.G. When our meetings recommence it would be grand if someone active in a U.S.A. F.G. were on holiday over here and able to talk to us. Good luck to your forth coming publication on F.G. and thank you so very, very much for writing to us in the way you did. I would have written earlier but preferred to wait and see how we progressed.

Yours most sincerely,
Margaret [redacted]

Care on file

As from A.A.
60, Dublin Rd.
Belfast.

8 Ch[redacted]
Be[redacted] Road,
Belfast, N.I.
30. 10. 52.

Dear Lois,

If anyone can help us, I am sure you can, i.e. with a problem pertaining to our Family Group. No doubt you hear of other F.G. problems from time to time and we wonder if you have come across one like ours.

We have been functioning for over a year now and have a regular but small bunch of devotees about 12. Its chairman, I ... to follow along lines such ... have laid down, and make ... discussion group, with a selected ... with the Lord's Prayer ... conclusion, to keep our thoughts ... a spiritual line of ... enjoy our laughs in between ... comes at the end usually ...

Well now, a number within our ... who might be want this ... not seem to considered the ... thing and be out for ... ought to etc. etc. this ... socials the fact that there ... of the Saturdays when ... Club on a very jolly ... can have ...

A.A. members, ... others do seem suspicious, and so on.

We are trying to ... matter out here and ... seems necessary, but w... so much like, to have ... verdict may be, from ... experience "over there."

We enjoy taking que... the Family Forum. Do you not think it would be a great idea if you formulated 50 or so possible group questions for practical use?

Our warm wishes, as ever to you and your husband.

Yours very sincerely,
Margaret C[redacted].

P.S. Am sure you will note in this some urgency for a personal reply.

Mrs. Margaret C[redacted]
8 C[redacted]e Road
Belfast, N. I.

JUN 22 1953

November 12, 1952

Dear Margaret:

It was so nice to hear from you. I remember our visit with you all with so much pleasure. I do hope sometime we will be able to be with you again.

But I am sorry to hear that your group is not doing so well. Don't be discouraged. The interest and attendance in most groups fluctuates. As for the social activities - I should think those who wanted more social contact could have it as long as it did not interfere in any way with the more serious meetings of the Family Group.

Many A.A.s over here also have been very slow in understanding the benefits to them of the Family Groups but lately they seem to be appreciating more and more the help they can be. Some Family Groups hold an open meeting every so often and invite one or two A.A.s to speak, telling in what way they think the Family Group help themselves and help A.A. This often breaks down any resistance the A.As may have felt. After all it is only natural for A.A.s to be wary of anything they may take to be an encroachment on A.A. - until they understand.

Under separate cover we are enclosing some literature. There are some suggestions for meetings among them. Maybe some time I will get down to listing 50 questions for discussion but there is so much material in inspiration books, the Bible of course heading the list, that it hardly seems necessary. In the literature we are sending, there is a list of inspirational reading. Some groups read a chapter of one of these and then discuss it afterwards. Is there any group near enough to exchange speakers with them? New ideas and new blood are always stimulating.

I'm afraid I haven't been a great deal of help but do write us and tell us how things progress.

Bill joins me in all good wishes to you and your family personally, as well as to the Belfast groups, both A.A. and Family Group.

Cordially yours,

4, Hi[redacted]
G[redacted]R ROAD,
EALING. LONDON W.5.

Hullon Louis + Bill

Just a line to wish you both well + to let Louis know we have started a group in connection with our West London Groups for the NON ALKIES.

Could you suggest a title for this. We have suggested "The Family Groups", The Non AA's The AA Mates Groups The World's Society of Health, Happiness + Peace but nothing seems to be fitting and as simple as ALCOHOLICS ANONYMOUS.

Three ladies, wives of members are starting this + already we have had a successful day out at the Seaside, + any suggestion you might have for a social evening will be welcome. Everything they do is ... sanctioned by our AA West-L... + we are having some fine ... We shall be pleased to know ... Molly, Holly, Dolly, Helen ...

August 13, 1952

Mr. Bill D. T.
4, H[redacted]
65[redacted]r Road
Ealing, London W. 5, England

JUN 22 1953

Dear Bill:

Bill and I were so glad to hear from you and to learn that you are starting a Family Group in West London. In the many places these groups are established they have proved themselves of great help to the alcoholic as well as the non-alcoholics. An understanding home atmosphere is of such great help to the alcoholic.

We call these groups here the Al-Anon Family Groups and we have founded a Clearing House for answering inquiries, getting our literature and helping groups get under way. Enclosed is some literature and we shall be glad to send you more free of charge until you can get your group well established.

Do keep in touch with us and let us know how the group progresses.

Our best to Molly, Dolly, Helen and yourself,

Cordially

md

Lois B. W[redacted], Chairman
The Al-Anon Family Groups

The spread of Al-Anon to other countries (in 1985 there are 81 countries) is truly remarkable. One such story is that of Swiss-born Frieda, and her American husband, John, who moved to England in 1948. John had found AA in Washington, DC. In many respects, their British experiences paralleled those of early members in the United States:

"In London at the time, our life was quite different from the one we had left behind—there were no AA meetings nearby. John tried to meet other AA members, but there were only about eight of them scattered all over England. John and I had our own modest meetings, and once another English member, Bill H. invited us to travel up to his house. A German AA member left London soon after we arrived, so John had to have new AA contacts. In desperation, John stopped a policeman to inform him about AA in the pouring rain. I did actually murmur, 'Must you?' to John. He was in a real pink cloud state.

"Next, John tried to do some Twelfth-Step work. He was asked to visit Donald C., which he tried to do right away. At first he couldn't find him because Donald was too busy visiting pubs. We asked him to come and stay with us for a couple of weeks. We thought we could look after him because our employers were going away, and we had the house to ourselves.

"But Donald turned up a week too soon. We simply couldn't hide such a big fellow, so we asked our employers if Donald could stay, explaining the work of AA. To our

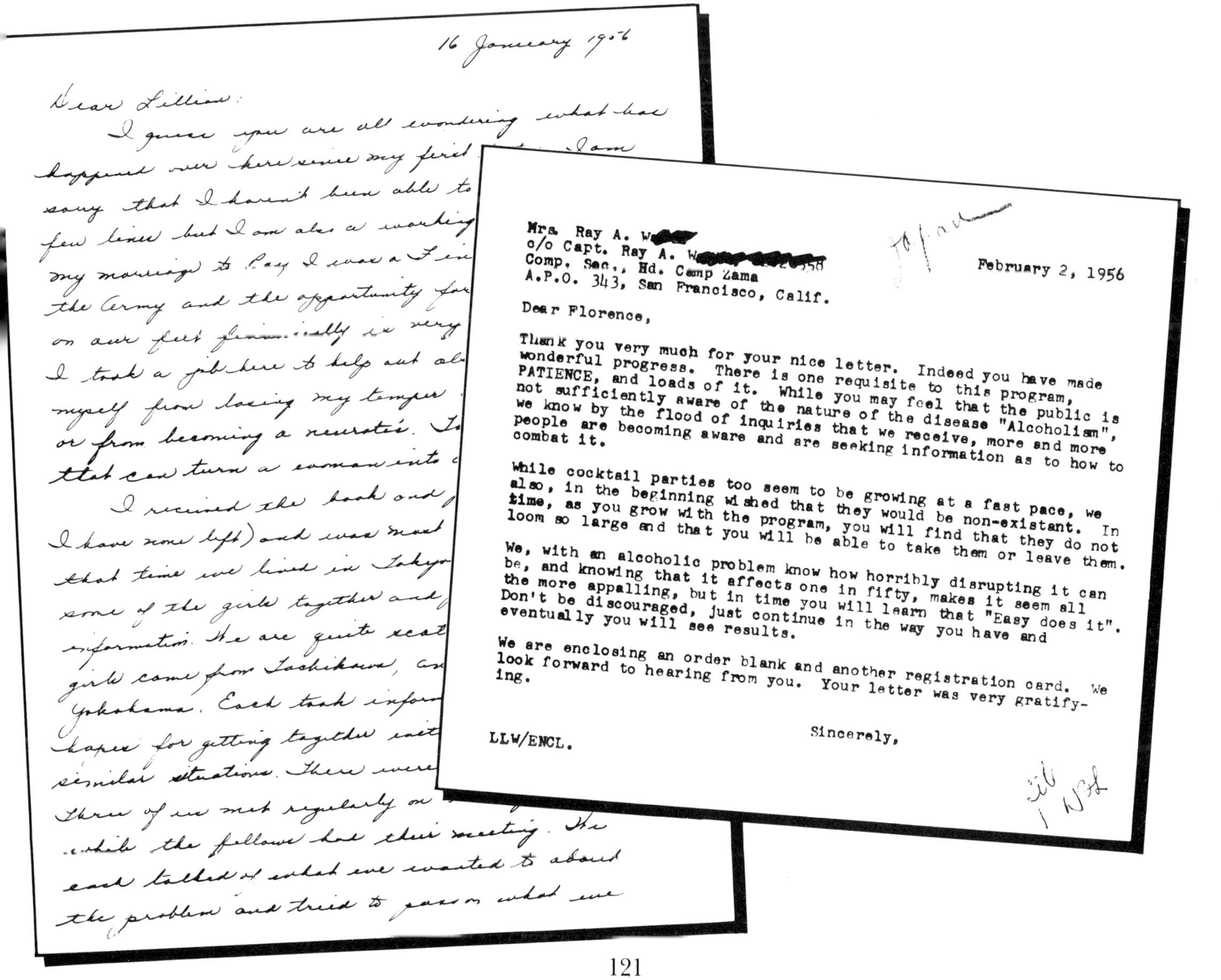

16 January 1956

Dear Lillian:

I guess you are all wondering what has happened over here since my first ... I am sorry that I haven't been able to ... few lines but I am also a working ... my marriage to Ray I was a ... the Army and the opportunity for ... on our feet financially is very ... I took a job here to help out al... myself from losing my temper ... or from becoming a neurotic. ... that can turn a woman into ...

I received the book and ... I have none left) and was most ... that time we lived in Tokyo ... some of the girls together and ... information. We are quite scat... girls came from Tachikawa, an... Yokohama. Each took infor... hopes for getting together ... similar situations. There were ... Three of us met regularly on ... while the fellows had their meeting. We each talked of what we wanted to about the problem and tried to pass on what we

Mrs. Ray A. W[redacted]
c/o Capt. Ray A. W[redacted]
Comp. Sec., Hd. Camp Zama
A.P.O. 343, San Francisco, Calif.

Japan

February 2, 1956

Dear Florence,

Thank you very much for your nice letter. Indeed you have made wonderful progress. There is one requisite to this program, PATIENCE, and loads of it. While you may feel that the public is not sufficiently aware of the nature of the disease "Alcoholism", we know by the flood of inquiries that we receive, more and more people are becoming aware and are seeking information as to how to combat it.

While cocktail parties too seem to be growing at a fast pace, we also, in the beginning wished that they would be non-existant. In time, as you grow with the program, you will find that they do not loom so large and that you will be able to take them or leave them.

We, with an alcoholic problem know how horribly disrupting it can be, and knowing that it affects one in fifty, makes it seem all the more appalling, but in time you will learn that "Easy does it". Don't be discouraged, just continue in the way you have and eventually you will see results.

We are enclosing an order blank and another registration card. We look forward to hearing from you. Your letter was very gratifying.

Sincerely,

LLW/ENCL.

great surprise they agreed, and told us they thought it was wonderful that we helped one another.

"Donald was in very bad shape. He had delirium tremens. John had to sleep with him, and I had to clear out of the bedroom. Donald has not had a drink since. When Donald sobered up, another AA member, James joined us. In time there were so many AA's our place became too small for meetings:

"The very first AA Convention in England was held at Cheltenham. There we met many others with whom we became firm friends—Archie, Frank, and Connie, who got sober in Washington too, although she had never met John. Connie told us later how she had feared returning to England because there were so few AA members there. But she was told, 'There will be John and Frieda, so don't you worry.'

"We had no Al-Anon program in Washington as such. We did have the Steps as a guide. When we moved to Bath in 1954, I worked as a hairdresser. John would hold his AA meetings downstairs, and tell any wife who turned up to come upstairs to see me. We did start an Al-Anon meeting on the same night as AA had its open meetings. It happened this way.

"In August, 1953 at an AA open meeting, the chairman shook the hand of the one Al-Anon member there—me. I was allowed five minutes to explain to everyone there what Al-Anon was all about. No one seemed interested with the exception of one wife present. She wanted to know when the meetings were going to start, to which I replied, 'Right away.' That is how my first Al-Anon meeting in England took place. First we held them in a tea room, and later we got a community hall."

Al-Anon grew rapidly in English-speaking countries during the 1950's. Without the barrier of language, the literature came into its own as a useful tool in helping new groups to get going. The *FORUM* provided a two-way communication for the entire membership, and Headquarters was on hand to answer group problems, just as real overseas as at home. Of interest was the registration of loners—members who, for one reason or another, were without a group. Numbering 51 in 1960, they steadily increased along with Al-Anon. "World Hello," a meeting-by-mail for loners and other members wishing to correspond began in June, 1960 as an offshoot of AA's counterpart.

For new members overseas, Headquarters was a listening ear. Such was the case for Florence W., who experienced all the isolation and boredom of being a serviceman's wife in Japan in 1956, prior to her discovery of Al-Anon. In correspondence with a volunteer, she poured her feelings into a letter in which she talked of linking Al-Anon loners in Yokohama, Zama, and Tokyo. She finished her letter by saying, "If we can help anyone in any way, we are only too glad to do so. Al-Anon can do so much for people like myself." From Florence's small beginnings, two pamphlets translated into Japanese were received by the WSO in 1967 from the Mukogawa Hospital Al-Anon Group, and by 1985 Al-Anon in Japan numbered 26 groups.

Translation of the literature into Spanish and French owes much to Mimi H., a volunteer, and Harriet L., former Chairman of the French Literature Committee now called PFA. Both reported to the Conference for a number of years on the development of foreign language Al-Anon. Mimi started her pioneer work with Henrietta's by translating letters and literature into Spanish. First came *Purposes and Suggestions,* completed in 1962. In two years she had tackled the hardcover book, *Living With An Alcoholic.* She reported enthusiastically in 1965:

"This was the most exciting and rewarding year for our work with the Spanish-speaking groups. The challenge of quiet but effective attraction met in the past two or three years, by writing letters and answering questions finally began to show results. From last April to December, 20 new groups have been slowly but steadily increasing in attendance and in good Al-Anon. Mexico, until recently tightly closed to our efforts, bloomed with six new groups. Peru, which had been barren territory for Al-Anon, came forth with two groups. The Lima "Comprension" Group has provided us with a most excellent translation of *Freedom from Despair,* now part of our regular Spanish Al-Anon literature. Colombia has five new groups, and Spain has one group registered. The rest of the groups are scattered over Central America except for one in New York City and one in Los Angeles, California. There are also a few loners.

"According to my records for 1965, 90 letters were written, 29 free books and 264 pieces of free literature were sent out, plus three new group packets in English." Mimi's valuable contribution continues to grow with a current Spanish-speaking staff at WSO of three, serving 3,000 Spanish-speaking and 800 Portuguese-speaking groups in 20 countries."

Harriet L. explains how her function developed. "The first French-speaking group was founded in Montreal in 1955. Versions of the Twelve Steps and Traditions, *Purposes and Suggestions* and *Freedom from Despair* were submitted and approved by the Clearing House. As we needed a

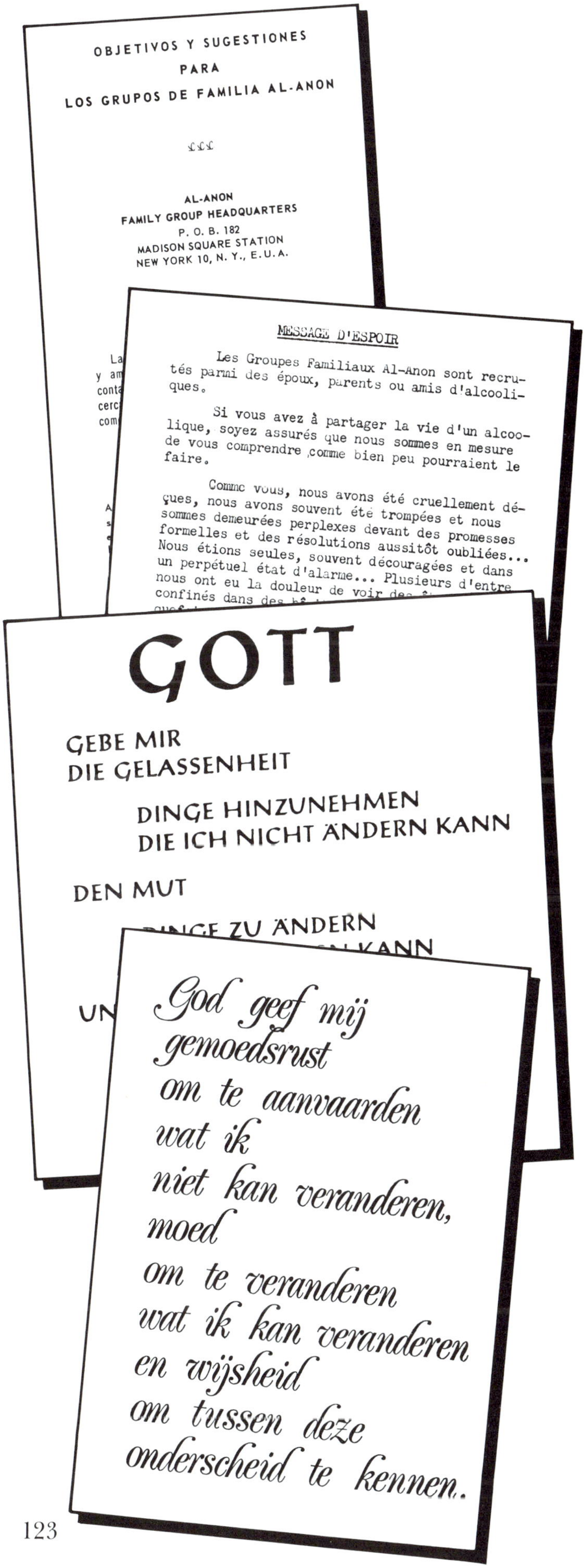

FOREIGN LANGUAGE AL-ANON

French

As the agent of the WSO in the translation and production of the FORUM and CAL, the French Literature Committee in Montreal services French groups around the world.

Harret L., who translates the FORUM, is making good progress on the French version of ODAT. A number of new and many revised pieces were produced during the year by Alberte, the chairman, and a volunteer committee. Harriet translated the script of LOIS'S STORY; a French adaptation of the film was ready in time for the 1972 Bilingual Conference in Quebec. Alberte produced the descriptive sheet which was sent to the groups.

Several requests from groups in France asked about forming an Intergroup. The Tenth Anniversary of Al-Anon in France was celebrated in October by the Paris Intergroup. Two members of the U.K. and Eire General Services attended and wrote us glowing reports of the occasion. The Intergroup Secretary sent copies of the Anniversary talks.

* * * * *

Spanish

The General Service Committee in *Argentina* made great progress in 1972, renting an office within easy reach of any part of Buenos Aires. Fifty members were needed to pledge support; by year's end 109 were contributing regularly. Addition of a much-needed staff member is now being considered.

Many pieces of literature were reprinted with WSO permission. By mid-September, 1,000 copies of VIVIENDO CON UN ALCOHOLICO were off the press; production was made possible by members paying for their orders in advance.

The Secretary of the Argentine GSC, Lilian C., asked us to send a circular letter to all 45 registered groups enlisting their cooperation with the national General Services.

An earlier attempt to form a *Mexican* GSC had failed, but in 1972, 12 members of Mexico City groups joined in establishing a GSC. It is now helping groups in different sections of the country with program suggestions and literature. By mid-summer, eight Officers and Committee Chairmen had been elected and an office was leased in the heart of the city. The Chairman of Group Relations wrote to every group in Mexico. Committee members are working to unify the groups by speaking at joint meetings in nearby states. The WSO notified the 116 Mexican groups that sole literature distribution rights had been assigned to the Mexican Al-Anon GSC, suggesting that groups order directly from the Mexico City office.

At an AA Convention in Puebla in November, the GSC announced plans to hold an Al-Anon Assembly in 1973 and asked for volunteers from various states to act as Delegates, to help unify the groups in their states and to promote interest and support for the GSC office. The WSO supplied information on structure and the *World Service Handbook*. We told them how the U.K. and Eire had adapted the latter to their own needs and suggested that Mexico might follow a similar procedure.

Susy K., the Secretary, submitted a translation of Louise M.'s CAL presentation at the 1972 WSC which was included in *"CAL—Al-Anon/Alateen"* The complete piece is now available in Spanish. Laura, a bilingual member of the Committee, is trying to unify the Alateen groups and has translated sections of *"For Teenagers . . ."* for distribution in Mexico.

The director of a government school for social workers in Mexico City arranged to have Al-Anons address more than 1,000 students at several meetings; Mexican Health Authorities want to start a council on alcoholism and have invited an Al-Anon member to join the planning board.

"Twelve Steps and Twelve Traditions" taken from LIVING WITH AN ALCOHOLIC, was produced in *El Salvador*. *"Alcoholism, the Family Disease,"* revised by our Spanish staff member with the help of Father Roberto C. of California, will be produced by the WSO. *El Salvador* was given permission to reproduce our Al-Anon poster.

Numerous other letters from Spanish-speaking countries related to literature, service structure and group problems. Consuelo de S, Secretary of the GSC in *Costa Rica*, sent an updated meeting list of groups and wrote of plans to meet Angela de V. of the *El Salvador* GSC in Panama at the AA Congress Easter week-end.

An item by an AA in Tegucigalpa, *Honduras*, in the September issue of *"Al-Anon/Alateen En Accion"* brought excellent response to his plea for Al-Anons to write letters to his arthritic housebound wife. A *Venezuelan*-born member in Erie, Pa., asked permission to translate occasional pages of ODAT to send to the Spanish Al-Anon group in *Caracas*. A group in *Peru* requested permission to reprint Spanish literature. We suggested that thought be given to starting a GSC and sent guidelines for overseas service structure. The Secretary of the group in *Aviles, Spain* requested "How-Tos" for PR projects and information on establishing a national General Service. We also sent her the Spanish version of *"The Al-Anon Information Service—What It Is—How It Serves"*

Opal B. (WSO N. Mex.) recommended a valuable assistant in Spanish translation. She is a professor in a University Language Department who has volunteered to revise the translation of ODAT, begun by Theresa, our bilingual staff member, and Fr. Roberto.

The U.S. Department of HEW published a pamphlet titled *"Spanish Language Health Communications Teaching Aids"* in which our literature is listed second, just after AA's.

* * * * *

Dutch/Flemish

After a long silence the WSO heard from Karel M., Secretary of the ADB Nederlandstalige in *Belgium* who sent us file copies of the Flemish *"So You Love an Alcoholic"* and 25 copies of the sponsorship pamphlet as a contribution. Permission was given to publish two Alateen pieces and *Al-Anon and Alateen Groups at Work*. There is great interest in spiritual growth and in the quality of the progra which Karel feels is due to CAL. He reported growing interest in Alateens in Belgium. No progress has been made in establishing a General Service for the *Netherlands*, but he keeps in touch with their groups.

* * * * *

Finnish

During 1972, translations of the pamphlet *"A Merry-Go-Round . . ."* and the book, AL-ANON FACES ALCOHOLISM, were sent the WSO, reviewed by our Finnish AA friend Mikko L., were returned to Helsinki, and were off the press before year's end! Twenty complimentary copies of each were forwarded to the WSO as a contribution. Mikko also corrected the translations of *"Al-Anon IS for Men"*—*"Questionnaire for a Step Four Meeting"* and the cartoon booklet. In September, we were visited by a Finnish newspaper woman, an Al-Anon member whose husband had died of alcoholism at thirty. She was in the U.S. to research treatment methods.

* * * * *

German/Swiss

After more than a year's effort, the Al-Anon Zentrale Kontaktstelle (General Services) in Germany obtained registration as a society and as a charity organization. This made possible the publication of much-needed literature. A number of pieces have been reviewed and approved for publication by WSO volunteers.

Henrietta and Henny, our Office Manager and bookkeeper, attended an Al-Anon meeting in June in Lucerne where Jean B., Secretary of the Swiss-German GSC, gave us her translation of the minutes of the April 15 meeting of the GSC in Frankfurt/Main. Much of the discussion revolved around literature problems. Al-Anon literature gets much valuable publicity in AA's monthly *"Informationen."*

At the October meeting of the GSC in Munich, it was decided to publish *"A Guide for the Family"—"Freedom from Despair"* and *"Homeward Bound."* Publication of LIVING WITH AN ALCOHOLIC, approved more than a year ago, was postponed for financial reasons.

All publications will be available at cost to the Swiss GSC and the WSO.

The November appeal letter to overseas groups was reproduced in Switzerland's Al-Anon publication, M&F, which is sent each month to all German-speaking groups.

Opportunities in radio and TV are opening up for Al-Anon in Switzerland.

Five additional translations were revised by Margaret R., WSD Va., a WSO volunteer and Ursula P. a Utah member who had offered her services after hearing references to foreign language literature in Lois's film.

* * * * *

Japanese

Harumi K., the member responsible for our three Japanese pieces, started translating the leaflet *"Lois's Story."* She sent us copies of articles about Al-Anon to be used in a bulletin for families of patients in the alcoholic ward at the Tokyo hospital where she works. These are being reviewed by a Japanese member in New York.

* * * * *

Portuguese

The Secretary of the GSC in Sao Paulo, *Brazil,* has written that after six years' effort, Al-Anon is taking hold. Ten new groups were formed in 1972. She asked us which CAL should be published first with profits from the sale of the Portuguese LWAA. (Neither Al-Anon nor AA groups contribute to their service centers.)

* * * * *

Other Languages

A member of a new English group in Oslo, *Norway,* was given permission to translate, mimeograph and distribute CAL in Norwegian.

A priest who started an Al-Anon group at a family health agency in Valencia, India, sent us a copy of his book on alcoholism, written in *Konkani* (a dialect of one area of India) in which he refers to Al-Anon as a resource for the family.

An Al-Anon group in *Ceylon,* whose members speak *Sinhalese,* was started by an AA who had written to the WSO for information.

* * * * *

ENGLISH AL-ANON OVERSEAS

U. K. & Eire

Dorothy H., Conference Chairman of the General Service Board, wrote us that this was a record year for visitors from the U.S. Henrietta and Henny visited the London office in June: later there were several former Delegates, and staff members Evelyn, Timmy and Holly. Evelyn brought back two copies of the *District Representatives Handbook* prepared for the Third Al-Anon U. K. & Eire Service Conference held in October.

Dorothy is also chairman of the Southern District and active in the Chichester Hospital Group; Gloria D., originally of Bogota, Colombia, now living in London, has assumed Dorothy's office responsibilities.

The Conference Chairman reported on the success of their third Conference of which we will receive a Summary. Thirteen out of seventeen Districts, (equivalent to our Areas) were represented. The DRs had voted overwhelmingly to again send Helen M-S as Representative to the WSC and to underwrite the expenses.

After many frustrating delays, registration as a charity organization was finally obtained.

* * * * *

Australia

At the Third Australian Trial Conference held in Brisbane, Queensland, Easter week-end, Delegates from the six Australian states attended. They returned home to suggest election of subcommittees in their respective states to study the *Twelve Concepts* and the *World Service Handbook*. The Chairmen were to communicate with each other before the next meeting in Perth, Western Australia, 1973, for further discussion on the adoption of a constitution for Australia.

Victoria and New South Wales will continue to sell their CAL to other states. Reprints of *"Purposes and Suggestions"* and *"This is Al-Anon"* were forwarded by Victoria. They supply new groups with sample literature for a start with CAL before our gratis packet arrives from WSO. Professional inquiries have increased, According to the Secretary, "this indicates the growth of Al-Anon's reputation as an agency of help to the families of alcoholics. I sometimes think we take for granted the service WSO provides to all groups. The visit of Lois and Evelyn made us all feel so much closer."

There was much correspondence with all the Australian states during the year; the WSO regularly receives copies of their monthly newsletters, and minutes of the various Central Service committee meetings.

* * * * *

New Zealand

An Al-Anon "Field Worker" was appointed to serve on the Board of the N. Z. Al-Anon Service Conference to visit groups on invitation, to guide them in PR, group practices, use of CAL, etc. We were asked what her responsibilities should include. An Auckland member inquired if there was any precedent for such an officer in the Al-Anon structure, questioning the need for this office.

As a result of our replies, the Secretary forwarded a copy of the N. Z. Al-Anon S. C. Guidelines, minutes of their latest national conference and descriptions of their structure. Area Delegates (two each from four Areas in the country) serve three years and may be re-elected for a second term. In-town Service Delegates serve indefinitely, producing an annual magazine, a monthly newsletter, PR, literature and plans for the annual conference and convention.

New Zealand rented a copy of Lois's film for one year.

* * * * *

South Africa

The Al-Anon General Service in Pretoria was also sent a copy of the film and information on distribution. The Secretary asked how they could make their monthly business meetings more stimulating and suggestions were offered. They explained the structure of their General Service body and agenda usually planned for meetings. They were perturbed about the possibility that neighboring Johannesburg might start an Al-Anon Information Service Office because this might adversely affect their contributions. We suggested that this would be only temporary; eventually the increase in the size and number of groups in Jo'burg could *increase* support of the national office.

A Johannesburg member sent lengthy correspondence relating to this matter, and was sent a copy of *"The Al-Anon Information Service—What It Is and How It Serves."*

* * * * *

Europe

Major John Squires of the *School of Aero-Space Science,* Lackland Airforce Base, Texas, Social Actions Officer responsible for European installations, visited the WSO in November and asked us to write to the Social Actions officers at 31 bases in Europe. Letters and literature were sent with a view to forming Al-Anon groups at the bases, and to suggest that officers at bases where there are groups, provide families with information about Al-Anon.

* * * * *

qualified translator, I registered at Montreal University for a complete course, but kept on translating in the meantime. The groups were serviced on a voluntary basis with the help of the Intergroup Committee. By 1963, Al-Anon had grown to such an extent that the servicing had become a full-time and expensive job. Headquarters then suggested forming a committee to carry on the work. I was employed as their agent to service the French groups."

Testimony to the effectiveness of Harriet's work and that of the French translations is given in Henrietta's report to the 1965 Conference. "The Group D'Orsay in Paris, which now has 70 active members, with never less than 20 at a meeting, originally heard about Al-Anon through the *AA Grapevine,* then from American visitors—both AA and Al-Anon, whom members met at AA meetings. They wrote to us for information, but now are in frequent contact with the French Literature Committee, from whom news of their activities is relayed to New York. Last October, a Spanish couple from San Sebastian visited the Paris group. Upon his return to Spain, the non-alcoholic husband, a doctor, wrote us for help with starting a Spanish group, which is flourishing. So it is an ever widening circle,with Al-Anon established in more than 35 countries around the world."

As Harriet suggests, translation was done at first by anyone who was more or less fluent in a second language and anxious to carry the Al-Anon message. Finnish and Swedish translations were lovingly carried out by Veikko K., AA secretary in Finland, who first translated *Purposes and Suggestions* in 1953. Over the years, a policy developed whereby WSO permission had to be sought in order to ensure the quality of the translation. Another refinement was the creation of the handbook, *Al-Anon Groups at Work,* written especially for foreign language use. By 1973, reports on foreign language Al-Anon indicate that the Al-Anon message had reached as far as India and Ceylon. Translations still continue to disseminate Al-Anon information to an incredible diversity of people. The literature can so far be read in 24 languages, including Afrikaans, Punjabi, Icelandic, Korean, Polish, Greek, and Chinese. At the time of writing, a translation is being worked on in Aborigine, for the people of the Australian outback.

General Service Meetings between overseas Delegates and the WSO staff were initiated in 1980 in New Orleans. Two more trial meetings were held in 1982 in New York, and 1984 in Stamford, Connecticut. To encourage participation by overseas delegates, the WSO pays 75 percent of their expenses. The 1986 discussions will determine whether subsequent gatherings are held in New York or overseas, but the meetings themselves have now become a permanent part of the World Service structure.

Chapter Ten
The Conference

The creation of the first trial World Service Conference in 1961 significantly changed the face of Al-Anon.

The Conference was to be the "wider group conscience" of Tradition Two, besides a more elaborate service structure. Made up of Delegates, Board of Directors, Advisory Board (later known as Board of Trustees and Executive Committee) and WSO staff, the Conference was and is representative of the Al-Anon membership and can focus on the mainstream of Al-Anon experience, helping to keep the movement on course. Sue L., who served as chairman of activities for AA Delegates' wives during the 1950's, piloted the Al-Anon Conference through three experimental years, to the Conference proper in 1964. Sue L. was named first Al-Anon World Service Conference Chairman and served through 1968.

By 1960, events had begun to show that problems of growth could occur with a small, New York office servicing a worldwide fellowship through mail polls and general correspondence alone. The suggestion for an Al-Anon General Service Conference states, "if a serious error were made by the New York Headquarters, and there had been no general authorization of the decision involved, confidence would be lost and contributions would suffer. The whole vital service effort might then have to be seriously curtailed, or it might collapse entirely. Having no direct linkage with Al-Anon as a whole, the repair of such a condition might be impossible. Al-Anon could thus suffer heart failure at its very core."

AA's General Service Conference had been initiated in 1951, and Al-Anon was to draw on that experience. WSO staff had gained a working knowledge of Conference operation since Al-Anon had been hosting activities for AA Delegate wives since 1952.

Al-Anon participated in AA's second Conference when Lois talked about the Family Groups and the AA Delegates gave the new movement a standing vote of support. Al-Anon also chaired a panel discussion on children of AA members at that 1952 Conference and Lois entertained the AA Delegates' wives at Stepping Stones.

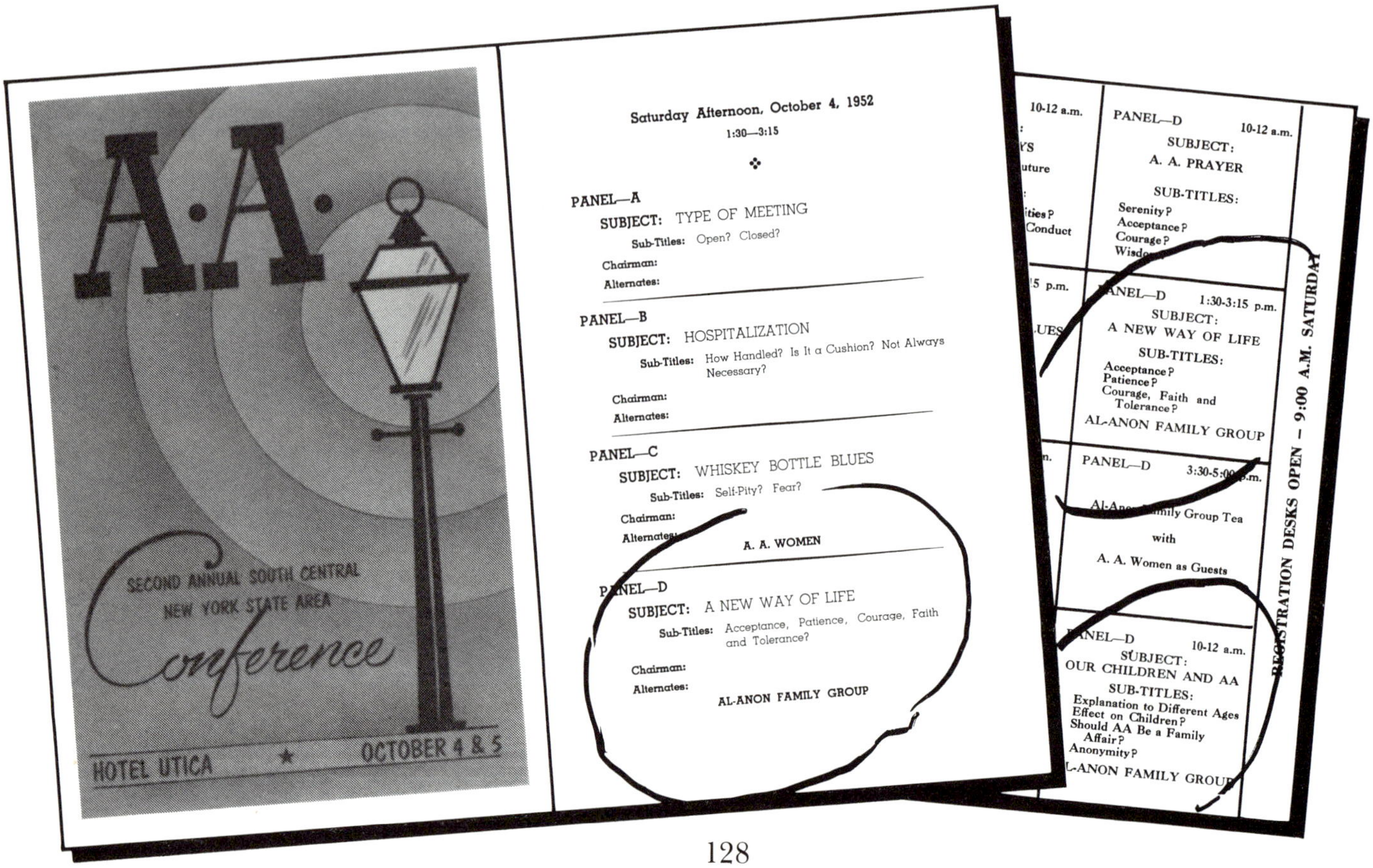

A year later, Lois and Anne B. were busy preparing a program for the AA Delegates' wives which was to turn into something of an adventure. All the volunteers at the Clearing House were asked to pitch in to help, and help they did. Dot L. brought in a tablecloth which she laid over a table placed in front of the Clubhouse fireplace. On it she laid her own silver service. Anne B. brought in vases and candleholders, and Lois arranged flowers from the garden at Stepping Stones. Carrie and Helen made 100 sandwiches each, which proved to be more than enough for the 35 guests. The leftovers were donated to the Clubhouse.

The following day, all the volunteers accompanied 46 AA Delegates, Trustees, and wives on a bus to Stepping Stones. This time the menu included spaghetti and meatballs. A report to the Clearing House observes that 200 meatballs were not enough! To make matters worse, the chartered bus had a flat tire on the way back, and with no jack on board everyone was delayed for four hours. Clearing House volunteers were hot and weary, but AA Delegates' wives said warmly that New York hospitality was just fine.

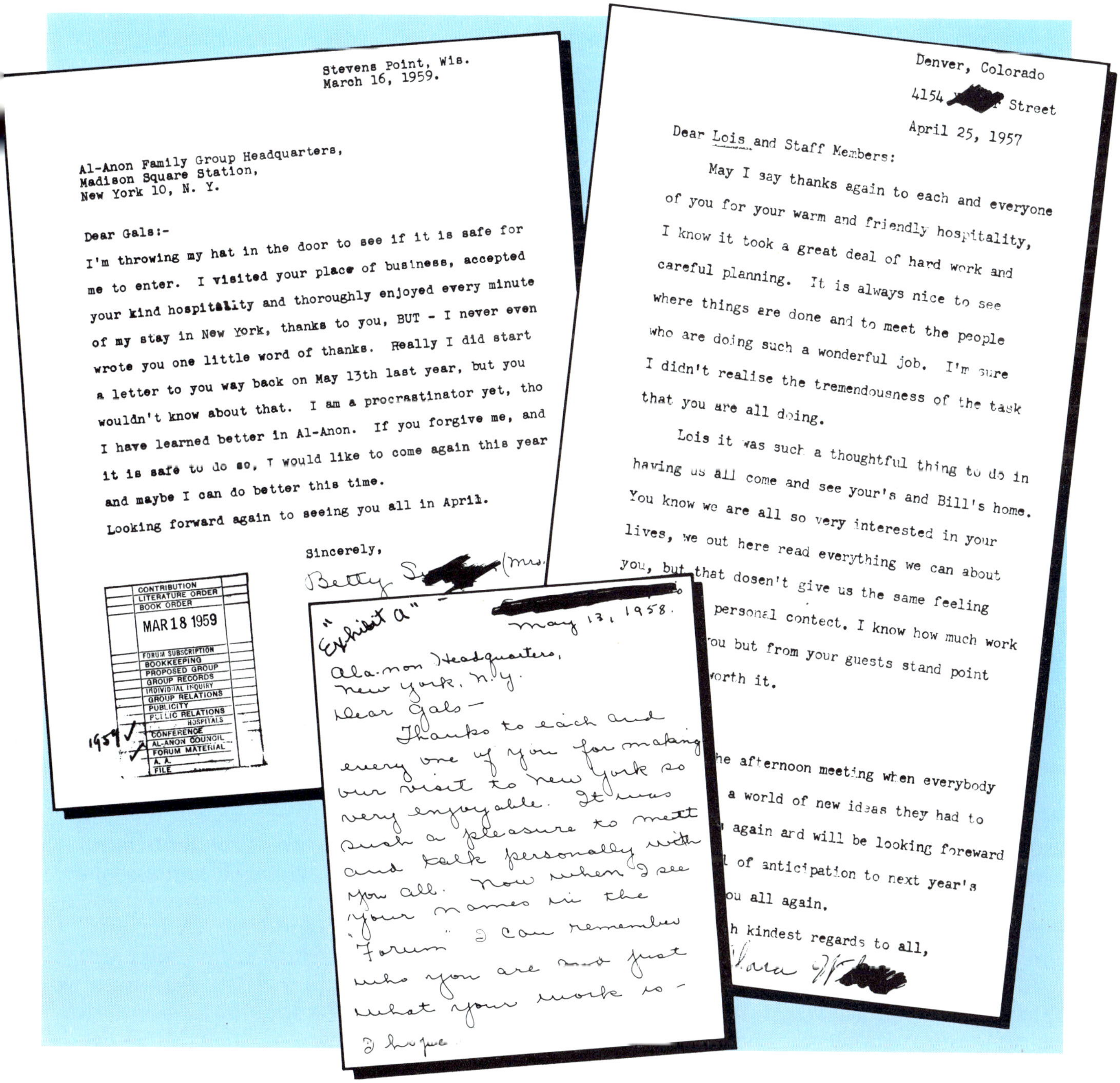

Stevens Point, Wis.
March 16, 1959.

Al-Anon Family Group Headquarters,
Madison Square Station,
New York 10, N. Y.

Dear Gals:-

I'm throwing my hat in the door to see if it is safe for me to enter. I visited your place of business, accepted your kind hospitality and thoroughly enjoyed every minute of my stay in New York, thanks to you, BUT - I never even wrote you one little word of thanks. Really I did start a letter to you way back on May 13th last year, but you wouldn't know about that. I am a procrastinator yet, tho I have learned better in Al-Anon. If you forgive me, and it is safe to do so, I would like to come again this year and maybe I can do better this time.

Looking forward again to seeing you all in April.

Sincerely,
Betty S[redacted] (Mrs.

CONTRIBUTION
LITERATURE ORDER
BOOK ORDER
MAR 18 1959
FORUM SUBSCRIPTION
BOOKKEEPING
PROPOSED GROUP
GROUP RECORDS
INDIVIDUAL INQUIRY
GROUP RELATIONS
PUBLICITY
PUBLIC RELATIONS
HOSPITALS
CONFERENCE
AL-ANON COUNCIL
FORUM MATERIAL
A. A.
FILE

1959 ✓

"Exhibit A" [redacted] May 13, 1958.

Ala-non Headquarters,
New York, N.Y.
Dear Gals—
Thanks to each and every one of you for making our visit to New York so very enjoyable. It was such a pleasure to meet and talk personally with you all. Now when I see your names in the "Forum" I can remember who you are and just what your work is—
I hope

Denver, Colorado
4154 [redacted] Street
April 25, 1957

Dear Lois and Staff Members:

May I say thanks again to each and everyone of you for your warm and friendly hospitality, I know it took a great deal of hard work and careful planning. It is always nice to see where things are done and to meet the people who are doing such a wonderful job. I'm sure I didn't realise the tremendousness of the task that you are all doing.

Lois it was such a thoughtful thing to do in having us all come and see your's and Bill's home. You know we are all so very interested in your lives, we out here read everything we can about you, but that dosen't give us the same feeling
personal contect. I know how much work
ou but from your guests stand point
orth it.

he afternoon meeting when everybody
a world of new ideas they had to
again and will be looking foreward
of anticipation to next year's
ou all again.

h kindest regards to all,
Clara [redacted]

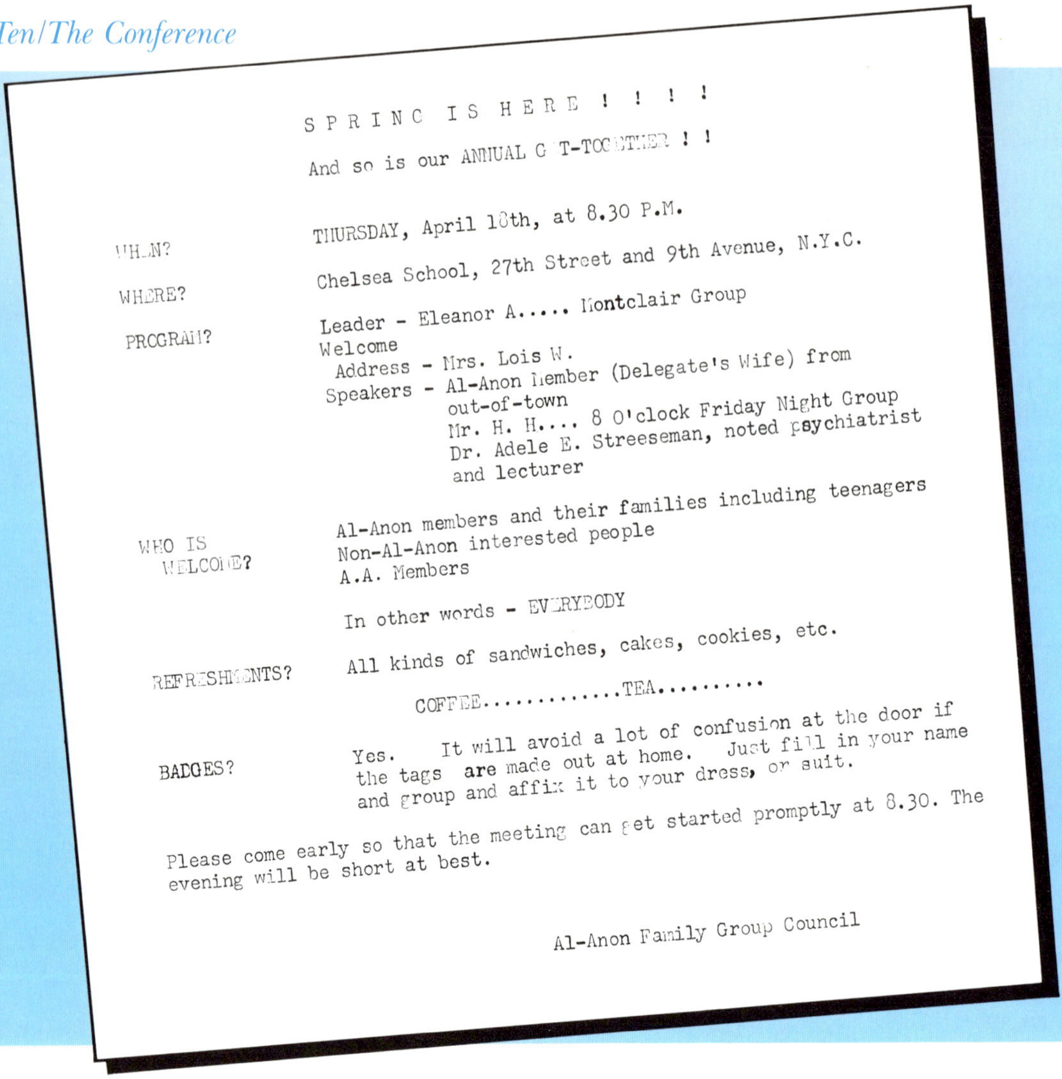

S P R I N G I S H E R E ! ! ! !

And so is our ANNUAL GET-TOGETHER ! !

WHEN? THURSDAY, April 10th, at 8.30 P.M.

WHERE? Chelsea School, 27th Street and 9th Avenue, N.Y.C.

PROGRAM? Leader - Eleanor A..... Montclair Group
Welcome
Address - Mrs. Lois W.
Speakers - Al-Anon Member (Delegate's Wife) from out-of-town
Mr. H. H.... 8 O'clock Friday Night Group
Dr. Adele E. Streeseman, noted psychiatrist and lecturer

WHO IS WELCOME? Al-Anon members and their families including teenagers
Non-Al-Anon interested people
A.A. Members

In other words - EVERYBODY

REFRESHMENTS? All kinds of sandwiches, cakes, cookies, etc.

COFFEE.............TEA.........

BADGES? Yes. It will avoid a lot of confusion at the door if the tags are made out at home. Just fill in your name and group and affix it to your dress, or suit.

Please come early so that the meeting can get started promptly at 8.30. The evening will be short at best.

Al-Anon Family Group Council

Not surprisingly, Headquarters volunteers were asking for additional help by the next year, and the Al-Anon Family Group Council, later known as Intergroup, came forward to organize a Spring Get-Together at the Chelsea School in New York City. Like a large Al-Anon meeting or small convention, visiting Al-Anons, who were also AA Delegates' wives, could see for themselves how the Al-Anon movement was flourishing. In 1956, Hugh S., first Alateen Chairman, wrote a letter to Sue about the Get-Together.

"Incidentally, Central Westchester (or Scarsdale) Family Group is adjourning their usual Thursday night meeting to the Chelsea School for the Rally. I expect we will be down with about ten members with their share of sandwiches. See you Thursday."

Al-Anon members were on hand at the 1958 AA Conference registration desk to welcome the AA Delegates' wives and make them feel at home. Sue, with much insight, rented a separate Al-Anon room at the Prince George Hotel, where the AA Delegates' wives and local Al-Anon members could meet together during the AA Conference; 38 people registered with Al-Anon. The Al-Anon presence remained throughout the AA Conference. Four hundred attended the Spring Get-Together, and more than 50 went to Stepping Stones for Lois's luncheon. Sue's report begins to look rather wistfully to the future.

"The meeting and luncheon on Saturday climaxed the Al-Anon activities during the AA Conference. Lois again welcomed the guests, and said that the time had come when Al-Anon as a whole should be made aware of the importance of having its own yearly Conferences and that AA has just decided to hold its 25th Anniversary Convention in California in 1960. Although we may not be ready by then to have our first Al-Anon Conference to which Al-Anon

Delegates' could be sent, we should at least plan to hold preliminary meetings there."

An important pre-Conference step was added in 1959. At an Al-Anon sponsored luncheon at the Hotel Roosevelt for AA Delegates' wives, these guests were asked to talk about Al-Anon back home. Face to face communication about Al-Anon had been established for the first time. As they listened to one another, they collectively took a giant step forward for Al-Anon unity. Here is a sampling of what they heard:

Vancouver, B.C. "There are five Al-Anon groups in Vancouver. People in their twenties are showing a great deal of interest. They come in through contact with the Alcoholic Foundation (a government agency, not the first AA Service Office in New York). Each province has one. They were started by a grant from the government."

Minneapolis, Minn. "There are four groups in Minneapolis. This is our second year. We started with six members. Now, we have about 18, including the original six. An Alateen group has just been started with about 30 members."

South Dakota "We have an Intergroup started. They contributed to my expenses, both last year and this year. We attended the State Conference on our way here. A new state chairman was elected. There will surely be someone from our group at Long Beach, at the 1960 AA Convention."

Idaho "We are 85 or 90 miles south of Yellowstone National Park, and the region is sparsely populated. There are 20 at the AA meetings. The wives attend with their husbands. We then have a break, and the wives go into the kitchen to fix the coffee. We talk Al-Anon as we go along, and the AA's have a closed meeting. We go on Twelfth-Step calls with our husbands and also on our own. A group was started in Idaho Springs but didn't get support. Our Idaho AA Delegate would like to hold meetings and tell of Al-Anon in other states."

Ogden, Utah "There is no group in Ogden, but we would like to start one when we return."

Modesto, California "We meet the same night as AA. We put on an open meeting for AA to attend, and they asked for another one. We have alphabetical chairmen. We drop our planned programs whenever a newcomer attends and discuss the Steps and purposes of Al-Anon. The Northern California Council is very interested in Hospital and Institutions work. We have a chairman who contacts hospitals where AA is active."

Already, these AA Delegates' wives are anticipating the work of the Al-Anon World Service Conference.

By the time of the Long Beach AA Conference in 1960, Al-Anon members were ready to discuss a Conference plan of their own. A three-year trial plan provided for the election of Al-Anon Delegates by dividing the North American continent into four quadrants and naming Delegates from the most populated states or provinces. Each year, three more Delegates would be chosen from each quadrant, so that by the third year 36 Delegates would be attending. Group Representatives at Assemblies would elect Delegates to a World Service Conference thereafter. Meeting in New York with Al-Anon's Board of Directors, Advisory Board and WSO staff, the Conference would hear staff and committee reports, consider new business and vote on resolutions.

Expenses for the Conference were met through a Conference Fund established by Headquarters. All groups, whether participating in the Conference or not, were asked to contribute annually to this fund, over and above the semi-annual appeal for Headquarters funding. To meet Delegate expenses, Areas participating in the Conference were required to share in an equalized expense fund.

Four hundred Al-Anon members attended the Long Beach Conference Workshop, and voted unanimously to adopt the experimental plan. Sue, the Conference Chairman, contacted the groups and sent them a copy of the Conference plan, asking them to vote its acceptance, and they did. Sue wrote back proudly, "The voting on the World Service Conference was overwhelmingly in its favor. Therefore, we are proceeding with plans for our First Al-Anon Conference in New York City on April 21st and 22nd, 1961, to coincide with the AA Conference."

Conference manuals, later called *World Service Handbooks,* were sent out to the Delegates in October. Next, a Delegate brochure was prepared. Records show that six Representatives and 27 observers also attended the Conference. Representatives were non-voting participants whose expenses were paid by the Area, while observers were individuals paying their own way.

AA's Conference began at the Hotel Roosevelt on April 19th. The following day, the WSO had an open house. Then, at the Hotel George Washington, just up the street from Headquarters, Al-Anon's First Conference convened on the morning of April 21st, 1961.

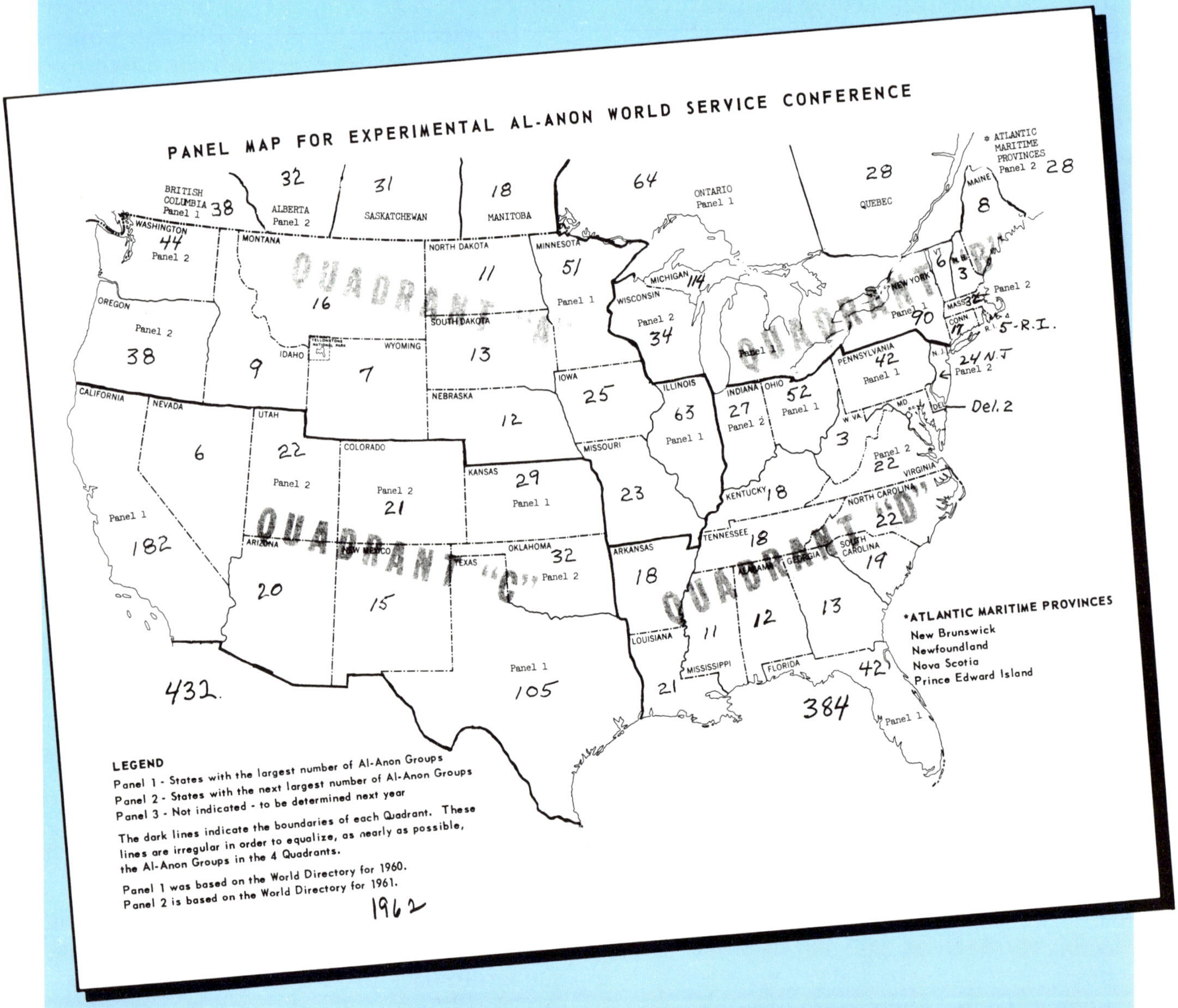

Count
October 11th, 1960
inclusive

States	Group Registered 1960		No. of Groups Voting: Yes	No
Alabama	8	---	--	--
Alaska	1	---	--	--
Arizona	8	---	6	--
Arkansas	14		3	1
California	117		34	--
Colorado	15		5	--
Connecticut	14		7	1
Delaware	4		1	--
District of Col.	5		1	--
Florida	34		5	--
Georgia	12		4	--
Idaho	3		1	1
Illinois	47		13	3
Indiana	27		4	1
Iowa	16		2	2
Kansas	26		9	--
Kentucky	12		6	--
Louisiana	20		3	--
Maine	3		2	--
Maryland	18		7	--
Massachusetts	26		6	--
Michigan	88		41	3
Minnesota	26		8	1
Mississippi	12		2	--
Missouri	16		6	--
Montana	14		4	1
Nebraska	8		5	--
Nevada	3		0	1
New Hampshire	1		0	--
New Jersey	19		10	--
New Mexico	5		3	--
New York	66		42	--
North Carolina	22		5	--
North Dakota	14		5	--
Ohio	34		9	1
Oklahoma	12		10	--
Oregon	21		12	--
Pennsylvania	41		15	--
Rhode Island	1		0	--
South Carolina	15		5	--
South Dakota	9		6	--
Tennessee			5	2
Texas			18	3
Utah				1
Vermont				--
Virginia				
Washington				
West Virgnia				
Wisconsin				
Wyoming				

Provinces	Groupgs Registered 1960	No. of Groups Voting Yes	No.
* Albertam Canada	23	10	-
X British Columbia	27	11	2
Manitoba	9	3	1
New Brunswick	4	1	-
Newfoundland	5	---	---
Nova Scotia	11	3	-
X Ontario	62	20	-
Prince Edward Island	2	0	-
Quebec	7	4	-
Saskatchewan	14	14	-
Yukon Terr.	1	0	-

HOTEL GEORGE WAS
WASHINGTON
HOTEL
GEORGE

A transcript of the proceedings records that Bill W. opened the first session with a flourish:

"I want to dwell for a moment on the vital necessity of this effort in service, of which you are the first token. Growth-wise, as a movement, you have exceeded anything that ever happened to AA in its early days. And this is, we all know, because you people have been intent on filling the vast vacuum that has long existed in family relations. Now comes the time when Al-Anon must function as a whole. So the deep significance of this small but wonderful meeting this morning is this: that you are now applying Tradition Two to Al-Anon as a whole. You Delegates, who have come here as Al-Anon's group conscience, are trusted servants. Sometimes you will come here to give advice, and indeed it is in your power to give active direction because the ultimate authority is yours. Then again you will offer new suggestions not thought of here, that which will make for greater progress. Sometimes you face momentous questions, in which your guidance and collective wisdom will surely manifest itself and save you from grievous error.

"At other times you will come here, and find internal troubles, and you will correct those. At still other times, you will have Conference meetings which will be so boring, so dull, that some of you will say, 'Why in heaven's name go to New York to say yes to what our public accountant has already verified? This is a lot of nonsense.' But no matter what happens, your presence will ensure the maintenance of the linkage. Each one of these yearly meetings, be they dull, be they controversial, is really an insurance policy which can guarantee the future unity and functioning of your society."

The work of the first 12 Al-Anon Delegates was to set some guidelines and lend support. There was much discussion on how future Conferences should be conducted. As one early Delegate, Anne V. from British Columbia was to remark, "There were no precedents. We were in on the beginning of all that we have today." These were to be exciting times, when plans were formulated for funding the WSO, instituting Conference-Approved Literature, and improving the *World Directory*. Delegates working on committees got to know one another and to see their individual contributions have an impact on Conference decisions.

A Conference Summary, mailed to all Group Representatives, meant that the membership too, could feel a part of the functioning of the Al-Anon movement. To quote from the 1963 Summary: "The conscience of Al-Anon on the North American Continent now has voice. The decision to make the Conference a permanent arm of Al-Anon was the most important action taken by the Third Annual Trial Conference held in New York City from April 25 to 28, 1963. The permanent Conference will watch over the policies of Headquarters. It will be the guardian of our Traditions and will hold all Al-Anon together in unity. Al-Anon's future is in dedicated hands."

First Al-Anon Delegates remember those early days fondly. Mary C., British Columbia's first Delegate says of her election, "Mine wasn't a popularity contest. There just wasn't anyone else to go, that's all." Anne V. says that actually B.C. Assembly voted 7-6 in favor of Mary. All 13 of them met in Edith A.'s cottage and the Assembly was really Vancouver Intergroup under a different name. All the GRs were also members of Assembly, as well as Intergroup volunteers. Mary was Assembly Chairman and Delegate, and Anne V. was Assembly Secretary and Treasurer. As Mary says, there were no guidelines back then.

Raising the $225 (Canadian) needed for Mary to travel to New York was quite a job. Passing the hat at that first Assembly netted a grand total of $13, with $212 still to go. Then the local AA group came up with a scheme whereby Al-Anon could have the collection at the AA meeting in return for making the coffee. Anne V. says they made $85 that way. Other funds came from Assemblies and Round-Ups all over B.C.—barnstorming, Anne V. calls it. She remembers Mission Round-Up with affection because she traveled with her two children in Mary's car. Visiting a farm belonging to a future Delegate, she came face to face with a pig in the bathtub! She also tells how Mary learned to undress completely inside a sleeping bag. But Al-Anon events like the picnic at Princeton were great fun, ending up with a barn dance and extra contributions for Delegate expenses.

Anne V. also adds, "We were very cautious out here in the west. We were going to put our Delegate in for one year only, out of a possible three year term. But when Mary came back from New York, we voted her in for another year." Then, at the Assembly held at the Royal Towers, New Westminster in 1962, she herself was voted Delegate.

Barbara, another B.C. Delegate, talks about what it felt like to be elected and how it was for her when she came to New York:

"When I was elected, the first thing that came into my mind was how could all these people who had helped me so much entrust me to be their representative and messenger to New York, and then back to them. I wept tears of joy for what Al-Anon had done for me, not in electing me Delegate, but telling me by voting for me to believe in myself.

"Once in New York—I am a very shy and retiring person—I decided to go and meet people one at a time, so that I could remember their names. I am terrible at names. I got to New York on a Saturday. I was the first one at the Conference. So I went down into the hotel lobby, and I decided to go up to the first person and say, 'Hello! I'm Barbara from B.C.' And that's just what I did.

"You know, we all loved one another then. There was a feeling of love and caring, and it's there in New York, just as it is here in B.C. It's no different now. You walk into the Conference and you are not talking about *you* and *me.* It's *We* in Al-Anon. It's a terrific feeling.

"It's so important to have this function of Delegate. As a Delegate it means you are in constant touch with the WSO and know what is going on in other Areas."

Knowing what is going on is what Conference and Convention participation in Al-Anon is all about. Today, the Conference meets for six working days each spring, and covers a broad range of Al-Anon business. Some topics covered are service planning, review of budgeting and fiscal matters, policy, and regional concerns. There is also time for open discussion. The 1985 Conference Summary is 48 pages. Overseas, a number of countries have their own Conferences. Among them are UK and Eire, Australia, Mexico and New Zealand.

Al-Anon's bid for unity has been taken very seriously by its Board of Trustees, and Conference members. The Conference is living proof that the "wider group conscience" has found a voice, when once a year, elected Delegates and volunteers (Trustees, Executive Committee members and Committee Chairmen) and WSO staff meet together to discuss the "business" of Al-Anon.

Chapter Eleven
Public Relations

Publicity about Al-Anon has had a slow start. Some of the reasons are built into the program itself, especially the Traditions. Unavoidable changes in the chairmanship of the first committee chosen to handle publicity also did not help. Called Publicity and Public Information, this committee had an extraordinarily broad function. A public information policy did not take shape until 1960, with its direction coming from the Al-Anon membership itself. Because misinformation about Al-Anon began to be reported in the press, Al-Anon groups put pressure on Headquarters to "set the record straight," so the concept of public education developed along with public information. Both were originally called publicity and later included, in a broader scope, public relations.

LONG[redacted]-TELEGRAM
1950
NON-ALCO[redacted]NYMOUS

Group Born in L. B. Expands U. S.-wide

From Flossie L[redacted] Ave. Long Beach Cal.

By BILL CONWAY

MOST of us know a little about Alcoholics Anonymous, a selfless group organized a few years ago, dedicated to mutual aid for those who were afflicted with the disease of alcoholism.

Comparatively few, however, know about another group which was organized here in Long Beach on March 1, 1945, called Non-Alcoholics Anonymous. Born here in our own town, the movement has spread over the nation and now, in most of the principal cities, there are Non-Alcoholics Anonymous groups.

These are the gallant women who walked with grief and bleak despair, seeking blindly a way to help their loved ones, their husbands and brothers, fathers and friends. This is not, in any sense, a "temperance" group. It is an organization of women who face, with forthright acceptance the problem that is deadly and real to "the Colonel's lady and Judy O'Grady" . . . who are sisters and comrades, when all is said and done.

AIMS EXPLAINED

The aims and purposes of the Non-Alcoholics Anonymous group are pointed up in a folder which is available to those who are interested. "To better understand what A. A. has to offer in a better way of living . . . With organization, and the guidance of the Higher Power, to stand ready at all times, to carry this message to all who seek it."

Basically, the program of this group of women is to encourage and aid the alcoholic. They do not permit their natural fear and worry to show through their shining shields of hope. They analyze their problems and meet them, head-on, with courage and confidence. Wives are coached to go along, shoulder to shoulder, with their mates and help wherever they can, but "nagging" is out.

They seek to show others who suffer how they were given the boon of hope and help.

They are humble, and, at the same time, gallant. They base their faith, their hope, their confidence, on prayer and conscious contact with a Higher Power. They admit their weakness, thereby displaying their strength.

They are willing and eager to work for "the serenity to accept the things we ca... change; the courage to chan... can, and the wis... difference."

FOUR WATC...

Patience, tol... ing and lov... words. "The... the reporter... American so...

The lady ... Anonymous... she said, "... synonymou...

And tha... about it. ... of hope ... way the ... hands o... their ey...

They ... meeting... lieve i... laught... en wh... ered ... ism, ... are ...

All ... Talk to ... ments and you'll ... cause you'll see, like a g... candlelight, love and loyalty and faith — and the glint of a dream held true. . . .

Page 20 — The Dallas Morning News — Thursday, April 22, 1948 — Section 1

READJUSTMENT COMES HARD

AA Helps Wives, Too, One From Ranks Says

By STEWART M. DOSS

The wives of new Alcoholics Anonymous members are usually sick, too, but they can get over their illness by adapting the AA program to their own use.

This advice was given 175 wives of AA members Wednesday by Lois, wife of Bill, the cofounder of the self-help program for problem drinkers. The meeting was at Hotel Adolphus.

"Usually, the wives are neurotic and they should hand their problem over to God," said she.

She told the women that from **personal experience she knew wives** of new AA members are often resentful, full of self-pity and unhappy when husbands first adopt the AA program.

"There is a period of readjustment after a husband sobers up. Previously the wife usually was the boss and had to take care of things. She had to mother her husband as she would a little boy. But the little boy grows up when he sobers up. Many wives resent this growing up.

Lois said her husband started AA in 1934 after talking to one of his friends, a former drinker who had become deeply religious.

"Just to think that someone had done for him in a half hour all that I had tried to do in seventeen years cut me deeply. He developed many outside activities. I was unhappy over these new companionships.

Bill became the head of the family again. Before he had needed me so badly. Before, I had taken all the responsibility. Now, I felt that I wasn't needed. So many of us have had to go through the same thing."

The talk to the women was one of a series by Lois and Bill, who included Dallas as part of a 3-month tour visiting Alcoholics Anonymous groups. Members of scores of Texas towns were represented at the 2-day meeting.

RICHMOND, VA.
NEWS-LEADER
Circ. D. 86,941

SEP 8 1949

AA Wives Credit Happiness To 12 Steps of Dedication

By JUNE RANDOLPH

Women of the Richmond Auxiliary to Alcoholics Anonymous look as happy and content as they say they are. They even enjoy joking about their trials as wives of drunkards in the dark days before their husbands found AA.

Observers incline to credit this to the elasticity of the human heart and mind.

The wives think otherwise. Their happiness is based on a deep sense of dedication to a better way of life—not just for their husbands, but also for themselves.

"We have found ourselves through the 12 steps of the auxiliary, similar to the 12 steps in AA," one explains.

ADMIT POWERLESS

The rigorous steps are a creed as demanding as that of any church. Each involves action. First step of the 12, "I admitted I was powerless over our alcoholic problem and that our lives had become unmanageable," is the most difficult, they say.

"I tried to make my husband over," an auxiliary member explains. "I didn't think of his drinking as anyone's problem except his own. I valued myself highly as a 'good influence' and was sure I could reform him. The idea that he was an alcoholic or that alcoholism is a disease just didn't occur to me. I sure got some surprises."

Her story helps interpret the evolution in personality of all auxiliary members who honestly follow the 12 steps.

Trained in a profession, this wife has worked since the early days of her marriage. She struggled with the problem of an alcoholic husband for years before she admitted she was powerless to cope with his drinking.

'BE A SPORT'

"First I scolded. Then I tried ignoring him until a friend told me she thought I was a prude and suggested a little drinking harms no one. She said I ought to take an interest in his drinking companions and be a good sport about it," the wife recalls.

"I tried being a good sport and our home became a club. Anyone who wanted a drinking companion was welcome. When I could stand this 24-hour open house no longer, we moved to an apartment. I thought so many people couldn't get into a smaller place. Soon I could hardly get in myself.

"The day I picked up the telephone to hear a long-distance operator say she had an interpreter ready for the person who wanted to talk to Mussolini, I decided we would move to another part of town. When my husband and his friends got drunk, they developed telephoneitis. Calls to Italy, London, Moscow and Shanghai were more than I could afford. In a new section of the city, I hoped his old pals wouldn't be able to find him. We could make a new start, find new friends.

"We moved. First thing I knew, the neighbors thought me stuck up. My husband drank as much as ever and I didn't dare accept invitations from our new friends because I never knew whether he would be able to go out. Usually he wasn't. I lived in fear of their discovering his drunkenness.

"Finally I sent him to a sanitarium. Instead of trying to understand him, I see now that I was trying to run him out. I refused to go to see him, but a friend told me he was having a marvelous time with all the other drunks.

"After the cure, I threatened if he ever got drunk again I would leave. He got drunk. I went home to mama. Then he found AA. I could hardly believe his plea for me to return. He said he had been sober for two weeks. I still loved him, and decided to give him another chance.

"He told me about the 12 steps and what a hard time he was having trying to follow them. I wanted to help." The wife investigated AA. Impressed by the 12 steps and the changes they were bringing about in her husband, she decided she had some changes to make herself.

After the first difficult acknowledgement, she went on to the auxiliary's step two: "I came to believe that a power greater than ourselves could restore me to normal living."

"I think I confused the AA with God for a while because it seemed a miracle had happened," she says.

After she made a searching and fearless inventory of herself, the third step. She was amazed to discover she had felt "put upon" during the years of their marriage and "self-righteous." She remembered how she felt when he called at 5 A. M. to tell her he would be late to supper.

"I realized that I had never understood my husband's problem. I had tried to get him to 'drink like a gentleman.' When that didn't work, I turned into a shrew. A shrew can't help a sick man. I began to understand him only after I realized he has an incurable disease which AA has helped arrest."

HUMILITY

Step three prepared for four: "I made a decision to turn my life over to God as I understand Him and to admit to God, myself and another human being the nature of my mistakes." That calls for real humility, she said.

Next is to vow, "I am entirely ready for God to remove these defects of character and humbly ask Him to remove my shortcomings."

To auxiliary members, step seven has a special meaning: "I shall try to put my life on a 24-hour basis and let God guide me as to how I shall spend this time. I shall pray, listen and thank Him at the end of the day."

They reason that the indebtedness their husbands feel to AA can only be repaid by helping other alcoholics. Calls at any hour of the day or night are the rule. A wife never knows when her husband will be away from home helping others or when she will be asked to put on another pot of coffee and set an extra place at dinner because he is bringing home an alcoholic in need of encouragement.

STEP EIGHT

Step eight, "I am willing to make amends for mistakes of the past, to be constantly on the alert for any destructive habits," is necessary because AA offers no miracle over night. It is a long process requiring continual adjustment and attention.

"When wrong, I will promptly admit it," is step nine. "This is mighty hard and I find myself making dead certain I am wrong before I admit it, even yet," said a wife who knows she needs to work on this step.

September 10, "I will continue to take personal inventory," keeps auxiliary members from becoming too proud, they say. "We get the idea that we have accomplished more than is humanly possible. We need to remind ourselves we have done nothing we can truly say we did alone."

KEEP CONTACT

"I will seek through prayer and meditation to improve my conscious contact with God or a Higher Power," is step 11—an action they conscientiously practice.

"Having had this spiritual experience through the help and fellowship of AA, having had my heart warmed and my soul fed by friendliness and love exhibited in this organization, it is my earnest desire to carry this message to others, and to practice these principles in all my affairs," is step 12.

Through the auxiliary, the women fulfill this step, helping each other and always on call to assist in AA work with wives or family groups.

Like AA, Al-Anon has labored under some popular misconceptions about alcoholism. Just as a traditional stereotype of the drunkard has seen him as a man, a comic figure at times, the stereotype of the nagging, scolding wife who is his counterpart is generally thought to be unattractive enough to get what she deserves. Information about alcoholism has slowly eroded these stereotypes by educating the public that neither is acting in accordance with a personal choice, but such a realization has been slow in coming.

Another Tradition that slows down public information about Al-Anon is the Twelfth Tradition. Anonymity is dear to Al-Anon, because it is the spiritual foundation of the Al-Anon way of life. Members believe that the common good is better served by a purpose higher than personal recognition. Al-Anon members shun personal publicity, and the anonymity of others, especially AA members, is closely guarded. Like AA, Tradition Eleven states that Al-Anon's public relations policy is "based on attraction, rather than promotion."

Despite the difficulty of remaining true to Al-Anon principles, individual members who have had contacts with the media did introduce the idea of Al-Anon to those able to communicate its message of hope. In 1953, Lois spoke on a television program called "Lamp Unto My Feet." This was followed by an article in the *Christian Herald,* and other magazines. A Wisconsin Area Archivist reports an appearance of Al-Anon members on the "Beulah Donahue Women's Show" on WTNJ-TV in 1955. Members actually appeared on the screen to answer questions on how they had been helped by Al-Anon, and what the aims and purposes of the fellowship were. In order to be faithful to the anonymity principle, they were wearing sunglasses!

AA had had its breakthrough with an article written by Jack Alexander in the magazine, *The Saturday Evening Post*, in 1941. Al-Anon's article in the same magazine came out in July, 1955, written by Jerome Ellison. But Al-Anon did not get the overwhelming response that AA had had. Lois worked with Ted Malone of WABC on a radio program to be broadcast to local stations across the country on the Al-Anon story, but Ted Malone left WABC before the broadcast date, and the show never materialized.

But whatever reference was being made to AA, the chances were that Al-Anon was being mentioned too, by helping professionals and by newspaper writers and columnists. The minutes of the Board of Directors meetings reveal the kind of publicity Al-Anon was receiving in 1957.

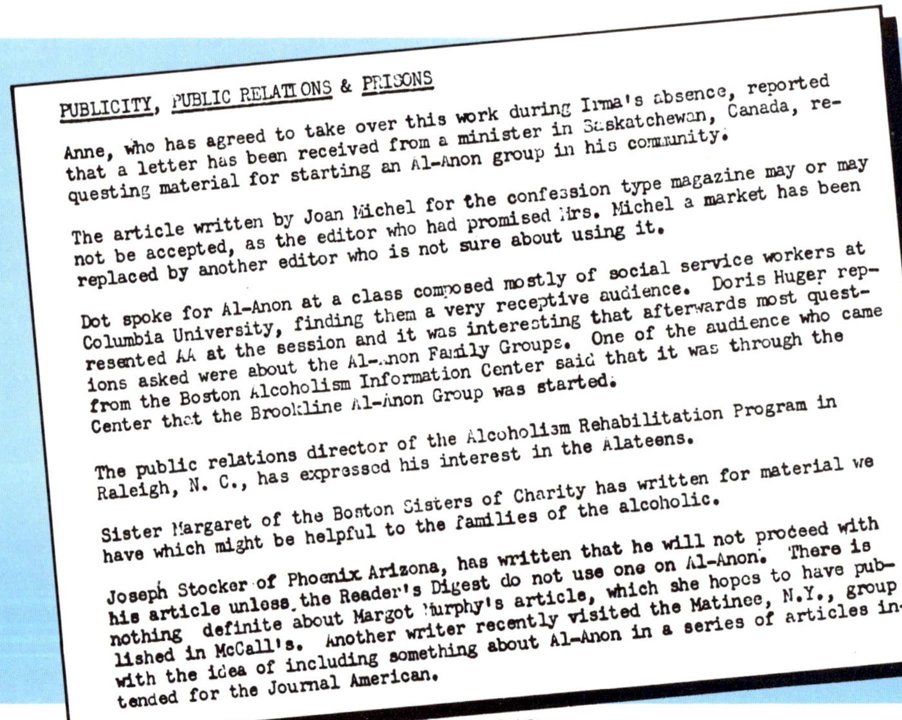

PUBLICITY, PUBLIC RELATIONS & PRISONS

Anne, who has agreed to take over this work during Irma's absence, reported that a letter has been received from a minister in Saskatchewan, Canada, requesting material for starting an Al-Anon group in his community.

The article written by Joan Michel for the confession type magazine may or may not be accepted, as the editor who had promised Mrs. Michel a market has been replaced by another editor who is not sure about using it.

Dot spoke for Al-Anon at a class composed mostly of social service workers at Columbia University, finding them a very receptive audience. Doris Huger represented AA at the session and it was interesting that afterwards most questions asked were about the Al-Anon Family Groups. One of the audience who came from the Boston Alcoholism Information Center said that it was through the Center that the Brookline Al-Anon Group was started.

The public relations director of the Alcoholism Rehabilitation Program in Raleigh, N. C., has expressed his interest in the Alateens.

Sister Margaret of the Boston Sisters of Charity has written for material we have which might be helpful to the families of the alcoholic.

Joseph Stocker of Phoenix Arizona, has written that he will not proceed with his article unless the Reader's Digest do not use one on Al-Anon. There is nothing definite about Margot Murphy's article, which she hopes to have published in McCall's. Another writer recently visited the Matinee, N.Y., group with the idea of including something about Al-Anon in a series of articles intended for the Journal American.

Then, on October 8, 1957, Lois reported to the Board of Directors that she had received a letter from Al S. of Southern California Intergroup saying the "Loretta Young Show" on television intended to feature Al-Anon. Al asked for an announcement to be made in the *FORUM*. Anne reported on the showing.

"The Loretta Young Show, 'The Understanding Heart' was broadcast over NBC TV on Sunday, November 10th, at 10 p.m. Lois sent Miss Young a copy of our book, autographed. A letter to the AA General Service Headquarters offering the film to them was turned over to us. We in turn contacted the sponsors, Proctor and Gamble. They agreed to make eight copies of this film available to us. A distribution program for these is being set up. The five Al-Anon Intergroups have been notified and an article will appear in the March *FORUM*."

The publicity given to Al-Anon by Loretta Young seemed to galvanize the membership into a recognition of Al-Anon as a fellowship that had now arrived. It was like dropping a pebble into a pond (later this thought was developed into a booklet for members in Public Information). Headquarters was besieged with requests to show the film at meetings for the next two years.

"March 11, 1958. Eleanor A. reported that since the Advisory Board meeting of February 11th, all seven films of the Loretta Young Show have been sent out. The responses coming in are most enthusiastic. There are many requests on file for the film when copies are available. The groups in the New York Council (Intergroup) who are planning to use the film are Staten Island, Levittown and Scarsdale in New York, and Westport, Connecticut."

"June 10, 1958. To date, 27 groups have received the Loretta Young film. Many of the copies have been shown more than once by the groups and also used at AA meetings."

"July 8, 1958. To date, the films of the Loretta Young Show have been sent out to over 40 groups, including Puerto Rico and New Zealand."

"October 14, 1958. The Loretta Young Show films are now all scheduled for use through February, 1959."

Finally, in January, 1959, Eleanor reports, "During the past year, the Loretta Young Show has been sent out to 50 Al-Anon groups. Ten have gone to the Canadian groups, and three to foreign groups—Ireland, New Zealand, and Puerto Rico. There are still 20 requests on file to be honored up through June. We would suggest no further publicity about the film in the *FORUM* as our copies are wearing out."

Later on, *"Lois's Story,"* a motion picture in sound and color was produced on the recommendation of the 1971 Conference. Group contributions covered 50 percent of the production costs. A truly beautiful and moving film, it stars Lois talking about the early days of AA and Al-Anon. Available for distribution in February, 1972, it is still shown throughout Al-Anon today.

What seems clear is that in-house publicity was needed before Al-Anon could launch outside publicity. As AA had rallied around the "Big Book" after six years of struggle, so Al-Anon, to a lesser extent, could first rally around a production called "The Understanding Heart." To simplify the whole task of public information and Institutions, Eleanor A. chaired the remaining two sections of the original committee. In March, 1958, a further split divided publicity between Ann N. who chaired Public Relations, while Eleanor A. continued with Public Information. An unwieldy committee had been subdivided into three specialized functions.

Al-Anon's public relations were given a boost by Alateen. General public sympathy with children, and especially children coping with parents' problems, gave Alateen almost overnight attention from the media. An article appeared in the May 16, 1960 issue of *Time* magazine, which was followed by another in *Life,* illustrated with sketches. These articles brought 500 inquiries to Al-Anon Family Group Headquarters about Alateen. "My Mother is an Alcoholic," which appeared in *Guideposts* magazine in March, 1960, was reprinted and 10,000 copies were distributed. Other articles about Alateen followed in *Parade,* a Sunday supplement, *American Weekly,* and *Seventeen* magazine. More reprints funneled requests for information.

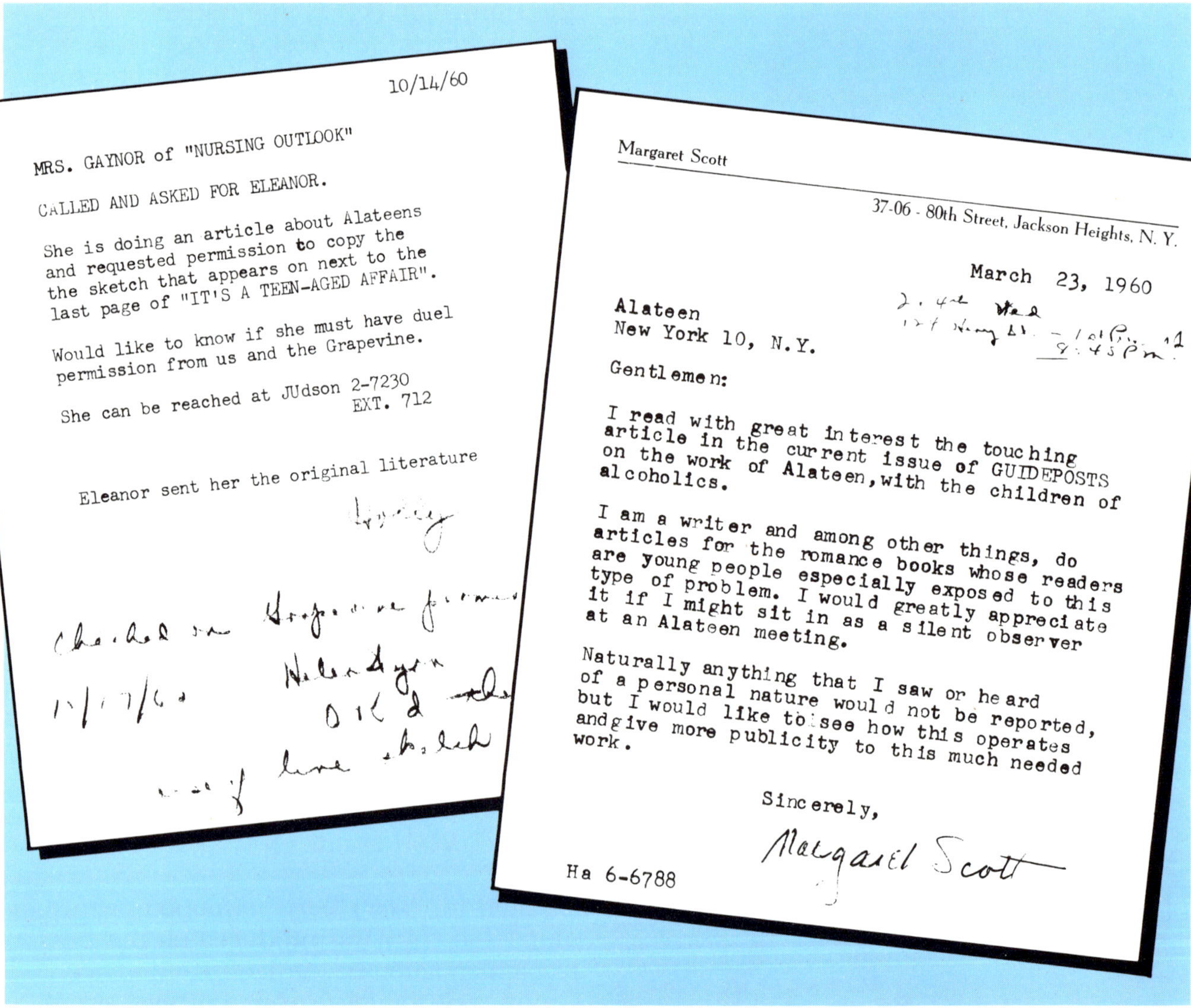
10/14/60

MRS. GAYNOR of "NURSING OUTLOOK"

CALLED AND ASKED FOR ELEANOR.

She is doing an article about Alateens and requested permission to copy the the sketch that appears on next to the last page of "IT'S A TEEN-AGED AFFAIR".

Would like to know if she must have duel permission from us and the Grapevine.

She can be reached at JUdson 2-7230 EXT. 712

Eleanor sent her the original literature

Margaret Scott

37-06 - 80th Street, Jackson Heights, N. Y.

March 23, 1960

Alateen
New York 10, N.Y.

Gentlemen:

I read with great interest the touching article in the current issue of GUIDEPOSTS on the work of Alateen, with the children of alcoholics.

I am a writer and among other things, do articles for the romance books whose readers are young people especially exposed to this type of problem. I would greatly appreciate it if I might sit in as a silent observer at an Alateen meeting.

Naturally anything that I saw or heard of a personal nature would not be reported, but I would like to see how this operates and give more publicity to this much needed work.

Sincerely,

Margaret Scott

Ha 6-6788

NORMAN VINCENT PEALE
EDITOR-IN-CHIEF

LEONARD E. LESOURD
EXECUTIVE EDITOR

JOHN L. SHERRILL
SENIOR EDITOR

Guideposts

STARR WEST JONES
SENIOR EDITOR

VAN VARNER
ASSOCIATE EDITOR

DINA DONOHUE
DEPARTMENTS EDITOR

EDITORIAL OFFICE • 3 WEST 29TH STREET • NEW YORK 1, N. Y. • TELEPHONE MURRAY HILL 9-4313

February 10, 1960

Al-Anon Family Group Headquarters
P.O. Box 182, Madison Square Station
New York, 10, New York

Dear Sirs:

We thought you would be interested in seeing the March 1960 issue of Guideposts which features the story "My Mother Is An Alcoholic" on Page 8.

Cordially yours,

LEL:jtl
Encl.

news

CLEVELAND CENTER ON ALCOHOLISM

2107 ADELBERT ROAD CLEVELAND 6, OHIO SW. 5-1616

Vol. 1 — DECEMBER-JANUARY, 1959-60 — No. 4

Alateens Visit Center

On November 21st a group of Alateens visited the Center and met with the editor of this publication. The members of Alateen are teen-age sons and daughters of alcoholic parents and they come together in an effort to understand and cope with the difficulties in their families. The meetings enable the members to "talk out" the problems that arise from the special impact of alcoholism on family life.

Obviously Alateen cannot give these young people sober parents or a normal home, but as one reporter observed, "it does help them to live with their problem, and to overcome the deep sense of shame, insecurity and resentment that haunts the children of alcoholics." The first lesson a new member learns is that alcoholism is an illness that can afflict the "nicest" of people. Basic to the philosophy of Alateen is the concept that "You are not alone in facing the problems alcoholism brings so don't waste time feeling ashamed."

One of the most striking characteristics of the organization is its realistic approach. The problems are real and tough but the best chance to conquer them lies in facing them squarely rather than running away. For example, the question that monopolizes the thinking of most members is: "How can I get my father (or my mother) to stop drinking?" The answer is always direct. "Perhaps you cannot alone. But you can help immeasurably by understanding the problem of alcoholism; by treating your parent as a sick person; and by adopting a tolerant attitude."

A reporter for a weekly news supplement visited groups in California and told about the discussions he had heard. A member groping for guidance asked, "Should a teen-ager obey an alcoholic when he's drinking?" An older member suggested that "it depends. If the request is reasonable, I don't see any reason to disobey. Like, well, if the family's finished dinner and he asks you to wash the dishes . . ."

Another question: "Should a child make special amends to a parent if he sobers up?" The answer from one boy was sharp and clear. "No! You should not kiss his feet just to keep him sober. You should feel real happy, treat him nice, but you shouldn't have to bend over backwards."

Every Alateen meeting includes two adult representatives—one from Alcoholics Anonymous and one from Al-Anon. They are available to answer questions and participate in discussion but the meetings are conducted by the boys and girls. One inflexible rule, according to our visitors, is the exclusion of parents. "We just can't talk if our parents are there," explained one girl, "because they are so much a part of the problem. But with other people and with each other we can really let our hair down." This was said without rancor or disrespect and her mother, standing nearby, agreed enthusiastically.

The first Alateen group was organized in Pasadena, California, in 1956. Today there are more than 30 active groups and many others in the formative stage. Our visiting group numbered only six and all were from the suburbs. They observed that it was "a new idea around here and hasn't really caught on in Cleveland." Our feeling was that it can't be too long before it does because it offers much needed help to those who can be hurt most severely by alcoholism.

News Briefs From the Center

Recently Governor DiSalle announced the appointment of D. Bruce Falkey, Director of the Center on Alcoholism, as one of the three members of Ohio's new Alcoholism Advisory Board.

* * *

Dr. Mildred Weiss is scheduled to appear on Dorothy Fuldheim's *One O'Clock Club* program on Channel 5 on December 24th.

* * *

The November 1959 issue of *The Bulletin* published by the Academy of Medicine of Cleveland had an article, *Alcoholism-Problem in Cooperation* by Herman E. Krimmel and Dieter Koch-Weser, M.D. Reprints of this article as well as other materials authored by members of the staff are available on request.

Minutes of the Board of Directors meetings show that the trickle of local and national newspaper articles on Al-Anon developed into a steady stream during the 1960s. Abigail Van Buren, "Dear Abby," wrote about Al-Anon in September, 1959. On March 24th, 1960, another article on Al-Anon appeared in the *New York Herald Tribune,* written by Dr. Margaret Bailey. An entry in the minutes is typical of the time:

"A letter was written to the Editor of *Business Week* after an article on AA appeared in a recent issue, suggesting that this magazine might like to do one on Al-Anon. Instead, the entire letter, minus the suggestion appeared in the June 6th issue." Whether riding on the coattails of Alateen or AA, the Al-Anon message was getting across, thanks to the efforts of Eleanor A. and Ann N.

Public relations were strengthened with the arrival of Al-Anon's hardcover literature. Free copies were distributed to libraries and professional organizations by the Publications Department, headed by Evelyn C. At first, this effort must have seemed like scattering seed to the four winds, but the policy bore fruit rather soon, as reference to Al-Anon appeared in professional journals and reference works, such as *RN Magazine,* or *The Encyclopedia of Mental Health.*

In March, 1962, a new public relations tool was devised. Trudy M. reported:

"A public relations kit has been completed for distribution on request. An announcement of its availability (free to Intergroups, 50 cents per kit to groups and individuals) will be made in the May issue

POST

Help for the Alcoholic's Family

By JEROME ELLISON

The exclusive story, with case histories, of a new group that is bringing hope to alcohol's most tragic victims: The wives, husbands and children of the drunkards themselves.

ONE night three years ago a wife in Long Beach, California, despondent over her husband's drinking, went to a meeting of the local Alanon—contraction of Alcoholics Anonymous—Family Group to see what, if anything, might be done. After an evening of intent listening to men and women who had served as spouses to other drinkers, she returned home with her strategy drastically revised.

Always one to pour the household liquor down the drain when a binge was on, she now purchased five imperials of the finest, lined them up on the kitchen sink and waved an invitation to her husband to help himself. Unmanned by this reversal, he sat down to hear her explanation. He was so impressed by what she had learned about his problem that he returned the bottles unopened and hasn't had a drink since.

Alanon Family Groups, of which there are now about 700 neighborhood units, have produced many recoveries which are hardly less remarkable. The society is not mainly organized, however, to effect such comebacks. This is the province of its parent organization, Alcoholics Anonymous, or AA, the international fellowship of former problem drinkers who keep sober by helping inebriates find sobriety. Alanon tackles the problem from the standpoint of the nonalcoholic who is hurt in the emotional and economic tornado which so often accompanies alcoholism. Its members are mostly wives and husbands of AA members or prospects.

The field for Alanon is larger, the statistics suggest, than that available to AA itself, and the need is scarcely less urgent. The National Committee on Alcoholism, an educational and fact-finding organization, estimates that of the 65,000,000 Americans who drink, 4,000,000 have well-developed cases of alcoholism. A Public Affairs Committee summary of the annual cost to the nation charges $31,000,000 to medical care, $25,000,000 to jail maintenance, $89,000,000 to accidents, $188,000,000 to crime, and $432,000,000 to wage losses. Other costs, such as the addling of good brains, the neglect and abuse of children, the disruption of families and friendships, are borne in large measure by those closely associated with problem drinkers. It is this population segment of 20,000,000 that Alanon Family Groups are intended primarily to help.

"And we need help," says the wife of AA's surviving founder. "After years of living intimately with an acute drinking problem, we've become as jumpy as the drinker, and as much in need of restorative measures."

As in AA, help is given mainly in the form of shared experience. Just as former drinkers are best qualified to appreciate inebriates' problems, so the harassments of the alcoholic's spouse—or brother, father, sister, mother, sweetheart, employer or

At the Alcoholics Anonymous clubroom in Des Moines, Iowa, an AA member (left) chats with a visitor who looked in on a meeting of the local Alanon Family Group. The group is an offspring of AA.

17

18

friend—can best be understood, Alanon members say, by a nonalcoholic who has had similar experiences.

The voices of experience are heard in the talks members give at meetings, during the refreshment period afterward, and through informal get-togethers betweentimes. Sometimes, as in the case of the Long Beach wife, a listener gains insight that results in an immediate improvement of the home situation. Of course, no one had suggested treating alcoholism with alcohol. But the principle that a desire to stop drinking is an inward thing that cannot be created by outside lecturing, threatening, scolding or deprivation, is one of the tenets embraced in a way of life that AA's and their mates call "the program." The Californian grasped it promptly, applied it daringly and achieved a seemingly miraculous recovery.

"Hang around," new members are advised. "Sooner or later, you'll hear a story that exactly matches your own." When this happens, a feeling of belonging is strengthened, isolation is ended, anxiety begins to ease off.

In a recent trip through the East and Midwest I met and talked with scores of Alanon members, attended their meetings and heard their case histories. There was a fantastic variety of family narratives, most of them having a happy ending. Families had been salvaged from circumstances seasoned counselors had pronounced hopeless. With the help of AA and Alanon, chronic drunks had been restored as dependable fathers, female barflies had made a comeback as conscientious mothers, families had been lifted from a special brand of hell to a special brand of peace.

"Stories," as members call their talks at meetings, briefly describe the family's condition before AA and Alanon, the circumstances that led to joining and the family record since. The "before" passages often recall days and nights of desperation and shame. "Our house was always a mess," a New York husband reminisced. "I could never be sure my wife would be sober when I came home; we could never entertain friends or go visiting. I hated all of it." A Westchester father said, "I dragged my son out of bars, argued with him, took his money and liquor away. Nothing worked."

Wives spoke movingly of what had happened to their loved ones and themselves. "He was changing before my eyes, losing his gaiety, growing irritable. He was a binge drinker and the binges came closer together."

"Our problem so filled my mind that I found myself forgetting appointments, riding past bus stops, looking at people and not hearing what they said."

"We live in a small, gossipy, party-line town. We tried to keep up a gay front, but were stingingly unhappy."

From a Western state: "You know the story: father'd get plastered and you'd retreat to a corner to commit mental suicide and murder. I could never know what turn things would take; there was never any security or sense of well-being or peace. Finally I built a wall around myself and retreated behind it. We didn't go out for months at a time."

The Alcoholic Doesn't Fool the Children

SOME had taken refuge in a dulled acceptance. "I had given up hope and become a martyr. We never talked much; we were almost strangers. He was sure I had stopped loving him; I was sure he had stopped loving me."

"The strain had affected my disposition, and this, in turn, affected the children. Our daughter avoided home like a plague and our son was in trouble at school. Bills at all the stores were long past due, we had no cash, our furniture belonged to a loan company. For a family accustomed to making its way, it was hard."

Others had lived at a high pitch of nervous protest. "When he was out, I'd jump out of my skin when the phone or doorbell rang, chain myself to the house so I'd be there when he returned, visualize accidents, extravagances, infidelities, arrests. When he was home there were spilt drinks, uneaten meals, insults, physical violence, interrupted sleep, ordinary filth, constant quarrels."

One wife said, "Our marriage was held together by a little hope, a large fear and two children."

The children were not fooled. "I always knew when daddy was drunk, by the way he put his key in the door," a drinker's daughter said. "When he was like that I ran to my room and locked the door."

Another recalled: "Kids notice things. I remember them stumbling around saying, 'This is the way Marilyn's daddy walks.'"

In some cases a family member took the first step toward family recovery through Alanon, drawing the alcoholic into the AA orbit later. "Our doctor suggested AA as a possible step for our son," one father said. "I began attending AA meetings on my own, and after a time Bob went with me. AA made sense to him right away, and he hasn't had a drink since his first meeting." Later, this father helped organize a family group and served as its chairman.

The alcoholic's response is not always so prompt. "Alanon welcomed my daughter and me and gave us new hope," one wife said, "but my husband didn't join AA until a year and a half later, when being fired for drinking finally opened his eyes."

In a New York City Alanon meeting it was the questing wife, one night, who received the eye opener. After hearing the symptoms of alcoholism described she jumped up, saying, "I don't belong here, but in AA. I'm an alcoholic!"

Some members report having been self-conscious and even suspicious in the beginning. "We had been referred to AA by our minister. I knew nothing about it, and my son was afraid it might let him in for some kind of enforced soul-saving program. He came home glowing after his first meeting, relieved of this and a great many other fears." This Midwest mother learned of the family group, joined and became an effective counselor to other families.

Family groupers like to compare notes about how they happened to "come in." Some are awed at the unlikely "chance" which brought help in a desperate hour. A husband said, "One day when I was at my wit's end about Mary's drinking, I ran into an old friend who had been a complete lush, and found out he'd been sober for several years. He told me about AA. Mary said she'd try it, and I joined the local family group to help her."

A wife reported: "During the last week of Jim's last bout, a ninety-seven-day affair, I knelt down in my flower garden and said what was probably my first really serious prayer. A few minutes later a neighbor called and suggested I phone AA."

PHOTOGRAPHY BY PAT COFFEY

Left: Alanon Family Groupers hear Judge C. Edwin Moore of Des Moines, a friend of AA. Right: AA's meet. Working together, AA and Alanon have reunited many families, sometimes when circumstances seemed hopeless.

AA provides the companionship and understanding that frequently cure dipsomaniacs.

Frequently the alcoholic joins AA and the nonalcoholic partner affiliates with Alanon at the same time. "While I was in the hospital for an operation, my husband drank himself into another hospital. The AA's called on him, and when he came out he was a member. When I came out I joined the family group."

More commonly the alcoholic pioneers in AA, and the spouse joins Alanon weeks or months later. One factor is curiosity. "Something had worked a profound change for the better in my husband," a Buffalo, New York, wife testified, "and I wanted to find out what it was." Another factor is a constructive kind of rivalry. In my visiting around the groups I heard frequent reference to the growth in understanding and maturity of the alcoholic spouse through AA. "We had to find out what it was all about or be hopelessly outdistanced."

Finding out what it's about sometimes comes as a shock. "I was quite put out at my first meeting," one wife said. "I expected to hear my husband's problem discussed, but there was hardly any mention of husbands. Instead we were invited to examine ourselves. I was huffed when one wife expressed the opinion that fear, worry, gossip, criticism, grudge-bearing, self-righteousness and self-pity might be as reprehensible as drunkenness, lying and thieving. This was a shock—it hit home." A more usual first reaction is one of relief. Again and again I heard of the newcomer's reassurance on discovering that others had survived all he now faced and more, and had emerged cheerful and with a solution.

The "after" portions of the stories did not always proclaim unqualified victories over the demon rum. AA claims to be able to help all sincere applicants except those who are "constitutionally unable to be honest with themselves." A number of these are represented in Alanon by their spouses. One wife felt that the Alanon program was successful in her case "simply because I have some degree of serenity and good health, and can feel respect and good will for my husband even though he's just come off a two-week drunk." Another reported dramatic relief from disabling headaches which she believed had been psychosomatic. A five-year member, she is successfully raising her two sons, though her husband remains a pathological drinker. One wife advised newcomers to be optimistic and patient about mates who were slow to respond. Her husband, now sober four years, had taken seven years to "make" AA!

Another group of "after" stories bears a restrained witness to improvement. "Has all disagreement ended in our household?" one woman asked rhetorically. "No, but friendly compromise has become possible."

After a year of Alanon, a wife reported: "The main difference in our family is that now we can talk. The two hardest people on earth to talk to are a drunk and an irritated wife. Now that we've broken the sound barrier, companionship is growing."

Generally, however, Alanon stories reflect a happily reconstructed family life. They are preponderantly enthusiastic. "I'll never forget those first meetings—seeing so many people I knew, never dreaming they'd had the same problem we'd had! I'd been a plain snob! We had all been so foolish to cover up our problem instead of solving it!"

"I've made such wonderful friends! We can laugh and even cry together and understand just what we're laughing and crying about."

"My advice to families with an alcoholic problem ls, don't try to do it alone; it's too big."

"We found this secret of harmony: When each partner is trying to remedy his own defects, there's nothing to differ about."

I recall particularly a meeting in Des Moines, which has a family group of the predominantly female variety. Since AA runs more than five-to-one male, this is the usual, but by no means invariable, complexion of the spouse groups. The main AA group in Des Moines has more than 200 members and holds meetings in its downtown clubrooms, over a store at 816½ Walnut Street, on Tuesday evenings. Saturday night is family night, and it is not unusual to have seventy for dinner and twice that many for the evening program of AA speakers. Family group meets on second Wednesdays at eight P.M.

At the meeting I attended I counted about eighty women. There were grandmothers and there was a babe in arms. The twenties and forties were well represented, with the thirties having a plurality. The members were smart in appearance and cheerful in demeanor, and the quarters were pleasant. The loft measures perhaps (Continued on Page 44)

AA's make a first call on an alcoholic. A factory worker, he was earning $25 a day, yet his home was a shambles and he was deeply in debt. He finally turned to AA when drinking cost him his job.

of the *FORUM*. The kit will contain *The Al-Anon Fact File* with basic information for outside public relations, social agencies, clergy, doctors and nurses, etc., a four page folio on 'Speaking at non-Al-Anon meetings', a montage of typical newspaper articles that have appeared, and a few suggestions for local press contacts.

"Indicative of a wider interpretation of our public relations program is a recent meeting at AA with Lyb S., their Public Information staff member, myself, and Dr. Carl Anderson, Director of the Community Services branch of the National Institute of Mental Health. Dr. Anderson wanted to learn more about the roles of AA, Al-Anon and Alateen in the community job of restoring greater mental health to alcoholics and their families. He also wanted to explore possibilities of closer and more effective cooperation at both the national and local levels of his organization and ours."

This broader spectrum of cooperation between outside agencies and Al-Anon is indicative of how Al-Anon handles public relations today. Three committees are closely related, but with clearly defined functions, as outlined in the 1972 Concepts of Service. Each is headed by a staff member, advised by a volunteer committee. Public Information handles media contact at national and local levels, advising groups on how to present the Al-Anon program to regional networks. Cooperating With The Professional Community, renamed in 1980, has contact with industry and professional organizations. CPC exhibits represent Al-Anon at conferences, such as those held by the American Bar Association and the American Management Association. Institutions makes contact with places such as hospitals, treatment centers, correctional and other residential facilities. Each committee aims at establishing Al-Anon as a resource of those in need, and educating those in charge to make referrals.

No response to Al-Anon's effort to carry its message to families, in keeping with Al-Anon's Twelfth-Step principle, can quite match the contribution made by Ann Landers. With a perceptive grasp of what Al-Anon is all about, and an unflagging ability to communicate effectively, this doyenne of syndicated columnists has made a superb contribution to Al-Anon. Ann first wrote about Alateen in 1962, and again in 1964. She covered Al-Anon extensively in 1967, and has been recommending it to her readers ever since, along with Alateen.

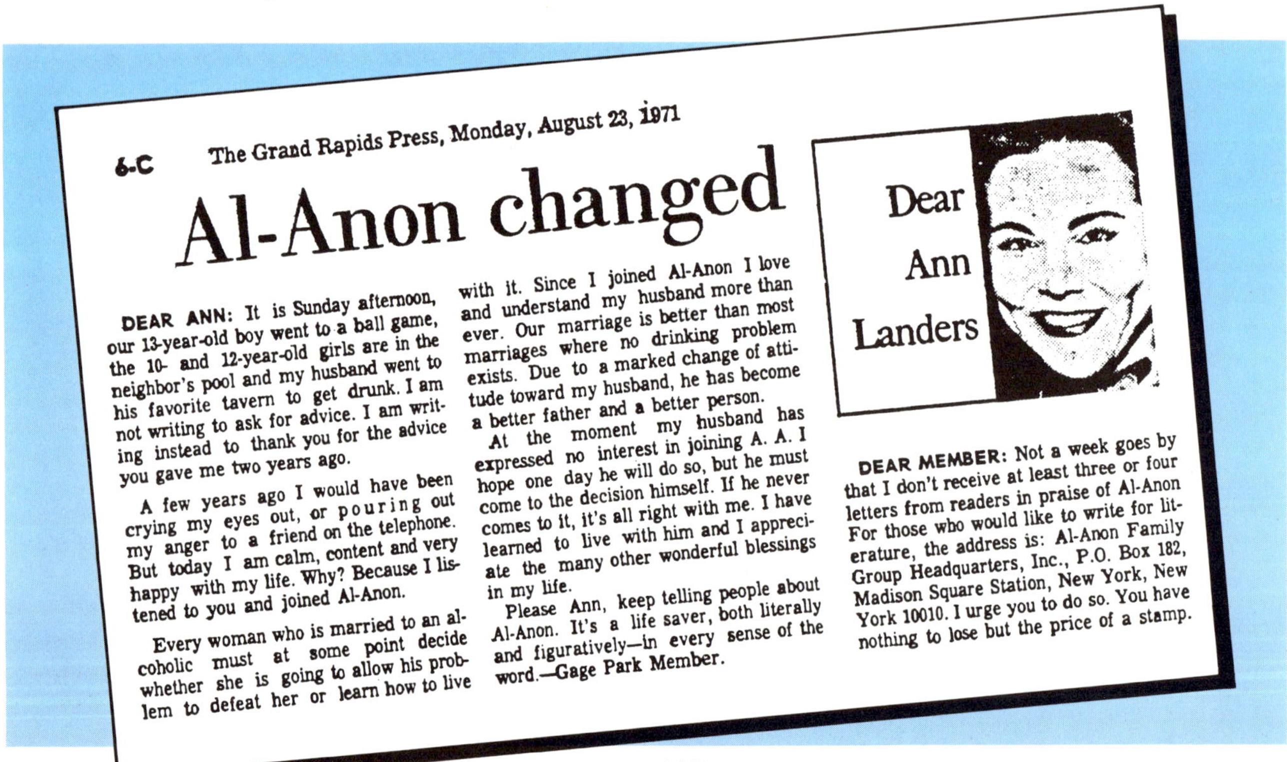

6-C The Grand Rapids Press, Monday, August 23, 1971

Al-Anon changed

Dear Ann Landers

DEAR ANN: It is Sunday afternoon, our 13-year-old boy went to a ball game, the 10- and 12-year-old girls are in the neighbor's pool and my husband went to his favorite tavern to get drunk. I am not writing to ask for advice. I am writing instead to thank you for the advice you gave me two years ago.

A few years ago I would have been crying my eyes out, or pouring out my anger to a friend on the telephone. But today I am calm, content and very happy with my life. Why? Because I listened to you and joined Al-Anon.

Every woman who is married to an alcoholic must at some point decide whether she is going to allow his problem to defeat her or learn how to live with it. Since I joined Al-Anon I love and understand my husband more than ever. Our marriage is better than most marriages where no drinking problem exists. Due to a marked change of attitude toward my husband, he has become a better father and a better person.

At the moment my husband has expressed no interest in joining A. A. I hope one day he will do so, but he must come to the decision himself. If he never comes to it, it's all right with me. I have learned to live with him and I appreciate the many other wonderful blessings in my life.

Please Ann, keep telling people about Al-Anon. It's a life saver, both literally and figuratively—in every sense of the word.—Gage Park Member.

DEAR MEMBER: Not a week goes by that I don't receive at least three or four letters from readers in praise of Al-Anon. For those who would like to write for literature, the address is: Al-Anon Family Group Headquarters, Inc., P.O. Box 182, Madison Square Station, New York, New York 10010. I urge you to do so. You have nothing to lose but the price of a stamp.

The impact of Ann Lander's column hit the WSO with something like a shock wave. Letters simply poured in. Present WSO staff members remember back to those days when the desire to meet the challenge of helping so many, so desperately in need, was zealously undertaken. Al-Anon General Secretary, Myrna H., remembers too:

"I was on hand on three occasions when Ann Landers published letters about Al-Anon and Alateen. In 1967, I was supervisor of Group Records when several thousand letters from teenagers were carted into our small office in huge mail sacks. We didn't know what hit us! Everyone on our staff, regardless of what the jobs were, was asked to pitch in and help. Each letter was given loving attention. We searched the maps and our records to find a nearby group for each young person who had written looking for Alateen's help. Most of us toted letters home in shopping bags, as we all felt the need to provide some answers as soon as possible.

"On another occasion, a letter was published from an Al-Anon member in Illinois telling Ann Landers' readers about how much she was being helped by Al-Anon. This brought in a response of 10,000 letters. At the WSO, we were inundated, and yet happy, because we knew that more people would be finding Al-Anon. Once again, we drew out our maps and made our referrals. Local volunteers joined the staff as the job was monumental. When this same letter was published for the second time, we drew in another 11,000 letters. The fact that each person was given individual atttention on each of these occasions, made me feel that no matter how large our office grew, we should always do our best to maintain the personal touch."

Al-Anon archivist, Margaret O'B., then Henrietta's secretary, remembers that the atmosphere was electrifying, as volunteers arrived at the WSO to perform prodigious quantities of work.

"It was very touching to see and read these letters. Some pages were filled with vivid descriptions of the conditions at home. Others were simply a torn scrap of paper asking for help. One wondered which of these were the more desperate.

"The local volunteers were wonderful. They were so faithful and dedicated to the undertaking. Because the staff had to spend time on the usual day-to-day office work, the volunteers would sort the mail into categories. They divided it first by states, then large cities and lastly, into small towns. Some were not even on the map! Volunteers typed the group information provided by a staff person.

"Armed with a well worn atlas and a magnifying glass, I was eager to do my share. I personally received so much joy knowing I could help someone in this way. Often I would picture the writer going to the mailbox to find my letter."

The two desires, keeping the personal touch and confidentiality while pursuing a public relations policy that promotes the Al-Anon movement as a whole, continues to be a monumental task.

Chapter Twelve
Stepping Stones: A Spiritual Home

Thirty-five years after Al-Anon was established, it is clear that this fellowship has had many firsts—founders, pioneers, groups and regional leaders, without whose individual contributions this milestone could not have been reached. It is also clear that the work of the Al-Anon pioneers is now nearing completion. Many of the newer members look to them fondly as custodians of the Al-Anon heritage. Their contributions, which they have so generously shared, have been collected and held in trust in the Al-Anon archives. The storehouse of spiritual wisdom that all these beloved people represent is not so easily preserved, but there is one repository of tranquility and spirituality that can go forward with Al-Anon in the years ahead, and that is Stepping Stones.

The Stepping Stones Foundation was formed in 1979 for the preservation of the AA and Al-Anon heritage. The house and grounds are currently Lois' home, and the Foundation requests that her privacy be respected. Eventually this small and informal Foundation will supervise the house and grounds for use by both memberships. Meetings and small conferences will be held there, and the Foundation's charter calls for good works in the field of alcoholism. Fran H., executive secretary, says that the intention is to keep Stepping Stones much as it is today.

The entrance to Stepping Stones is unobtrusive and off the beaten track. Lois has reminisced about the day in March, 1941 that she and Bill saw the house for the first time:

"We had been hearing about this place for a long time, but we never thought a house of our own in Westchester County was within our means. We were visiting friends Ruth and Wilbur S. in Chappaqua, so we thought it a good opportunity to see the house for ourselves.

"It was a sunny day with patches of snow on the ground. The interesting brown shingled, hip roofed dwelling stood among trees on a hill, overlooking a valley. We looked at the house from the outside, but we couldn't tell much from that. A window was unlocked, and we clambered in. Although everything was covered with white sheets, the minute Bill saw the big fireplace in the living room, that was that. I found the surroundings to be very lovely. When Bill said he wanted to buy the house, I agreed immediately.

"We went back to the friend who had told us about the property. She was an AA member in real estate in New Jersey. She explained we could have the place for $40 a month with no down payment. As it was, we were paying $20 a month storage on our furniture which meant that we only had to add another $20 a month. Don V. offered to help us by paying our back storage bill and moving expenses. How could we miss such an opportunity?"

The surrounding woods are still charming. Beginning shortly after Bill and Lois moved in, they acquired several additional pieces of land, so that now the property totals 8.5 acres. Going up the driveway and through the woods leads to carefully cultivated gardens. There are stands of trees with groups of garden chairs beneath them, as if to invite conversation between friends. Here is "Stonehenge," named by Bill. This semi-circular seat of stacked stones formed the back drop to the outdoor AA and Al-Anon meetings he and Lois held. In summertime, flowers bloom while bees buzz lazily over the blossoms before coasting off on some private mission. Lois loves flowers. Her mother, who was quite a botanist, taught her the names of many varieties. In the garden, time stands still. There is a sense of uninterrupted tranquility. Like many other places of spiritual significance, the atmosphere has an almost tangible, physical quality.

Some of the stepping stones for which the property was named can be found on a rough path just beyond the porch that extends downhill from the kitchen door. The path was a shortcut off the original driveway, which wound up the hill from a garage at the lower part of the property. When Bill and Lois had put their old Studebaker in the garage, they would walk along the road and then the hundred or so yards up the stone walk to the house. Later Bill put in another garage up above the

house and drive that circled around to it. It was hardly completed when the town put in a street that made it largely superfluous, so that much of it is no longer in use. Paths have been cut through the dense undergrowth to give glimpses of what is close to forest. The remains of a bird box amongst some wild berry bushes mark the edge of where the original stone walk led to the house. Now it keeps watch over the encroaching woods.

Up the gentle rise beyond the garage on the south side of the property is Bill's study, a concrete cabin standing alone in the woods. Here he wrote all but the "Big Book."

Bill's large walnut desk, acquired from his former partner, Hank P., is near a broad expanse of windows. It gleams softly in the lamplight. On the walls hang oil paintings of Bill and Dr. Bob, early Convention photographs, and other AA memorabilia. There is a large, white embroidered sombrero hanging on a peg over what would have been Bill's right shoulder as he sat at his desk. A row of file cabinets line the wall in front of the desk. An overstuffed leather armchair, in back of a desk near the windows, a brown wicker armchair, two straight-backed chairs with cane seats and bedspreaded daybed complete the furnishings. Light streams in through windows on either side. Nothing breaks the silence. The room has not been occupied for a long time.

The entrance to the house is through the porch to the big central living room with its famous stone fireplace. The grand piano on which Lois used to accompany Bill stands in the far corner. Lois says that Bill played the cello better than he played the violin. "We loved to play together, although we couldn't play awfully complicated things," Lois says. "We used to play Mozart for beginners, or something like that. We loved the classics." The wooden floor with its open grate hot air heating system creaks under the tread today as it must have creaked in those early days when visitors combined a social visit to Lois and Bill with a meeting at Stepping Stones. The room has a residual glow.

Lois says that most of the furniture comes from her mother's family. An exception is a drop-leaf dining table that was made by Bill's great-grandfather from a butternut tree that stood in his front yard. Lois designed the patterns for the upholstery on a mahogany chair beside the fireplace and some friends did the embroidery. Here are the six tall windows over which Lois painted valances in the days before she could afford draperies. There is soft lamplight in this rather dark interior, and many books, paintings and flowers belonging to Lois. From the wooden staircase that does an about face halfway up, it is possible to peer over a wooden railing for a bird's eye view of the living room. It is easy to imagine Bill sprawled before a winter fire. Lois allows that Bill never stood when he could sit, and he never sat when he could lie down. "He was always thinking," Lois confides, "And he was very unconventional."

In a large room at the top of the stairs is Lois' desk. Very different from Bill's, its utilitarian steel top is piled high with the stacks of papers, boxes and other paraphernalia of someone who is so very involved with others.

It was here that Lois and Anne B. worked to answer the first family group inquiries before they established the Clearing House. On the walls are illumined photographs, early maps of AA groups, embroidered slogans and other memorabilia along with many tokens of affection received from AA and Al-Anon members the world over. The letter to Bill from Dr. Carl Jung hangs on the wall. The six windows in the room are dormered, and each has a distinctive alcove. One houses a ewer and pitcher, another an extension to a bathroom. Another speaks to Lois' training as an occupational therapist and interior decorator, because here is her sewing machine, dressmaker's model and threads. Books occupy the lower part of the walls between the alcoves, up to where the photographs take over. The books are neatly organized into subject headings such as psychology, healing, Bibles. Lois and Bill loved to read out loud to one another. Lois said her mother used to read out loud to her children, and so she got into the habit. "Bill and I read Shakespeare together and

all the classics," she says.

Lois and Bill's bedroom is at the end of the house opposite the staircase. Next to the mahogany bed is a night stand with radio, and the telephone. Lois has a mirror and dresser with silver brushes against a wall opposite a bathroom. Beneath the window looking south is a comfortable day-bed covered with cushions, and in the opposite corner a rocking chair sits next to a closet with glass-covered doors.

With your eyes closed, you can almost hear the late night ring of that telephone, to which a half asleep Bill would respond. (Lois would explain such a call as just another drunk in trouble.) This time Bill would perhaps have dressed again to go out on a Twelfth-Step call. As an Al-Anon wife, Lois long ago had come to accept such absences as a part of Bill's ongoing recovery in AA. Most members arrive at Lois' acceptance through practicing the program principles as outlined in the Twelve Steps. Talking of Al-Anon principles and spirituality, Lois says:

"I don't know that Al-Anon is a unique program. So many other organizations have the same general principles. Al-Anon's principles are a replica of AA's—in fact, all I did was copy AA. There is very little that is original to Al-Anon. So I quibble with the word, 'unique.' These Al-Anon principles are to live by, not just to wear on Sunday. They are for every day, every week, every year. You cannot change them to suit your mood.

"The word spirituality means so much it is hard to define it. It is wonderful to feel that tremendous sense of purpose, sympathy and brotherhood amongst so many people. It kind of takes you off your feet. I think that spirituality is living a life that has a deeper meaning than the search for daily necessities. If we live spiritually in our daily life, then we find a deeper fulfillment for ourselves. I don't think there is a spiritual part of the program. I think Al-Anon *is* a spiritual program. Every activity can have a spiritual motive.

"I don't think you stress spirituality to the newcomer. In the beginning they used to talk about trying to convey the spirituality, but not anymore. You let it develop on its own. If you talk about it to a newcomer learning about Al-Anon, he or she is apt to pooh-pooh the whole idea. Let the person discover it for themselves.

"Spirituality is the whole of Al-Anon. It is overwhelming, overpowering to see thousands upon thousands of Al-Anons gathered together at a Convention, all with the same motivation. There isn't any Al-Anon without the spirituality. Carrying the message is done best by example. There's nothing that works as well.

"Al-Anon grows because these principles are universal. I believe that they can save the world. Bill was out to save the world, and I don't think that was an exaggeration. It could really happen with people living by these principles."

The past 35 years in Al-Anon speak to this universality. People drawn together by adversity have found a collective spiritual wisdom which of itself has spurred the membership to reach beyond the limits of personal experience and create together a new order. This book has touched on the milestones along the Al-Anon journey so far. The celebration of this year's anniversary is only a beginning. At 35, Al-Anon looks to the years ahead with anticipation and vitality. A maturing fellowship goes forward to meet the future.

Acknowledgments

Al-Anon Family Group Headquarters, Inc. gratefully acknowledges the following sources for their tremendous contributions, both for the use of personal and copyrighted material presented in this book and to the growth of the fellowship worldwide.

The *AA Grapevine, Inc.*
Al-Anon Family Group Headquarters Inc.
Alateen Tell It Like It Is, © Al-Anon Family Group Headquarters Inc. 1984
Alcoholics Anonymous "The Big Book", © Alcoholics Anonymous World Services, Inc., 1939
Alcoholics Anonymous World Services, Inc.
American Weekly Magazine
Dr. Bob and The Good Old Timers, © Alcoholics Anonymous World Services, Inc. 1980
Christian Herald Magazine
Cleveland Center on Alcoholics, Cleveland, Ohio
Dallas Morning News, Dallas, Texas
Reverend Yevlin Gardner
The GRAIL Magazine
Guideposts Magazine
Reverend Joseph L. Kellermann
Ann Landers
Life Magazine
Lois Remembers, © Al-Anon Family Group Headquarters, Inc., 1979
The News-Leader, Richmond, Virginia
Parade Magazine
Pass It On, © Alcoholics Anonymous World Services, Inc., 1984
The Press-Telegram, Long Beach, California
Saturday Evening Post, Jerome Ellison, July 1955, © Curtis Publishing Co.
Seventeen Magazine
The Stepping Stones Foundation
Texas Commission on Alcoholism
Time Magazine
Loretta Young TV Show, "The Understanding Heart"
Abigail Van Buren

The primary source of material for this book was taken from the Al-Anon World Service Office Archives: correspondence, longtimers' tapes or written accounts, newsletters, reports and other memorabilia.

Chronology of Major Historical Firsts

June, 1935—Annie S. and Lois W. meet for the first time in Akron.

1939—family groups begin to form.

March, 1941—Lois and Bill W. purchase Stepping Stones.

1948—"One Wife's Story," by Lois W. published in the *AA Grapevine.*

1949—Ruth G. starts *The Family Forum.*

1950—Bill W. asks Lois to open a service office for family groups.

1950—Members with active alcoholics join family groups.

Spring, 1951-Lois W. asks AA Delegates' wives to lunch at Stepping Stones.

May, 1951—Lois W. makes a decision to open a service office at Stepping Stones. She asks Anne B. to help her.

May, 1951—AA General Service Office gives Lois W. a list of 87 Family Groups and individuals on record with AA.

1951-1954—Al-Anon, as the name for the Family Group movement gains acceptance.

November 17, 1951—Lois W. and Anne B. call a meeting at Stepping Stones with local chairmen and secretaries to discuss expansion.

January 9, 1952—Clearing House established at 334½ West 24th Street, New York City.

1952—"Purposes and Suggestions" written by Lois W.

1952—Al-Anon Traditions written by Lois W.

September, 1952—First Al-Anon literature price list published.

1952—First *Al-Anon World Directory* published.

1953—Henrietta S. becomes first Clearing House paid part-time worker.

1954—Al-Anon Literature, Budget and Publicity Committees form.

1954—Al-Anon Clearing House incorporates into Al-Anon Family Group Headquarters, Inc.

1955—*The Al-Anon Family Groups,* Al-Anon's first hardcover book published.

1957—Al-Anon Headquarters move to 125 East 23rd Street, New York City.

1957—Alateen meetings begin in California.

August, 1957—"It's a Teenaged Affair", published in the *AA Grapevine.*

1960—Al-Anon plans own Conference at AA Long Beach Convention.

April 21, 1961—First Al-Anon Trial Conference convenes.

1961—Conference-Approved Literature (CAL) concept voted.

1962—Ann Landers writes her first article on Al-Anon.

1962—*The Stag Line,* first pamphlet for men, published.

1962—First Alateen Conference held.

1968—*One Day At A Time In Al-Anon* (ODAT) published.

1971—World Service Office moves to 115 E. 23rd St., New York City

1972—*Lois's Story,* motion picture, produced.

1978—WSO moves to 1 Park Ave., New York City.

1980—First General Services Meeting for overseas delegates and WSO staff.

1985—Al-Anon first International Convention held in Montreal

1986—WSO moves to 1372 Broadway, New York City as Al-Anon celebrates 35th Anniversary.